T0327003

POPULATION, DISEASE, AND LAND IN EARLY JAPAN, 645–900

Harvard-Yenching Institute
Monograph Series, 24

Population, Disease, and Land in Early Japan, 645–900

WILLIAM WAYNE FARRIS

Published by the Council on East Asian Studies, Harvard University, and the Harvard-Yenching Institute, and distributed by the Harvard University Press, Cambridge (Massachusetts) and London, 1995

The Harvard-Yenching Institute, founded in 1928
and headquartered at Harvard University, is a foundation dedicated to the advancement of higher educa-
tion in the humanities and social sciences in East and
Southeast Asia. The Institute supports advanced research at Harvard by faculty members of certain Asian
universities, and doctoral studies at Harvard and
other universities by junior faculty of the same universities. It also supports East Asian studies at Harvard through contributions to the Harvard-Yenching
Library and publication of the *Harvard Journal of
Asiatic Studies* and books on pre-modern East Asian
history and literature.

Library of Congress Cataloging in Publication Data

Farris, William Wayne.
    Population, disease, and land in early Japan,
645–900.

    (Harvard-Yenching Institute monograph series ; 24)
    Bibliography: p.
    Includes index.
    1. Japan—Population—History. 2. Epidemics—Japan—
History. 3. Land use—Japan—History. I. Title.
II. Series.
HB3651.F37 1984   304.6'0952   84-22576
ISBN 0-674-69005-2

TO MY PARENTS

Contents

Tables

APPENDIX TABLES

A. Extant Population Records of the Nara and Heian Periods
   (Chapter 1)
B. Epidemics in Japan, 698–898 (Chapter 2)
C. Agricultural Development in Etchū Province, 759 and 767
   (Chapter 3)

Maps

Figures

Chronological List of Translated Court Orders

Acknowledgments

I first became interested in early Japan after reading Basil Chamberlain's translation of the *Kojiki* as an undergraduate. Since then, many people have helped to deepen my understanding of Japanese history. Foremost among them has been Professor Albert Craig, who opened my eyes to the importance of social and economic history and proved a stimulating and rigorous thesis director. His suggestions for revisions and further research were invaluable to both the thesis and the book. Professor Donald Shively encouraged my early interests in ancient Japan. He reviewed my initial translations of the law codes, and perused the thesis with an editor's eye. Professor Edwin O. Reischauer drew on his own research experience to correct my misconceptions about the early period. Professor David Herlihy aided in points of comparative history. Professor Ansley Coale of Princeton University kindly read the chapter on population and offered valuable comments, while Professor Denis Twitchett of Cambridge University supplied insights into East Asian disease patterns.

A Japan Foundation dissertation grant and a Japan Institute grant supported my research in Japan. I owe a great debt of appreciation to all my Japanese colleagues for the kind treatment I received there. A few scholars merit special mention: Professor Kishi Toshio, now retired from Kyoto University, who enthusiastically supported my research into population and disease; Professor Iyanaga Teizō, who willingly answered my questions and included me on his walking tour of the area north of Nara; Professor Kobayashi Kazumasa and Dr. Harashima Akira, without whose help the chapter on population could not have been written; Professor Hayami Akira, who generously commented on the same chapter; Professors Nishiyama Ryōhei, Kushiki Yoshinori, and Inoue Mitsuo, who introduced me to the fascinating world of *ritsuryō* records; Kamata Motokazu, Hara Hidesaburō, Sakaehara Towao, Kinda Akihiro, and many others. Of course, any mistakes are the responsibility of the author.

Finally, I would like to thank my wife, Jane Park, who edited and typed this manuscript uncounted times, and whose encouragement supported me throughout.

EDITORIAL POINTS

1. *Administrative Terminology.* There are no standard translations for many *ritsuryō* offices or documents. I follow the renderings of George Sansom, "Early Japanese Law and Administration," *Transactions of the Asiatic Society of Japan* (Series 2), 9: 67–109 (1932); 11: 117–149 (1934) for translations of many offices. In cases where no translation was available, I have tried to be as literal and reasonable as possible.

2. *Citations of Primary Sources.* I observe Japanese convention in noting all primary sources. When using the *Six National Histories,* I indicate date of the entry (reign period, year/month/day) as well as page number. For the *Ruijū sandai kyaku,* I include date of the regulation as well as its form. Citations of the law codes and other legal sources list chapter, article, page number, and commentator if relevant.

3. *Transliterations.* The Japanese language of the early period contained two more vowels than the modern tongue. For convenience' sake, I have not attempted to reconstruct the original phonology but have rendered names of persons, places, and things according to the conventions established by modern Japanese historians. When no conventional reading was available, consistency has been my sole concern. The Hepburn system is used throughout.

Map 1. The Provinces and Circuits of Early Japan

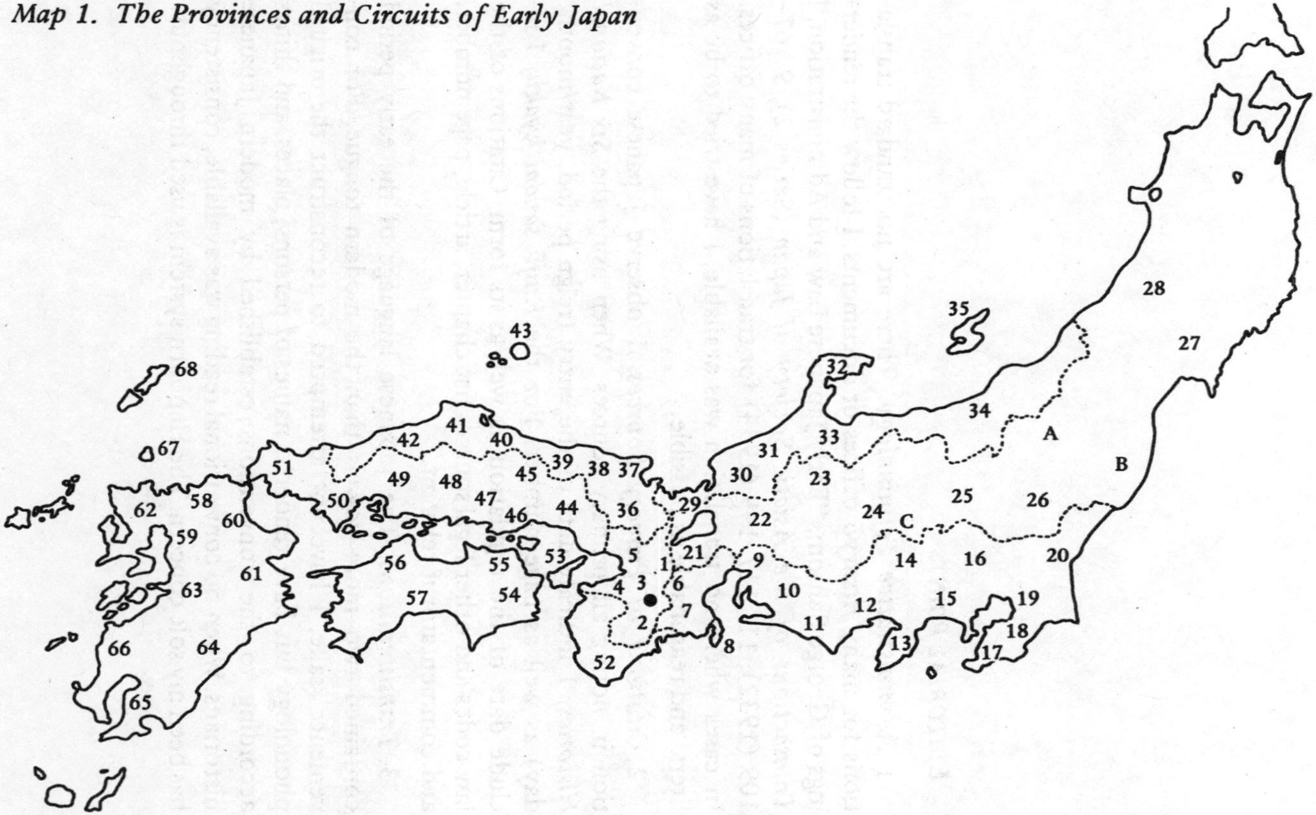

The Provinces and Circuits of Early Japan

Kinai	Tōsandō	San'indō	Nankaidō	Islands
1. Yamashiro	21. Ōmi	36. Tamba	52. Kii	67. Iki
2. Yamato	22. Mino	37. Tango	53. Awaji	68. Tsushima
3. Kawachi	23. Hida	38. Tajima	54. Awa	
4. Izumi	24. Shinano	39. Inaba	55. Sanuki	
5. Settsu	25. Kōzuke	40. Hōki	56. Iyo	A. Iwashiro
	26. Shimotsuke	41. Izumo	57. Tosa	B. Iwaki
	27. Mutsu	42. Iwami		C. Suwa
	28. Dewa	43. Oki		

Tōkaidō	Hokurikudō	San'yōdō	Saikaidō	
6. Iga	29. Wakasa	44. Harima	58. Chikuzen	
7. Ise	30. Echizen	45. Mimasaka	59. Chikugo	
8. Shima	31. Kaga	46. Bizen	60. Buzen	
9. Owari	32. Noto	47. Bitchū	61. Bungo	
10. Mikawa	33. Etchū	48. Bingo	62. Hizen	
11. Tōtōmi	34. Echigo	49. Aki	63. Higo	
12. Suruga	35. Sado	50. Suō	64. Hyūga	
13. Izu		51. Nagato	65. Ōsumi	
14. Kai			66. Satsuma	
15. Sagami				
16. Musashi				
17. Awa				
18. Kazusa				
19. Shimōsa				
20. Hitachi				

Source: Aoki Kazuo, *Nihon no rekishi 3 Nara no miyako,* appended map.

Most provincial offices were created in the late seventh or early eighth century and existed continuously thereafter. Until 750 or so, however, boundaries were uncertain and temporary amalgamation and subdivision of units took place frequently. Iwashiro, Iwaki, and Suwa (a, b, and c) were transitory provinces which had vanished by the 730s. Kaga (31) was established in 823 as the last of Japan's traditional sixty-six provinces.

Introduction

This book examines population, disease, land clearance, agricultural technology, and rural settlement in Japan between 645 and 900. These variables shape a society and its economy; their interplay has furnished the foundation for institutional life and political power in most premodern cultures. At the same time, these factors affect the individual; family, food, and community have been the chief concerns for almost everyone throughout history.

Previous historians of early Japan have studied population, disease, and land, often in great detail and with notable success.[1] Most works, however, have dealt with these factors in isolation, at best discussing a few of them, but never linking all together in a comprehensive fashion. As a result, a structure of assumptions about early population and agriculture has evolved which has gathered authority over time but has not been rigorously tested. This book reexamines these basic assumptions by applying to Japan new perspectives developed by Western social scientists and historians, and attempts to show the most vital interconnections among all of these factors.

Modern demographic techniques can be employed to analyze early Japanese population. How long could the average person expect to live? At what ages were the risks of dying greatest? When was a woman most likely to bear children? While historians have little hope of answering these questions for Western society before the year 1000, relatively copious census data could provide some clues for Japan.

A critical new insight concerns the role of disease in history.

1

Scholars have established that infectious killers had a lethal impact on preindustrial Western civilization.[2] Examination of evidence on disease in early Japan raises numerous questions. What was Japan's relation to the disease pools of Europe and Asia? Did insularity protect Japan? How firmly entrenched was disease in China and Korea, and what was their role, if any, in the transmission of pestilence to Japan? Once a virus was transmitted, how high was mortality? What social, economic, and institutional implications would ravages of disease have had?

Inquiries about population and disease naturally require an investigation of agriculture. Most Western studies portray the eighth and ninth centuries as an era of widespread land clearance; the opening of new fields is seen as a concomitant of population growth. Recent Japanese scholars have criticized this relationship. How much wilderness was converted to rice paddies? Did the creation of new parcels necessarily signify an expanding population?

Land clearance cannot be fully understood without exploring the ways in which the soil was worked. What were the tools and techniques of the first rice farmers? How important were other forms of agriculture? How did land use affect the system of tenure? Many writers tend to read back into the past what is known of Japanese farming in later eras. Recent research by Japanese historians suggests that agriculture from 645 to 900 was much more diverse and primitive than hitherto realized.

Research on population and farming stimulates a reassessment of early settlement. Western studies depict villages as compact habitats from which cultivators seldom strayed. By applying techniques of European geographers to estate maps and archaeological sites, Japanese scholars have raised doubts about conventional assumptions. As more evidence and better methods have appeared, new views of local administration have also gained approval.

Population and farming cannot be examined in isolation from institutional developments. What was the relationship between demographic and agricultural conditions in Japan and the adoption of a Chinese-style centralized state in the late seventh and early eighth centuries? Population was denser and agriculture more advanced in Tang China (618–907) than in Japan. Were Chinese institutions adapted to fit the radically different Japanese context? If so, what were those changes, and how do they illuminate social and economic conditions in Japan? What does modification of the Chinese system reveal about the motives of the Japanese court?

The time frame of this book is the two and one-half centuries of Japanese apprenticeship to Chinese civilization known as the *ritsuryō* period. Study of this epoch contributes to knowledge of later eras as well. How long did the population and farming conditions of the *ritsuryō* age prevail? How and why did they change? A proper understanding of the early economy is essential for building a model of development for the premodern era.

POPULATION AND AGRICULTURE BEFORE 645

Peasant life in the *ritsuryō* age evolved from subsistence patterns established during the Yayoi era (200 B.C.–A.D. 300). At that time, two innovations affected the lives of Japanese people. First, bronze and iron articles were introduced from Asia; residents of the islands soon learned to forge metal tools and weapons to substitute for the stone and wooden ones employed previously. Second, settled agriculture, particularly wet-rice cultivation, became a common livelihood in many regions, replacing and supplementing the hunting, fishing, and gathering habits of preceding generations. The alteration in subsistence patterns prompted a dramatic population increase, the formation of social classes, and the appearance of primitive forms of political organization.

A comparison of population figures for the Yayoi period and the preceding Stone Age, called the Jōmon era (10,000–200 B.C.), testifies to the impact of better technology and more profitable vocations. Archaeologist Yamanouchi Sugao estimated Japan's population before the advent of Yayoi civilization at about 120,000 people.[3] Serizawa Chōsuke proposed a figure of between 150,000 and 350,000.[4] By the end of the Yayoi era, Japan contained 1.5 to 4.5 million inhabitants, a tenfold increase over Jōmon population.[5] The greatest increase occurred during the first century A.D., with a gradual slowing of growth over the next two centuries. The Yayoi period marked a true demographic watershed not matched until the Industrial Revolution in the Meiji age.

Although new techniques meant a profound improvement for many Japanese, regional responses to the influx of skills from the continent varied markedly. Sahara and Kanaseki have described five zones of Yayoi civilization (see Map 2).[6] Zones II (northern

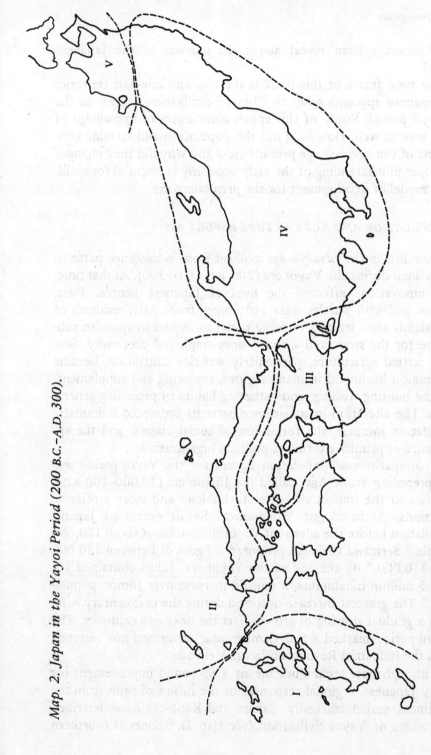

Map. 2. Japan in the Yayoi Period (200 B.C.–A.D. 300).

Source: Kaneseki and Sahara, *Inasaku no bajimari*, p. 88. By permission of Kōdan sha.

Kyushu and southwestern Honshū) and III (the Kinai and Inland Sea region) reacted most favorably. Rice agriculture was adopted early, metal tools and weapons were first forged there, and population grew rapidly. Skeletal remains reveal that settlers of Zones II and III were similar, although sample skulls suggest some anatomical differences. The earliest traces of social distinction and political organization come from those areas.

Other zones were less receptive to the transformation. Zone IV (Honshū extending from Nagoya to Morioka) resisted the encroachment of wet-rice agriculture. Salmon fishing remained an important livelihood for many locals. Even when rice farming did take root, stone or wooden implements were used. Human skeletons uncovered from that area are almost identical to Jōmon remains. Zones I (southern Kyushu) and V (the northern tip of Honshū and Hokkaidō) were virtually untouched by Yayoi influences and developed their own unique cultures.

Toro village in Shizuoka, on the border between Zones III and IV, presents one of the most detailed pictures of iron-age Japan. Discovered in the 1940s, Toro is a fine example of a third-century community that made the transition to wet-rice farming. It consisted of 12 dwellings and 2 storehouses, and about 8 hectares (17.4 acres) of paddies. Archaeologists estimate that about 60 persons resided at Toro. Living quarters were pit dwellings with floors dug to a meter or so below the surface. The lay of the land was so low that levees were constructed around the outside walls to keep seepage to a minimum.

The high water table made wet-rice cultivation simple. Fields were carved out of swampy land, with primitive sluices and dikes; no irrigation ponds were necessary. Although a great advance over earlier forms of subsistence, this type of rice agriculture was primitive. Cultivators broadcast seeds over the soil in spring and waited for rain to provide sufficient water for a crop. If there was too much or too little rainfall, the harvest failed and famine beset the villagers. Even under optimal conditions, yields were much lower than from the intensive, artificially irrigated rice farming practiced today.

Other archaeological evidence illustrates the primitive character of Yayoi agriculture. Hoes and spades excavated from Toro are all wooden. Such tools were softer and less durable than metal ones and limited the ability of the Yayoi farmer to cultivate richer,

more productive soils. Because no harvest tools have been uncovered at Toro, reaping techniques remain a mystery. But archaeologists believe that the two storehouses were constructed to
hold rice ears, not grain.[7] The reaping of individual panicles is a
time-consuming task usually associated with the cropping of less
productive low-lying lands.

The rice grown by Yayoi farmers was a direct ancestor of the
modern grain (*Oryza sativa japonica*). But, unlike present varieties,
Yayoi rice was awned.[8] In the Philippines, awned rice is still cultivated by methods strikingly similar to Yayoi techniques.[9] The
Filipino rice is prized for its resistance to blight and drought and
its ability to thrive in poor soils, properties that would have benefited Toro cultivators.

Two signs of progress appeared toward the end of the Yayoi
age: iron farming tools and more sophisticated irrigation techniques.[10] The use of iron for farm tools was potentially a great advance over earlier technology. Metal hoes and shovels could bite
more deeply into the soil, and were necessary for escaping the
cropping of swampy lowlands and unlocking thicker and more
fertile soils. Some peasants in northern Kyushu may have forged
iron blades for reaping sickles as early as the late first century
B.C.[11] Farmers outside northern Kyushu took much longer to become familiar with iron implements. Cultivators in the Kinai and
Kantō regions did not learn to manufacture metal pieces for harvest
implements or iron blades for hoes and shovels until the end of the
fifth century A.D.

Farmers also began to build more sophisticated irrigation works.
The *Nihon shoki*, Japan's earliest court history, describes the new
technology:

The Emperor commanded his ministers: "Viewing this land, moors and
marshes extend far and wide, and cultivated fields are few and rare. Moreover, river waters spread out to each side, so that lower streams flow slug-
gishly. Should there happen to be continuous rains, the tide from the sea
flows up against them so that one may ride in boats through villages: and
highways, too, are covered with mud. Therefore you as ministers should examine this together and, having ascertained the source of divergence, make a
channel for them to the sea, and, staying the contrary flow of the tide, pre-
serve fields and houses."

. . . The plain north of the Palace was excavated, and water from the south di-
verted into the Western Sea. Therefore that water was called by the name Horie.

... To prevent the overflowing of the Northern river the Mamuta embankment was constructed. [12]

Other chapters of the *Nihon shoki,* usually dated at the fourth and fifth centuries, contain similar stories. [13]

It is uncertain how widely these techniques were known. Engineers were normally of Korean descent, and labored for the ruling elites in the Kinai and other areas. An excavation at Kodera near Matsuyama City in Ehime reveals a fourth-century embankment more than 10 meters long made of spliced branches and logs. [14] At Makimuku near Sakurai City in Nara prefecture, a complex network of ditches, dams, and sluice gates was discovered dating from the fourth or fifth century. [15] Historians will never know who cropped the lands at Kodera or Makimuku, but local cultivators must have received some advantage from this new technology.

Horses and cattle were first domesticated in Japan during the fourth and fifth centuries. Initially, livestock had only a minor effect on farming. The Japanese already had a plentiful and long-standing supply of protein from wild boar, deer, and fish. Farmers did not yet use the plow, nor had they learned to cover their fields with manure. Animal husbandry was at a primitive stage. [16] Castration was unknown, making large herds unmanageable. Horses and cattle served primarily as individual beasts of burden, transporting supplies and humans over Japan's mountainous terrain. As with iron implements and the new irrigation techniques, the contribution of livestock to agriculture unfolded slowly over centuries.

Population trends from 300 to 645 are unknown. One archaeologist, Mori Kōichi, points to changes in burial practices as evidence of explosive demographic growth in the fifth and sixth centuries. [17] During the fifth century, tombs were few and large, as exemplified by giant mounds in the Osaka region. These burial practices were discontinued by the year 500, and numerous small mounds appeared instead. Mori believes these small but ubiquitous tumuli testify to a great population increase and an improvement in the level of subsistence. Although moderate gains may have occurred during these two centuries, archaeological evidence alone does not seem to justify the claim of dramatic growth. The role of disease and famine is unclear for this period.

By the mid-seventh century, Japan was a land with a bewildering variety of subsistence patterns. Its peasants practiced wet-rice agriculture in the more primitive Yayoi form and with the use of irrigation ponds and ditches. Other modes of agriculture, such as dry or swidden farming, were also employed. Fishing, hunting, and gathering still provided food for many people, especially in the north and the far south. As the *ritsuryō* era opened in 645, about 3 to 5.5 million inhabitants dwelt in the archipelago, an enormous figure compared to European populations at the same time.[18]

ESTABLISHMENT OF THE RITSURYŌ STATE

A growing crisis confronted Japanese political leaders in the mid-seventh century. The court's anxiety focused on the expanding might and ambitions of China's Tang empire, proclaimed in 618 by Li Yuan. Soon after quelling domestic uprisings, the new emperor turned his attention to securing China's borders (see Map 3). He was especially eager to subjugate the warlike kingdom of Kogŭryŏ, which had contributed to the downfall of the preceding Sui dynasty (589–617) by defeating several Chinese expeditions. If Tang armies conquered Kogŭryŏ, Japanese rulers worried that Japan's ally, the kingdom of Paekche, might be the next victim. If Paekche fell, the kingdom of Silla, Japan's mortal enemy and Tang's ally, could inherit control of the peninsula. Hostile forces would come perilously close to Japan.

In 631, the new Tang emperor, Taizong, commenced hostilities against Kogŭryŏ. He dispatched an expedition to Liaodong to gather the remains of Chinese soldiers who had perished during previous campaigns, and ordered Tang troops to pillage Kogŭryŏ settlements. The Tang military presence threw Korean domestic politics into upheaval. In 641, a palace coup rocked Paekche, the most unstable of the three Korean states, and the martial King Ŭija assumed power. In 642, on the eve of the Tang invasion of Kogŭryŏ, a military dictator named Ch'ŏngae Somun massacred more than 180 aristocrats to seize Kogŭryŏ's throne. The new regimes in Paekche and Kogŭryŏ sealed an alliance against Silla and Tang and made preparations for war.

Emigrés to Japan from Paekche and Kogŭryŏ recited tales of the Tang invasion and bloody coups.[19] This news from the mainland intensified Japanese feelings of vulnerability. In the 6th month of 645, Imperial Prince Naka (later the Emperor Tenji,

Map 3. The Battle of the Paekch'ŏn River, 663.

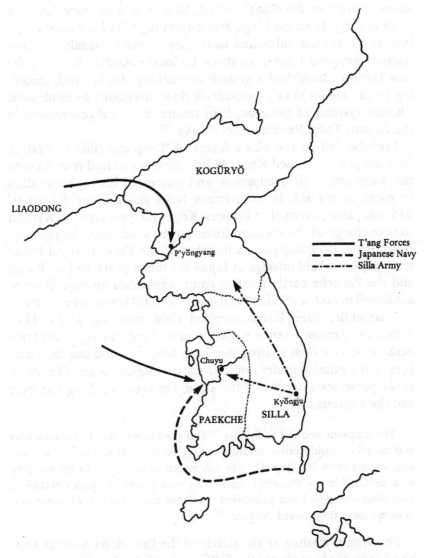

Source: Naoki Kōjirō, *Nihon no rekishi 2 Kodai kokka no seiritsu*, p. 259.

r. 661–671), Prince Karu (later the Emperor Kōtoku, r. 645–654), and Nakatomi no Kamatari (later Fujiwara no Kamatari, 614–669) assassinated Soga no Iruka, the leader of the court's dominant faction, before the eyes of a startled Empress Kōgyoku (r. 642–645).

As in Paekche and Koguryŏ, the first concern of the victors was military preparedness. Less than two months after the coup, emissaries arrived in the Kantō, which had been a military base for sixth-century Japanese kings. Messengers registered the local populace and recorded cultivated land; they erected arsenals and confiscated weapons from untrustworthy local notables. At court, the new faction established a system for ranking officials and, according to the *Nihon shoki*, announced their intentions to implement Chinese systems of taxation, land tenure, and local government in the famous Taika Reform Edict of 646.[20]

Paekche fell to the allied forces of Tang and Silla in 660. A Paekche general named Kwisil Poksin survived to lead resistance to the Tang armies of occupation, and convinced his Japanese allies to come to his aid. In 661, Prince Naka and Empress Saimei (r. 655–661, also governed as Empress Kōgyoku) journeyed to Kyushu to take charge of the invasion force. In the same year, the Japanese court freed Yŏ P'ung-jang, a member of the Paekche royal house who had been held hostage in Japan for thirty years, to join Kwisil and the Paekche partisans. The court dispatched an expedition to aid Kwisil in 662, and reinforced it with 27,000 troops a year later.

Meanwhile, Tang leaders devised their own war plans. They feared the Japanese court might learn of Tang strategy from Japanese emissaries then visiting the Tang Emperor, and put the members of the mission under house arrest at Tang Chang'an. The *Nihon shoki* preserves a record of the scene between the Tang Emperor and the ambassador:

... The Emperor decreed as follows: "This government has determined next year to take administrative measures in regard to lands east of the sea, and you, visitors from Wa [Japan], may not return to the east." In the end they were detained in the Western capital. They were placed in separate seclusion, their door was closed and prohibited, and they had no liberty of movement. In such misery they passed the year.[21]

The armies clashed at the Battle of the Paekch'ŏn River in 663. The *Nihon shoki* recounts the full impact of the disaster:

The hostile generals arrived before Chuyu [the former Paekche capital] and encompassed the royal city. The Tang generals, in command of 170 fighting ships, drew up in line of battle in the Paekch'ŏn River. The Japanese warships that first arrived engaged the Tang fleet, but had not the advantage, and therefore retired. Great Tang stood on its guard in strict order of battle.

. . . The Japanese generals and the Paekche King [Yŏ P'ung-jang], regardless of the aspect of affairs, said to one another: "If we struggle which shall be first, they will naturally retire of themselves." So they again led forward the routed Japanese ranks, and troops of the Middle Division of their force, to attack the Great Tang fleet. But Tang closed upon their vessels from right and left, and engaged them from all sides. In a short space of time, the imperial force was defeated, and many fell into the water and drowned. The ships were unable to maneuver either astern or ahead. Echi no Takutsu [a Japanese general] looked up to heaven and made oaths; he gnashed his teeth, and in his rage slew several tens of men. He then fell fighting. At this time, King P'ung-jang of Paekche with many others embarked in a ship and fled to Kogŭryŏ. [22]

In 668, Kogŭryŏ was destroyed and the Korean peninsula was united under powers hostile to the Japanese court.

The new balance of power in East Asia provoked a national emergency in Japan. After the loss at Paekch'ŏn, the Emperor Tenji ordered guards and beacon fires established at Tsushima, Iki, and the northern coast of Kyushu, the path the Chinese and Koreans would take for an invasion. He transferred the capital to modern Ōtsu on Lake Biwa, a safe distance from the Inland Sea and Japan's enemies. Castles and lookout stations were constructed in Yamato (Nara prefecture) and Sanuki (Kagawa prefecture) provinces. Tenji made tours of these sites, where military drills were a common sight. Ironically, many engineers and drill masters were Korean refugees. [23]

The defeat in Korea supplied fresh motivation for a Japanese court eager to expand and rationalize its power. According to the *Nihon shoki*, Tenji proclaimed a new and more systematic organization for the state bureaucracy within six months of the catastrophe at Paekch'ŏn. Regulations were handed down restricting privileges of senior members of powerful clans and limiting the number of retainers and slaves they could hold. [24] In 670, Emperor Tenji commanded that a census be made to "suppress robbers and vagabonds." [25] According to Inoue Mitsusada, the census of 670 (*Kōgo nenjaku*) enrolled people of all classes and regions then under Tenji's hegemony, and served to establish the surnames of the populace.[26] Registration was a necessary precondition for taxation and conscription.

The Emperor Tenji died before his policies were fully implemented. In the power vacuum that arose after his death in 671, two men vied for the throne. Prince Ōtomo was Tenji's son and designated successor, but Prince Ōama, Tenji's younger brother, also had legitimate claims to power, and was more politically astute. Prince Ōama went into hiding at Yoshino in modern Nara prefecture, where he pretended to become a Buddhist monk. Secretly he enrolled support for his cause. When civil war erupted in the spring of 672, Ōama's planning resulted in several quick, smashing victories. Within six months, Prince Ōtomo had strangled himself and Ōama had ascended the throne as the Emperor Temmu.[27]

Temmu benefited from Tenji's unpopularity. Tenji had incurred the wrath of many regional lords by his centralizing policies, particularly by placing limitations on aristocrats and instituting a census. Tenji's foreign policy was disastrous, and many notables in western Japan refused to provide troops for yet another war. Temmu himself won the throne without relying on many local or court magnates. Those details of the war not directed by Temmu himself were handled by a trusted band of lieutenants, many of them close relatives. Temmu owed few political debts to those who might oppose further centralization, and possessed the military power to crush reluctant courtiers.

The Emperor Temmu had learned the lessons of his age well. Born in 631, he was a young boy when Prince Naka and his cohorts assassinated Soga no Iruka and seized the reins of government. When the Emperor Tenji journeyed to Kyushu to direct Japan's invasion of Korea, Temmu was left behind to oversee affairs at court. Upon Tenji's return, Temmu watched as his older brother feverishly prepared Japan for an invasion by Tang and Silla. Through émigrés at the palace, Temmu recognized that Japan's defeat and the eventual destruction of Kogŭryŏ and Paekche were due only partially to the superior military strength of Tang and Silla. He understood the key to military might was a stable, centralized government that was clearly defined in a set of law codes. If he needed further proof of the advantages of the Chinese system, it was provided in 676 when Silla used knowledge it had gained from the Chinese to oust Tang from the Korean peninsula. Temmu knew Japan had to follow Silla's example to survive. [28]

After his victory in 672, Temmu immediately began to effect sweeping changes following the Chinese model. [29] Only three years after his accession to the throne, he issued an edict abolishing the private economic bases of the aristocracy, including their control of peasants, "mountains, marshes, islands, bays, woods, plains, and artificial ponds." [30] Many Japanese historians believe Temmu was much more effective than previous rulers had been in reducing the private power of the nobility. [31] Elimination of aristocratic control over people and land was a critical step in securing centralized management of the economy and establishing a national bureaucracy.

Temmu's unprecedented authority affected local government. The *History of the Sui Dynasty* discloses that Japan was divided into about 120 regional units (*kuni*) in the early seventh century. These units were supervised by local notables (*kuni no miyatsuko*) who held complete military, political, and religious power over their regions. Following the Taika coup, the Emperor Kōtoku and Prince Naka had attempted to reduce the authority of local magnates by appointing court emissaries to oversee local affairs. The *Hitachi Gazetteer* and other sources indicate that imperial power made some inroads in local areas, but court emissaries often became a new class of regional lords. [32]

The Emperor Temmu prevailed over local leaders through a policy of divide and conquer. First, he stripped former court appointees of their fiscal and military powers. [33] He then took advantage of local rivalries to stimulate more competition for regional posts, and made loyalty to the court an important qualification for office. By raising new candidates to positions of authority, Temmu carved up traditional bailiwicks and broke down old lines of influence. He also divested local magnates of their military and religious functions and created new positions to fulfill those duties. His policies continued in the 680s and 690s under his consort, the Empress Jitō (r. 686–697). By the year 700, Japan contained 555 local units, about five times as many as a century earlier. [34]

Temmu reorganized the court bureaucracy along more despotic lines (see Figure 1). [35] Unlike his predecessors, he gave little voice to aristocrats. The emperor could bypass the court and issue edicts directly to any office he pleased, and his own personal staff was

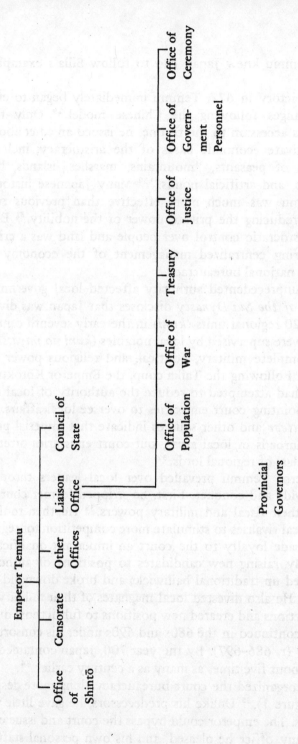

Figure 1. Polity of the Emperor Temmu.

Emperor Temmu

- Office of Shintō
- Censorate
- Other Offices
- Liaison Office
- Council of State
  - Office of Population
  - Office of War
  - Treasury
  - Office of Justice
  - Office of Government Personnel
  - Office of Ceremony
- Provincial Governors

Source: Hayakawa Shōhachi, *Nihon no rekishi 4 Ritsuryō kokka*, p. 37. By permission of Shōgakkan.

outside the jurisdiction of any regulatory body. Temmu instituted a new system of bureaucratic ranking, appointment, and promotion modeled on the Chinese example. His bureaucracy was evaluated on rational, objective grounds, and served as the model for later ministries. As a buttress to his rule, Temmu formulated a political myth that the imperial line had been unbroken for ages eternal and declared himself a god.

Temmu was mortal, and many tasks were left for his consort, the Empress Jitō. Her reign is noteworthy for three accomplishments. First, she oversaw the implementation of Japan's first systematic law codes, the Kiyomihara Codes.[36] These statutes spelled out Japan's initial efforts to adapt Chinese institutions to its own milieu, and were the direct forebear of the Taihō Codes. Second, she initiated comprehensive population registration, tax collection, and state land allocation. These institutions were interrelated, and had the dual purpose of raising sufficient troops to defend Japan's borders and supporting a bureaucracy competent to lead the nation. Third, as a symbol of her authority, Jitō ordered construction of Japan's first Chinese-style capital at Fujiwara, due south of Nara.

The promulgation of the Taihō Codes in 701 under Emperor Temmu's grandson, Mommu, was the zenith of Japanese efforts to adapt the Chinese model to their country. The polity authorized in the Taihō Codes included most offices created by Temmu, with several changes in jurisdiction and status wherever actual practice showed the Kiyomihara Codes wanting (see Figure 2). The most important adjustment was subordination of the imperial household to the Council of State, a consultative body composed of court aristocrats. The Taihō Codes also revised Temmu's system of official ranking, and refined and systematized procedures for selection and promotion of bureaucrats.[37] The Codes specified perquisites of power and required semiannual payment of salaries based on rank and office. Officials in the capital numbered about 10,000 in the early eighth century.

Regional administration was hierarchical. In the top tier were court aristocrats, who served as provincial governors for a term of six years. The Taihō Codes returned to governors the broad powers Temmu had taken from them in the 670s.[38] Their new mandate included tax collection, storage, and shipment, the adjustment of landholdings every six years, regular census-taking, and direction

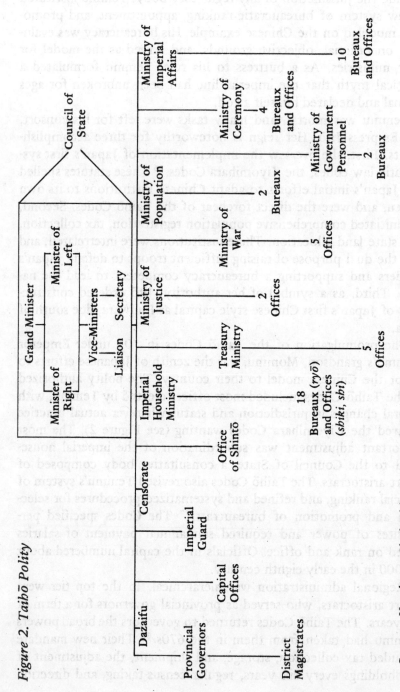

Figure 2. Taibō Polity

Source: Hayakawa Shōhachi, *Ritsuryō kokka*, p. 36. By permission of Shōgakkan.

of the provincial militia. Ordinarily, a provincial administration was staffed by about 600, many of local origin.[39]

District magistrates (*gunji*) comprised the second level of local administration. These officials were chosen from among families of local notables residing in the province. The Taihō Codes specified that district magistrates give obeisance to provincial governors, but district magistrates had certain advantages unavailable to other officials. They held their posts for life, and received land and military powers which they could transfer to their offspring. Because they were residents of the area they administered, their hold over the local peasantry was strong, and their cooperation was an invaluable asset in such government activities as census-taking, land allocation, and tax collection.

The lowest level of regional authority was the administrative village (*ri*, or *sato*). Each village was composed of 50 households (*ko*), according to the Taihō Codes, and was monitored by a headman. Within the administrative village, units of 5 households (*goho*) policed crimes. The household of the Taihō Codes should not be confused with the nuclear family, but was an administrative device organized to facilitate troop conscription and tax collection. An administrative village averaged about 1,000 people in the early eighth century.

The purpose of the elaborate structures established in the Taihō Codes was control of the peasantry, which comprised over 99 percent of Japan's population in 700. Most adult males paid a variety of annual taxes, such as local and national labor services, a products tax, and military duty. Landholders also owed a 3 percent grain tax, which was usually stored in neighborhood warehouses and was used to finance provincial government. According to the Taihō Codes, every person aged 6 and older was granted a parcel of land by the state to crop for his lifetime. The government adopted this system of tenure, not out of benevolence, but to ensure that each taxpayer could bear his share of the burden. A regular census and the compilation of detailed tax documents were essential to the fiscal and military well-being of the court.

CHAPTER ONE

Fertility, Mortality, and Life Expectancy in the Early Eighth Century

The purpose of this chapter is to describe early Japanese population as accurately as possible by applying modern demographic techniques to *ritsuryō* census data. The method used is stable population analysis, first conceived by Alfred Lotka and later developed by Ansley Coale and Paul Demeny in *Regional Model Life Tables and Stable Populations*. Demographers use stable population analysis to derive vital statistics such as birth rates, death rates, and life expectancy from the age and sex structure of a population. This procedure has been employed to investigate populations in medieval and early modern Europe and modern non-Western societies; Susan Hanley has analyzed Tokugawa (1600–1868) village records using the Coale and Demeny paradigms.[1]

Early Japanese census data present both problems and potential for demographic study.[2] The fragmentary nature and unknown quality of the census materials are the major problems. Although difficult to assemble and evaluate, these data are plentiful for an era that ended over a millennium ago. European feudal principalities have nothing to rival Nara (710–784) population records. The abundance of census data is due almost entirely to the effectiveness with which Japan borrowed Chinese registration techniques.

POPULATION REGISTRATION IN EAST ASIAN HISTORY

The census originated in China during the Warring States period (403–221 B.C.), when Prince Xian of Qin ordered the registration of his subjects to facilitate taxation and military conscription.[3]

18

The first Qin emperor continued the practice of enrolling peasants after uniting the Middle Kingdom in 221 B.C., and rulers of succeeding empires copied the Qin institution. A survey made in A.D. 2 listed China's population at about 60 million.[4] The oldest extant population records date from China's Dark Ages (A.D. 220–589), when civil strife made a regular census vital for the state's survival.[5]

Anxious to expand their power, rulers in other parts of East Asia eagerly adapted the Chinese model to their own countries. References to the Korean system of population registration are scarce, but the first nationwide census of Koreans probably occurred in the late seventh or early eighth century.[6] A fragment of a Silla record conventionally dated at 755 has been found in the Treasure House (Shōsōin) of Tōdaiji. On the basis of this single record, Japanese historians have inferred that Silla officials compiled registers every three years, the same frequency specified in the Chinese law codes.[7]

The earliest reference to population counts in Japan concerns Korean immigrants. According to the *Nihon shoki,* Japan's first Chinese-style history, kings of the sixth century decreed that the names of certain Korean artisans be kept in population registers.[8] Later, a similar proclamation was announced for the cultivators of royal lands (*miyake*). Calls for a nationwide census in 646 and 652 appear in the doctored Taika and Kōtoku chapters of the *Nihon shoki;* the reliability of these two entries is doubtful.[9]

The real impetus for the regular registration of peasants stemmed from Japan's need to bolster its defense after the crushing defeat at the Battle of the Paekch'ŏn River in 663. Emperor Tenji oversaw the first nationwide census in 670; Emperor Temmu and Empress Jitō systematized census-taking in their reigns. The enrollment of the populace at regular six-year intervals began under Jitō in 690 and was implemented throughout Japan for more than one hundred years thereafter.[10]

CENSUS-TAKING IN THE LAW CODES

The most important document drafted for the census was the household register (*koseki*). Both the Taihō Codes and the Yōrō Codes, a refinement of the Taihō Statutes written in 717, provide the following guidelines for compilation of this record:

Compile household registers once every six years. Beginning in the first 10 days of the 11th month conduct an investigation and compile registers according to the legal format. The registration of each administrative village [*sato*] shall comprise one scroll. Altogether make three copies. On each seam note the province, district, administrative village, and date of the register. By the 30th of the 5th month of the following year complete the registers. File two copies with the Council of State and leave one in the province. (For Miscellaneous and Imperial Mausolea Households [*zakko; ryōko*] make an additional copy and send each register to the office to which the household belongs.)

The concerned household shall furnish all the materials used in making paper and brushes for the registers. The provincial office shall conduct an investigation and calculate the amount used for these items, and take extraordinary circumstances into consideration. The provincial office shall not overburden the people.[11]

Once the provincial scribes finished their work, official messengers conveyed the household registers to the capital.

The law codes require the Council of State to review provincial registers carefully:

When registers reach the Council, collect and examine them. If the ages of the registrants are inconsistent with last year's record, previous registrants are omitted, or living persons are noted as dead, make inquiries of the provincial staff according to the situation. If the province admits an error, then note fully the reason for the inaccuracy in the registers of the Population and Imperial Affairs Ministries. The province also shall make note in its copy of the document.[12]

After the Council of State verified provincial findings, the records remained on file for thirty years.

The household register served three purposes. First, it listed all those eligible to receive a state land grant (*kubunden*). According to legal commentaries, compilation of new registers preceded the allocation of rice paddies by one year.[13] Second, the household register documented surnames for the populace. Because a person's surname indicated his social status, the household register distinguished slaves from free men. An eighth-century annal called the *Shoku Nihongi* records numerous legal battles in which a slave was manumitted on the basis of information discovered in a household register.[14] Third, this document acted as a tax record. Household registers were used to conscript soldiers for guard duty in Kyushu in the late seventh and early eighth centuries.

In addition to the household register, provincial officials compiled a second document called a tax register (*keichō*). The law codes contain the following provision on the tax register:

When compiling tax registers, offices in the provinces and capital shall demand draft returns [*shujitsu*, handwritten by the household head] of their respective jurisdictions every year before the 30th of the 6th month. Note fully the ages of the household members in the draft returns. If the whole household is not in the area, then transcribe entries as in the previous register and make clear the reasons for any absences. After collecting the returns, compile the tax register in compliance with the prescribed legal format. Countersign it and file it with the Council of State before the 30th of the 8th month. [15]

The tax register was conveyed to the imperial capital by a special messenger (*keichō shi* or *daichō shi*) in the summer and early fall. Upon arrival in the capital, the messenger delivered the tax register to the Bureau of Accounts (*shukei-ryō*) of the Population Ministry for calculation of the next year's budget.

The tax register never attained the importance of the household register. [16] During the late seventh and early eighth centuries, provincial officials may not have filed tax registers at all, but instead submitted only estimates of total population and taxes due. In 717, the court attempted to enforce the Taihō statute by instructing provincial officials on the proper legal format for the tax register. [17] The 717 format, reproduced in the *Ordinances of Engi,* appears to have been lengthy and complex; registers of the 720s preserved in the Shōsōin attest to the diligence of provincial scribes in meeting official standards. [18] Yet, by the 730s, provincial and capital bureaucrats reduced their paperwork by sending the draft returns compiled by each household head directly to the central government without composing a proper tax register.

Household and tax registers share similar formats and contain almost the same information (see Figures 3 and 4). Both documents are organized by household, with the name of the head followed by the names of members and their relationship to the head. For each registrant, the record states a full name and tax status based on the law codes. Exemptions due to disability or old age are also noted. Registers always provide the name and sex of each member of the household, information especially useful to demographers.

Figure 3. A Household Register from the Taihō Era (701–704)

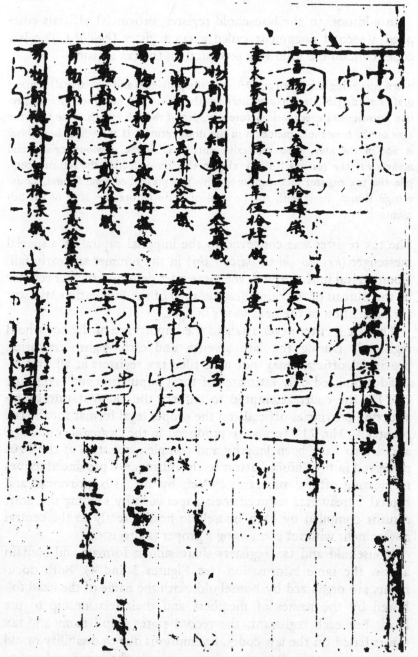

Source: *Guidebook to the Asuka Historical Museum*, p. 17.

A Household Register from the Taihō Era (701–704)

Land Allocation [for previous household]: 3 *chō*, 7 *tan*, 300 *bu*

[11.35 acres or 4.54 hectares]

Household Head: Mononobe no Hirafu, age 64
                      Tax Status: Elderly
                      Taxed household.

Wife: Ōyakebe no Metsu, age 54
                      Tax Status: Adult

Son: Mononobe no Kafuchimaro, age 34
                      Tax Status: Adult
                      Heir.

Son: Mononobe no Nami, age 30
                      Tax Status: Crippled

Son: Mononobe no Miwayama, age 28
                      Tax Status: Adult

Son: Mononobe no Takeru, age 24
                      Tax Status: Soldier

Son: Mononobe no Kuromaro, age 21
                      Tax Status: Adult

Son: Mononobe no Hotari, age 17
                      Tax Status: Young adult

The aforementioned five persons are Younger Brothers of the Heir.

[The four squares read: Chikuzen Provincial Seal.]

Figure 4. A Tax Register of the Tempyō Era (729–749)

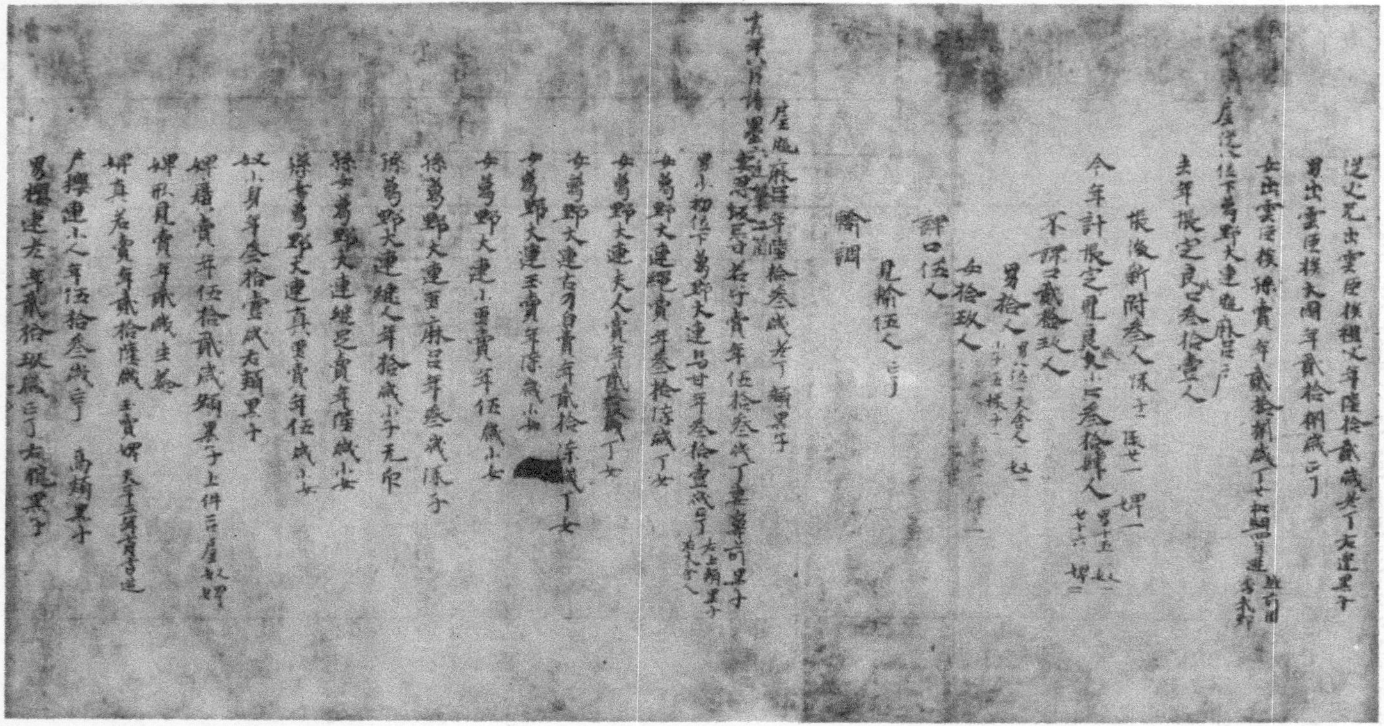

Courtesy of the Office of the Shôsô-in Treasure House

Household Head: Junior Eighth Rank, Lower Grade Kadono no Ōmuraji Mikamaro

Free [written in: and servile] Household Members Enrolled in Last Year's Register: 31 persons

Newly Appended Since Last Register: 3 persons
                                     Infant Boy: 1 person
                                     Infant Girl: 1 person
                                     Female slave: 1 person

Free [written in: and servile] Adults and Children in This Year's Tax Register: 34 persons

                 Males: 15   Females: 16
                 Male slaves: 1   Female slaves: 2

Untaxed Members: 29 persons   [written over erasure]

         Males: 10 persons
                 Male holding Eighth Rank: 1 person
                 Ōdoneri [government worker]: 1 person
                 Children: 5 persons
                 Infants: 1 person
                 Slave: 1 person

       Females: 19 persons
                 Adult: 9 persons
                 Elderly: 1 person
                 Young Adults: 1 person
                 Children: 4 persons
                 Infants: 2 persons
                 Slaves: 2 persons

Taxed Members: 5 persons

Presently Liable: 5 persons
                 Adult Males

Liable for Local Products Tax.

Household Head: Mikamaro, age 63
                 Tax Status: Elderly Adult, mole on forehead

[Written in from reverse: Received in the 8th month, 19th year 6 blocks of ink and 2 brushes.]

Wife: Oshisaka no Imiki Wakugome, age 53
                 Tax Status: Adult   mole on tip of nose

Son: Lesser Initial Rank, Lower Grade Kadono no Ōmuraji Umakai
    Age: 31   Tax Status: Adult   mole on upper part of right cheek
    Migiōdoneri [government worker]

Daughter: Kadono no Ōmuraji Nawame, age 37
    Tax Status: Adult

Daughter: Kadono no Ōmuraji Tojime, age 29
    [over erasure] Tax Status: Adult

Daughter: Kadono no Ōmuraji Kotoshime, age 27
    Tax Status: Adult

Daughter: Kadono no Ōmuraji Tamame, age 7
    Tax Status: Child

Daughter: Kadono no Ōmuraji Omushime, age 5
    Tax Status: Child

Grandson: Kadono no Ōmuraji Mushimaro, age 3
    Tax Status: Infant

Grandson: Kadono no Ōmuraji Tsuguhito, age 10
    Tax Status: Child   No distinguishing marks

Granddaughter: Kadono no Ōmuraji Tsugutarime, age 6
    Tax Status: Child

Granddaughter: Kadono no Ōmuraji Mamushime, age 5
    Tax Status: Child

Male slave: Omi, age 31
    Mole on right cheek

Female slave: Hirome, age 52
    Mole on forehead
    Aforementioned two persons are slaves of household head.

Female slave: Katamime, age 2
    New arrival

Female slave: Mawakame, age 26
    Tamame's slave. Absconded on Tempyō 3/10/10 [731]

SELECTION OF THE POPULATION DATA

Forty-eight tax and household registers survive from the years 702 through 1004 (see Appendix Table A). They describe the populations of at least 27 different administrative villages stretching from Kyushu to the Tōhoku. These records vary considerably in quality and content. The most complete register includes over 50 households and lists almost 1,100 people, while others are fragments containing only one or two households and less than a dozen names.

Most registers do not have enough reliable data for use in stable population analysis. For example, tax registers from Furuchi in Ōmi province (just south of Lake Biwa) portray eighteen years in the life of Ōtomo Tamba no Fubito no Miyatsuko Kibimaro in fascinating detail, but the 20-odd people in his household represent too small a sample to be useful in this study. Tax registers from the capital at Nara (documents 32–34), which list merely 5 households and 50 persons, are also too fragmentary. Most records from the second half of the eighth century share this limitation.

Documents from the Heian period (784–1185) present another problem. Household registers from Awa, Suō, and Sanuki provinces include a large number of persons, but the proportion of females is too high. For instance, there were 47 people in the household of Hatabito no Hiromoto of Kuga administrative village in Suō province (about 30 miles southwest of modern Hiroshima), but only 8 were male.[19] Heian registers belong to an era when adult males avoided taxation by lying to census-takers about their age and sex, and are too unreliable to aid in population analysis.[20]

Five sets of documents remain after excluding the records that listed too few people or came from the Heian era when the census was declining: the Mino, Hanyū, Kyushu, Shimōsa, and Yamashiro registers. Even these registers are far from perfect; due to their fragmentary character, the sex and age of many people are unclear. To guard against bias, only data from households for which the age and sex of every member are available are used.[21]

The first document set is composed of household registers compiled in Mino province in 701 (see Table 1). These administrative villages were located in what is today Gifu prefecture, within a day's hike or a short train ride of Gifu City. In the eighth century, rice farming was probably the dominant livelihood of the region,

Table 1. The Mino Records

District, Administrative Village	No. of Households	No. of Males	No. of Females
Ahachima, Kasuga	26	274	319
Motosu, Kurisuta	16	126	142
Katagata, Katagata	2	19	21
Unclear	1	9	11
Yamagata, Miita	6	47	62
Kamo, Hanyū	52	537	543
Unclear	2	10	7
	105	1,022	1,105

although the rolling terrain was also appropriate for dry and swidden cropping. Hunting, gathering, and fishing were important, especially in the isolated mountain communities of Kasuga. The Mino villages were rather remote; only Katagata was situated on a state road, the Eastern Mountain Route (Tōsandō).

The format of the Mino registers is unique (see Figure 5). All male commoners are listed first, followed by female commoners and slaves. No provincial stamp has been applied to the records. Households are graded into 9 levels of wealth, and ranked by the number of troops available for conscription into the army. The format of the Mino registers complies not with the Taihō Codes, but with the Kiyomihara Statutes of Emperor Temmu and his consort Jitō.[22]

Data from Hanyū administrative village in Kamo district comprise the second set (see Table 1). The Hanyū register was included in set one, but merits separate analysis because it lists over a thousand people and is in near-perfect condition. By testing Hanyū alone, a demographic picture of one village, free from biases introduced by data from other more fragmentary records, can be reconstructed.

The third set consists of household registers from northern Kyushu in 702 (see Table 2). Kawabe, Tō, Kashiguya, and Takebe were scattered throughout modern Fukuoka prefecture. Livelihoods undoubtedly varied considerably from village to village. Located less than 15 kilometers west of Fukuoka City on the Tsushima Strait, Kawabe was a seaside village important for its salt, fish, and seaweed. Some farming was also practiced. In contrast, Takebe was a relatively fertile region for rice farming. Both

Table 2. The Kyushu Records

Province, District, Administrative Village	No. of Households	No. of Males	No. of Females
Chikuzen, Shima, Kawabe	13	137	175
Buzen, Kamutsumike, Tō	3	48	53
Buzen, Kamutsumike, Kashiguya	2	19	24
Buzen, Nakatsu, Takebe	12	111	100
Bungo, unclear	1	6	9
	31	321	361

Kawabe and Takebe were near major thoroughfares: Kawabe was on the route to Tsushima and Asia, while Takebe was within 2 kilometers of Buzen's provincial capital.

Kyushu registers adhere to the format mandated by the Taihō and Yōrō Codes (see Figure 3).[23] Household members are listed by degree of kinship to the household head, men and women mixed. Kyushu registers record only one person per line instead of three per line noted in the Mino records.

The Kyushu documents have a few distinctive local traits. The paper used is of a peculiar white color, and provincial seals have been applied unevenly.[24] The land allotment of each household is entered in the Kyushu documents, which may imply that the year 702 was the first time the *ritsuryō* system of land allocation had been implemented in Kyushu.

The fourth set includes two household registers from Shimōsa province dating from 721 (see Table 3). Ōshima was located in what is now Tokyo, across the Edo River from Matsudo, while Obu was situated near the present town of Abiko. Although both villages were served by the Eastern Sea Route (Tōkaidō), and were close to Shimōsa's provincial capital, they were still more than two weeks' journey away from Nara. Jōmon livelihoods like hunting, fishing, and gathering must have been prominent in this region, especially in Ōshima which was on Tokyo Bay. Obu residents may have relied more on rice farming.

The 721 Shimōsa registers contain a few variations from the Taihō format. Two levels of village administration are listed in compliance with the Ordinance of 715.[25] As a result of this order, the average size of a household was reduced from about 20 to 10 members. The smaller household was used in this analysis. Another

Figure 5. A Mino Household Register

下政戸伊福部大庭戸主　正丁一　大丁一　小子三　緑兒二　并廿　正女三　丁女一　小女女一　緑女二　耆女一　并八

下々戸主大庭　年卅　大丁　嫡子牛麻呂　年二　緑兒　戸主兄廣多　年廿七　正丁

戸主甥多麻呂　年五　小子　次諸ル　年二　緑兒　戸主甥雲麻呂　年十三　小子

寄人阿刀部安豆　年卅　小子　戸主母五百利部黒目賣　年七十七　耆女　兒五百木部志急良賣　年卅二　正女

次意志波賣　年卅九　正女　次廣目賣　年廿二　正女　次若子賣　年廿　大女

戸主兒手手賣　年一　緑女　廣多兒屋波良賣　年四　小女　次古屋良賣　年三　緑女

Courtesy of the Office of the Shôsô-in Treasure-house.

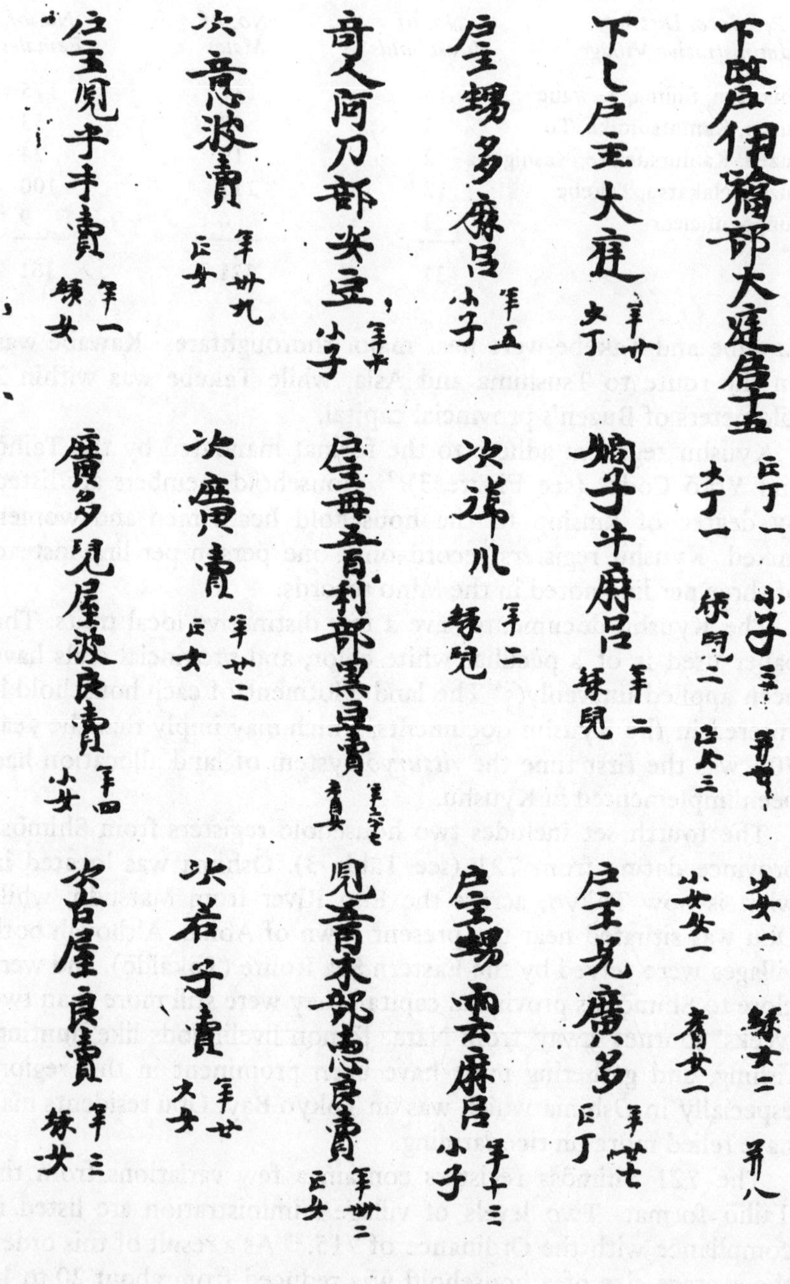

A Mino Household Register

Household with no Draftees (*geseiko*)

Head: Ihokibe no Ōba

Members: 15

7 Males	8 Females
Adult: 1	Adult: 3
Young Adult: 1	Young Adult: 1
Children: 3	Children: 1
Infants: 2	Infants: 2
	Elderly: 1

Lowest Grade of Wealth (*gegeko*)

Head: Ōba
Age: 20   Tax status: Young Adult

Heir: Ushimaro
Age: 2   Tax status: Infant

Elder Brother of Head: Hirota
Age: 27   Tax status: Adult

Nephew of Head: Tamaro
Age: 5   Tax status: Child

Ditto: Mikawa
Age: 2   Tax status: Infant

Nephew of Head: Kumomaro
Age: 13   Tax status: Child

Dependent: Atobe no Atsu
Age: 10   Tax status: Child

Mother of Head: Ihokibe no Kurotsume
Age: 67   Tax status: Elderly

Child: Ihokibe no Erame
Age: 42   Tax status: Adult

Ditto: Ohame
Age: 39   Tax status: Adult

Ditto: Hirome
Age: 22   Tax status: Adult

Ditto: Wakugome
Age: 20   Tax status: Young Adult

Child of Head: Oteme
Age: 1   Tax status: Infant

Hirota's Child: Yaharame
Age: 4   Tax status: Child

Ditto: Koyarame
Age: 3   Tax status: Infant

Table 3. The Shimōsa Records

District, Administrative Village	No. of Households	No. of Males	No. of Females
Katsushika, Ōshima	13[a] (59)[b]	219	292
Sōma, Obu	2 (5)	24	23
	15 (64)	243	315

Notes: a. Household as defined in the Taihō Codes.
      b. Household as defined in the 715 Ordinance.

unique aspect of the Shimōsa registers is the notation designating the heir of each household, as specified in a special imperial edict of 721.[26]

The fifth set of documents consists of tax registers from Yamashiro province (see Table 4). Izumo was situated in what is now downtown Kyoto, a ten-minute walk north of Dōshisha University. Because the Kamo River flowed nearby, rice farming could easily have been a major occupation. Many people were also employed as government bureaucrats. Izumo was only a short distance from the capital of Yamashiro and was well served by the roads and waterways of the Kinai.

Table 4. The Yamashiro Records

Date	District, Administrative Village	No. of Households	No. of Males	No. of Females
726	Atago, Upper Izumo	9[a] (16)[b]	67	50
726	Atago, Lower Izumo	4 (7)	76	129
732	Atago, unclear	14 (24)	122	140
		27 (47)	265	319

Notes: a. Household as defined in the Taihō Codes.
      b. Household as defined in the 715 Ordinance.

The tax registers in the Yamashiro set vary slightly in format from household registers (see Figure 4). Detailed descriptions of the physical characteristics of the people are included, conforming with a statute on official examination of the population. Runaways are listed, along with deaths and new arrivals. The local products tax paid by each household is also recorded. The tax register from 732 contains notations from 733, implying that this register was used for more than one year.

Table 5. Characteristics of Five Document Sets

Set/Date	Households	Population (M-F)	Format	Location	Profile
Mino (702)	105	1022–1105	Kiyomihara household register	South central and southwestern Gifu	Isolated farming communities
Hanyū (702)	52	537–543	"	South central Gifu	"
Kyushu (702)	31	321–361	Taihō household register	North central and southeastern Fukuoka	Accessible farming and fishing communities
Shimōsa (721)	15	243–315	"	Eastern Tokyo	Remote but accessible fishing communities
Yamashiro (726, 732)	27	265–319	Taihō tax register	North central Kyoto	Easily accessible farming communities

The distinctive features of each document set are summarized in Table 5.

APPRAISING THE QUALITY OF THE DATA

Census data may be flawed in two respects: coverage and accuracy. Census-takers may have omitted people through oversight or negligence, or the people who reported for registration may have lied about their age or sex. Two tests (sex ratio and the percentage of people aged 15 and under) measure how thoroughly the population was registered; one test (Myers's blended method) checks age accuracy.

The sex ratio may be defined as the number of males per 100 females, and normally ranges from 90 to 105 (see Table 6).[27] The records from the year 702 list populations with fairly balanced sex compositions, although the Kyushu count falls slightly below the usual standard. The sex ratio of Hanyū administrative village indicates an almost equal number of men and women; in this respect, at least, the Hanyū data are of particularly high quality.

Suspiciously few males appear in the two rolls from Shimōsa and Yamashiro. Feminine sex ratios may result from imbalanced mortality and fertility or sex-specific migration, but a more plausible interpretation is that males were significantly underregistered in the two regions. Registers from the Heian period all contain a disproportionately high percentage of women; taxable males probably enrolled as untaxed women, or altogether escaped detection by local authorities. The low sex ratios of the Shimōsa and Yamashiro registers suggest that, in the 720s and 730s, the problem of registering enough taxable men already hampered the government.

The percentage of population aged 15 and under is a second test of census coverage (see Table 7). The Shimōsa and Yamashiro counts include about 8 to 13 percent fewer children than the 702 data. The relative shortage of children could result from a lower birth rate in these regions, but may also signify the underregistration of untaxed population. Taken together with the high percentage of females, the underenumeration of children suggests that census coverage in Shimōsa and Yamashiro was poor.

A third test shows the accuracy of ages recorded in eighth-century documents. Myers's blended method measures the propensity

Table 6. Sex Ratios for Five Sets of Population Data

Set	Place	Year	Sex Ratio (M/F)
1	Mino	702	92.5
2	Hanyū	702	98.9
3	Kyushu	702	88.9
4	Shimōsa	721	77.1
5	Yamashiro	726, 732	83.0

Table 7. Registration of Children Age 15 and Under

Set	Place	Year	Children (%)
1	Mino	702	41.3
2	Hanyū	702	42.1
3	Kyushu	702	40.3
4	Shimōsa	721	28.9
5	Yamashiro	726, 732	32.2

of age data to concentrate at each of the 10 digits from 0 to 9.[28] Ideally, the number of people whose ages end in each digit should equal exactly 10 percent of the population, and Myers's index should be 0. If everyone's age had the same final digit, Myers's index would be 90.

Calculation of Myers's index reveals that the ages in the Mino and Hanyū registers are somewhat inaccurate (see Table 8). Age distortion in the Mino and Hanyū sets has two characteristics. First, men's ages are more accurate than women's. Census-takers were apparently more careful when registering men, who were subject to corvée and military service, than women, who were not. Second, data from both Mino and Hanyū show an affinity for ages ending in the same digits. Except for Mino males, both registers overrepresent people whose ages have 0, 2, 3, and 7 as final digits. Demographers call overrepresented digits "age-heaps."

Japanese historians have long sought to explain age-heaping at these particular digits. Sawada Goichi, a pioneer social scientist of the 1920s, first noticed the irregularities in the age structure of females from Mino. He pointed out that the bulges in the age structure were most prominent among women over 20, and linked age-heaping to the marital institutions of the Taihō Codes.[29]

Decades later, Kishi Toshio of Kyoto University offered a more plausible explanation for the age-heaps.[30] When Mino officials

Table 8. Myers's Index for the Mino and Hanyū Populations

A. Mino Males (n = 1,022)		B. Mino Females (n = 1,105)	
Digit	Deviation from 10%	Digit	Deviation from 10%
0	+1.4	0	+1.3
1	-3.6	1	-4.4
2	-1.4	2	+9.4
3	+1.9	3	+0.5
4	-1.1	4	-1.0
5	+1.3	5	-0.9
6	-1.4	6	-3.8
7	+2.2	7	+4.3
8	-0.4	8	-2.9
9	+0.9	9	-2.5
Myers's Index =	15.6	Myers's Index =	31.0

C. Hanyū Males (n = 537)		D. Hanyū Females (n = 543)	
Digit	Deviation from 10%	Digit	Deviation from 10%
0	+2.7	0	+2.8
1	-3.7	1	-6.0
2	+1.2	2	+8.4
3	+2.0	3	+0.3
4	-1.0	4	+0.4
5	+1.0	5	-1.0
6	-2.1	6	-4.7
7	+1.0	7	+4.7
8	-0.3	8	-3.0
9	-0.7	9	-2.0
Myers's Index =	15.7	Myers's Index =	33.3

compiled their first census in 670 during Emperor Tenji's reign, they had no way of knowing people's exact ages. No previous records existed. Many people did not know their precise age; even if they did, they were unlikely to tell officials. Census-takers estimated the ages of most people by rounding them at five-year intervals. A registrant whose real age was 13 or 14 was enrolled as a 15-year-old; a woman of 19 or 21 was registered as 20. In this manner, a disproportionate number of registrants were listed at ages ending in digits 0 and 5 in the 670 census.

In 690, after a lapse of twenty years, Empress Jitō reinstituted the census. As Mino officials implemented the 690 registration, they referred to the 670 statistics. When officials enrolled someone counted in 670, they merely added twenty years to his or her age. When census-takers discovered a new resident or a previously undetected subject, they followed the previous practice and rounded registrants' ages at five-year intervals. The age-heaps at 0 and 5 grew even larger.

In 702, as Mino administrators compiled the registers that compose document sets 1 and 2, they repeated earlier routines. The ages of previous registrants were increased by twelve years from 690. A person who was 15 in 670 and 35 in 690 was automatically recorded as 47, while a person of 20 in 690 was listed as 32. Age-heaps at the final digits 2 and 7 in the Mino and Hanyū counts show the combined effects of age estimates made in 670 and 690. Preferences for ages ending in 0 and 5 arose as officials rounded the ages of heretofore unenrolled people at five-year intervals.[31]

The age-heaps at final digit 3 merit special attention. According to the traditional Japanese system of counting age, each newborn infant began life at 1, not 0. Census-takers counting babies in 670 could only round their ages to one year. Thirty-two years later in 701 the 1-year-old infants of 670 appear as 33-year-old men and women. Clusters of persons at age 33 are primarily responsible for the preference for the final digit 3.[32]

Table 9. Myers's Index for the Kyushu Population

A. Kyushu Males (n = 321)		B. Kyushu Females (n = 361)	
Digit	Deviation from 10%	Digit	Deviation from 10%
0	−3.1	0	+2.1
1	−1.8	1	−3.1
2	+4.0	2	+12.8
3	−3.8	3	−4.4
4	+6.5	4	+0.2
5	+1.1	5	−3.3
6	−0.3	6	−2.4
7	+4.2	7	+1.6
8	−4.1	8	−2.5
9	−2.8	9	−0.9
Myers's Index =	31.7	Myers's Index =	33.3

Tabulation of Myers's index reveals age-heaps in the data from Kyushu as well (see Table 9). Ages ending in 0, 2, and 7 are again among the preferences, confirming a nationwide trend in census-taking in 702.[33] Myers's index also shows that the ages of Kyushu males are almost twice as inaccurate as those of Mino males. Kishi believes the Kyushu age data to be especially flawed.[34]

Ages in the Shimōsa and Yamashiro registers are also heaped (see Table 10). Many age preferences in these sets might also derive from the five- and ten-year estimates first employed in the late seventh or early eighth century. The Shimōsa age data are apparently of high quality, while Yamashiro ages are almost as inaccurate as those from the Kyushu set.

Table 10. Myers's Index for the Shimōsa and Yamashiro Populations

A. Shimōsa Males (n = 243)		B. Shimōsa Females (n = 315)	
Digit	Deviation from 10%	Digit	Deviation from 10%
0	+3.5	0	−1.7
1	+4.3	1	+2.6
2	+1.0	2	+3.8
3	−0.6	3	+1.6
4	−0.2	4	−6.0
5	−2.8	5	+1.0
6	+0.1	6	−0.2
7	−1.3	7	−0.8
8	−0.4	8	−2.0
9	−3.7	9	+0.2
Myers's Index =	17.9	Myers's Index =	19.9

C. *Yamashiro Males (726)* (n = 143)   D. *Yamashiro Females (726)* (n = 179)

Digit	Deviation from 10%	Digit	Deviation from 10%
0	+4.9	0	+1.3
1	-3.2	1	+6.0
2	+1.3	2	-4.0
3	+3.0	3	-0.5
4	+1.6	4	+6.7
5	-1.2	5	-3.3
6	-0.7	6	+5.7
7	-0.1	7	-3.6
8	-4.5	8	-4.2
9	-1.2	9	-4.1

Myers's   Myers's
Index =   21.7   Index =   39.4

E. *Yamashiro Males (732)* (n = 122)   F. *Yamashiro Females (732)* (n = 140)

Digit	Deviation from 10%	Digit	Deviation from 10%
0	+2.2	0	-1.8
1	-1.0	1	-5.5
2	-5.6	2	+4.5
3	+3.6	3	-3.6
4	-3.4	4	-5.9
5	-2.6	5	-0.6
6	+2.8	6	+8.5
7	-1.3	7	+2.3
8	+6.6	8	-1.3
9	-1.3	9	-3.3

Myers's   Myers's
Index =   30.4   Index =   37.3

The comparative quality of the five sets of eighth-century data is summarized in Table 11. The Mino and Hanyū sets contain the best data; coverage is extensive and ages are relatively accurate. Although the ages contained in the Kyushu documents are the most imprecise, coverage was much better than in either Shimōsa or Yamashiro. The Shimōsa data rank next because of highly accurate ages. The Yamashiro documents are the least reliable.

Table 11. Reliability Ranking of Early Population Data

A. Coverage	B. Accuracy
1. Hanyū	1. Shimōsa
2. Mino	2. Mino
3. Kyushu	3. Hanyū
4. Yamashiro	4. Yamashiro
5. Shimōsa	5. Kyushu

The relative reliability of the five sets derives in part from the condition of the records. The Mino registers are the most extensive and complete; the Yamashiro registers are very fragmentary. Yet, the quality of the data was also dependent on geography and politics. Mino was near the capital, the villages were primarily settled agricultural hamlets, and census-takers were experienced in counting the populace. Officials in more distant regions like Kyushu or Shimōsa probably had less familiarity with the census and could not be closely supervised by the court. The poor quality of the Yamashiro data is surprising because of the area's proximity to the capital. One possible explanation lies in the character of the tax register, which focused on adult males. Another reason for the unreliable information could be that the system of census-taking had already started to decay by the time these documents were compiled in 726 and 732.

ADJUSTING THE DATA

Eighth-century population data require two adjustments before they can be used in stable population analysis. First, ages must be converted from the traditional Japanese system to the modern Western mode. Second, the age-heaps measured by Myers's index should be smoothed.[35]

According to the traditional Japanese method of counting age, a newborn baby was considered to be 1 year old. Each New Year's Day, every person added a year to his or her age. For example, a Japanese born in the 5th month of 718 would have been 2 years old on New Year's Day 719. To make a precise conversion from the Japanese to the Western system, a demographer would have to know the exact date of birth for each registrant and the date when each person was enrolled. Neither household nor tax registers identify registrants' birth dates; thus exact conversion of the traditional ages to modern equivalents is not possible.

Yet other evidence permits a rough adjustment of the age data. According to the law codes, household registers were compiled from the 11th month of one year through the 5th month of the next. Because the registers had to be copied and transported to the capital within six months, census-takers probably surveyed the populace some time in the 11th and 12th months of the year. The register from Ahachima in Mino province was dated the 11th month of the year 702, suggesting that the census was taken at the year's end.[36] Therefore, to obtain figures closer to the modern system of counting age, one year was subtracted from each person's age as it appeared in household registers.

Conversion of the ages in the Yamashiro tax registers was more complicated. The law codes dictated that the draft returns used to compile the tax registers be collected at the provincial office by the end of the 6th month. The tax register from Yamashiro province includes notations which hint that the new tax registers were in fact deposited at the provincial headquarters by the middle of each year. To adjust the ages in the Yamashiro tax registers, the total number of people of any given age was increased by half the sum of the people in the following age, and then one year was subtracted from all ages.

Once ages were converted to modern equivalents, the age structure of each population was smoothed. Because of the large age-heaps above 20, the age structures were divided and smoothed in two different ways. Smoothing of ages 1 through 17 was achieved using Greville's multipliers.[37] This method was chosen because it is considered more effective and reasonable for smoothing young ages than alternative techniques like the Sprague or Bacchi coefficients.

Smoothing of ages over 17 took place in two phases. First, the population was redistributed over five-year intervals (18 to 22, 23 to 27, and so on) on the basis of a fractional formula devised by demographer Kobayashi Kazumasa of Kyoto University.[38] Second, the appropriate Greville's multipliers were employed to derive single-year values. Smoothing of ages 18 and above was designed especially to reduce the age-heaps at the final digits 2 and 7.[39] The raw and smoothed age structures are presented in Appendix Figures A–E.

APPLICATION OF STABLE POPULATION ANALYSIS

Once the data have been adjusted to compensate for flaws and smoothed age structures have been obtained, an attempt can be made to derive vital statistics using stable population analysis.[40] This study utilizes *Regional Model Life Tables and Stable Populations*, designed by Ansley Coale and Paul Demeny. *Regional Model Life Tables* condenses humanity's demographic experience into four models entitled North, South, East, and West. Models North, South, and East are based on data drawn from northern, southern, and eastern Europe in the nineteenth and twentieth centuries. Model West is more diffuse, representing such areas as the United States, Great Britain, Taiwan, and Japan.

Each model has two parameters: life expectancy at birth, and the rate of population growth. Life expectancy starts at 20 years and rises by intervals of 2.5 years to 77.5. Growth rates begin at -1 percent per year and increase by 0.5 percent to a high of 5 percent. To obtain vital statistics for early Japanese society, a search was conducted to find the model, life expectancy, and growth rate that most closely fit the smoothed age structures of the eighth-century data.

The male and female data were analyzed separately for each of the five document sets. Only four of the ten tests yielded viable results (see Table 12). There were two technical reasons for the failures. First, the test on the Shimōsa males resulted in credible vital statistics (27.5 years life expectancy and no growth), but deviation from the models was over twice as great as for any of the successful analyses. Second, life expectancy at birth for Mino males, Kyushu and Shimōsa females, and Yamashiro males and females was considerably below 20 years, the lowest limit calculated in *Regional Model Life Tables and Stable Populations*.

The exceedingly low life expectancies obtained in these five tests may be explained in two ways. First, the models constructed by Coale and Demeny may include too narrow a range of human experience for use in analysis of eighth-century populations. Evidence from medieval Europe suggests that life expectancy was below 20 years during times of famine or pestilence.

Second, and more likely, the high rate of failure may stem from the poor quality of the data. Appraisal of the Shimōsa and Yamashiro documents revealed that the coverage and accuracy of the

*Table 12. Successes and Failures in the Search for
Eighth-Century Vital Statistics*[a]

A. Successes[b]	Growth Rate	Life Expectancy at Birth
Mino female, 702	1.1	27.75 years
Hanyū male, 702	2.2	32.50 years
Hanyū female, 702	1.4	28.75 years
Kyushu male, 702	1.7	30.50 years

B. Failures	Cause
Mino male, 702	Life expectancy less than 20 years
Kyushu female, 702	Life expectancy less than 20 years
Shimōsa male, 721	Poor fit
Shimōsa female, 721	Life expectancy less than 20 years
Yamashiro male, 726/732	Life expectancy less than 20 years
Yamashiro female, 726/732	Life expectancy less than 20 years

Notes: a. The method used to determine degree of deviation was least mean
squares. A computer tape of the calculations is available upon request.
b. All four tests fit Model West best.

census in those regions were highly suspect.[41] The failure of the
tests on Mino males and Kyushu females indicates that even
the best population counts from the eighth century are not completely reliable.[42]

The significant tests are not those that failed, but those that
succeeded. Despite the flaws in the data and the limitations of
modern techniques, four analyses provide some insight into the
nature of early Japanese population (see Table 13). The findings
from Hanyū administrative village, where census data show a
nearly equal number of males and females and the household
register is almost intact, are most heartening.

The picture of early Japanese population sketched in the four
successful analyses is a familiar one. Life expectancy at birth was
pitifully low, ranging from a mere 27.5 years for the female registrants of Mino, to 32.5 years for the Hanyū males. Total death
rates were frightfully high. The newborn were especially vulnerable; more than half the children born never reached age 5. Those
who did not die in infancy generally lived to about 40.

Even with this striking mortality, all tests indicate that Japanese
population was growing at a rapid pace in 702. If even a 1-percent
rate of expansion is assumed, populations in Mino and Kyushu

Table 13. Vital Statistics for Four Early Japanese Populations

1. Mino Province in 702[a]

Birth rate = 51.21 persons[b]
Death rate = 40.21 persons
Growth rate = 11.00 persons
Life expectancy at birth = 27.75 years
Infant mortality to age 5 = 53.39 percent
Average age at death over age 5 = 41.56 years

2. Hanyū Administrative Village in 702, females

Birth rate = 50.47 persons
Death rate = 36.47 persons
Growth rate = 14.00 persons
Life expectancy at birth = 28.75 years
Infant mortality to age 5 = 55.48 percent
Average age at death over age 5 = 40.57 years

3. Hanyū Administrative Village in 702, males

Birth rate = 57.14 persons
Death rate = 35.14 persons
Growth rate = 22.00 persons
Life expectancy at birth = 32.50 years
Infant mortality to age 5 = 61.69 percent
Average age at death over age 5 = 38.86 years

4. Kyushu in 702, males

Birth rate = 54.34 persons
Death rate = 37.34 persons
Growth rate = 17.00 persons
Life expectancy at birth = 30.50 years
Infant mortality to age 5 = 59.16 percent
Average age at death over age 5 = 40.00 years

Notes: a. Adjustment of the Mino female birth rate to include all the popula-
          tion assumed that the sex ratio at birth was 100 females to 105
          males.
       b. All figures are given per 1,000 population.

would have doubled in about seventy years. Because it is generally
accepted that population did not grow for long periods in the
premodern era, the dynamism displayed by all four populations
indicates that the late seventh and early eighth centuries may have
been a demographic watershed in Japanese history.

But before one can fully embrace the findings in Table 13, a
final obstacle must be overcome. Birth rates for villages in Mino

and Kyushu were about 50 per 1,000 population per year. Such high fertility is more than double the estimates for women in the Tokugawa era, and is rare even in a rapidly growing modern nation.[43] To achieve a birth rate of this magnitude, nearly all women of childbearing age (15 to 44) must have been producing children. Yet the registers indicate that 40 to 50 percent of women in these areas were childless (see Table 14).

Table 14. Childless Women in Three Sets of Household Registers[a]

A. Mino

Age	No. of Women	No. of Childless Women	% Childless Women
16–20	149	119	80
21–25	78	52	67
26–30	52	31	60
31–35	95	33	35
36–40	46	14	30
41–45	79	16	20
	499	265	53.1

B. Hanyū Administrative Village

Age	No. of Women	No. of Childless Women	% Childless Women
16–20	86	72	84
21–25	46	30	65
26–30	24	13	54
31–35	35	9	26
36–40	22	6	27
41–45	32	6	19
	254	136	55.5

C. Kyushu

Age	No. of Women	No. of Childless Women	% Childless Women
16–20	47	37	79
21–25	33	13	39
25–30	22	7	32
31–35	28	5	18
36–40	22	1	5
41–45	21	3	14
	173	66	38.2

Note: a. Ages have not been smoothed or converted to Western equivalents.

The high infant mortality rate explains some of the discrepancy between the high birth rates and the small number of women claiming children in the registers. Household registers usually do not list deceased family members; thus women whose offspring were no longer alive might appear to be childless. According to the statistics calculated for the Kyushu and Mino populations, more than half of all babies died before reaching age 5. An adjustment for infant mortality can be made by reducing the number of childless women by half. The total percentage of childless women decreases to about 27, 28, and 19 in Mino, Hanyū, and Kyushu respectively.

The adjusted percentages of childless women correlate more closely with the high birth rates. Adjusted figures indicate that four of five Kyushu women gave birth, and nearly all females (98 percent) produced offspring by the time they reached their late thirties. The higher percentage of childlessness among Mino and Hanyū women is less reassuring. Fifteen percent of Mino women aged 36 to 40 remained childless. Too much reproductive capacity is left unused to attain birth rates of 50 per 1,000.

An unexplained difference between birth rates and percentages of childless women persists even when an allowance is made for infant mortality. Two additional factors have some bearing on this discrepancy. One is a peculiarity in the registration of families. Census-takers often registered spouses separately: 54.1 percent of the 702 households contain only one spouse; the proportions of single parents in the Shimōsa and Yamashiro documents are 62.7 and 78.3 percent respectively.[44] However, because of a patrilineal bias written into the Household Statutes (Ko-ryō) of the Taihō Codes, children were often enrolled with their fathers rather than mothers. Many examples of households containing a father and children, but no mother, appear in the Mino registers; the mothers are presumably to be found in another census record. Conversely, many of the "childless" women may really have had children, but the offspring are enrolled on another register. Yet, since this explanation rests on speculation about the contents of household registers no longer extant, it is not very satisfactory.

The link between fertility and nutrition is also relevant. A poor diet delays the onset of puberty in women; the high incidence of childlessness in the age-groups 16–20 and 21–25 may simply reflect physical immaturity.[45] If many young women between the ages of 16 and 25 were indeed childless due to malnutrition, significant reproductive potential would have been lost and birth rates of 50 persons per 1,000 per year would still be too high. Malnutrition would also not explain the high percentages of childlessness at ages 30 or 35.

The remaining discrepancy between the high birth rates and the small number of childbearing women in Mino and Kyushu is probably due to inadequate registration of the populace. In particular, progressively greater omission of adults from registers or understatement of their ages are flaws that would make the population appear to have many more young people, and a much higher birth rate, than was actually the case.[46] The discovery of the inflated birth rates is discouraging, and means that the vital statistics for Mino and Kyushu can not be used as exact measures.

FERTILITY, MORTALITY, AND LIFE EXPECTANCY IN EARLY JAPAN

The villages described in the Mino and Kyushu registers represent a wide variety of peasant life, and vital statistics obtained for these populations provide a general indication of conditions in early-eighth-century Japan. The validity of my findings can be corroborated in three ways. First, life expectancy at birth corresponds well to longevity figures posited for populations in medieval Europe and Tokugawa Japan. At first glance, a life expectancy of 28 to 33 years seems shockingly low but, according to Harry Miskimin, life expectancy in Renaissance Europe ranged from 30 to 35 years.[47] Longevity in eighth-century Europe was probably the same or even lower than Miskimin's estimates for the Renaissance era. Susan Hanley has tabulated life expectancy at birth during the Tokugawa period at about 40 years, suggesting a gradual increase in longevity in Japan over the premodern era.[48]

Second, infant mortality was high. A study of changes in the system of land tenure strongly supports this conclusion. According to Torao Toshiya, the Japanese court first experimented with the state allocation of land in 690 during the reign of Empress Jitō.[49] Torao believes that, under the 690 system, all peasants were given grants of rice paddies at birth. In 702, the Taihō Statutes added a restriction: Infants aged 5 calendar years and under were disqualified from holding land. Kōchi Shōsuke has argued that the Taihō restriction was added because, under the 690 system, many newborn grantees died soon after receiving land, and local officials then had to confiscate the new land grants and allocate the parcels to someone else.[50] Torao has recently endorsed Kōchi's emphasis on the role of infant mortality in the reform of the land system.

Third, population was growing fairly quickly at the beginning of the eighth century. The first documentary evidence for population growth appears in 715, when Nara courtiers reformed the system of local administration by increasing the number of households in an administrative village from 50 to 100 or 150. According to Kishi Toshio, a major factor in the court's decision was a rapidly growing rural population.[51] It is hard to believe that demographic increase was the sole reason for the 715 reform. Even a high rate of expansion could not account for all the new households and villages created by this reform. Yet, Kishi is probably correct in citing demographic increase in the years since 702 as an important factor in the new law.

In 723, we find further indication of population growth. The *Shoku Nihongi* contains the following proclamation:

Recently the population has gradually increased and farmland has become congested. We request that the Empress Genshō encourage the people of the realm to open more lands.[52]

In the same year a change was made in the qualifications for land grantees. The Taihō Codes had permitted slaves aged 6 and older the right to receive paddy land. In 723, the age limit was raised from 6 to 12.[53] In the opinion of Miyamoto Tasuku, the decisive factor in raising the age qualification was rural overcrowding, which left little paddy land for commoners, much less slaves.[54]

In 729, another attempt was made to deal with the problem that population growth was causing in the countryside:

This year, it is impractical to allocate and confiscate land grants as recorded in the Land Statutes. We therefore request permission to seize all land and reallocate it on a new basis.[55]

The 729 law was a product of many forces, including political intrigue at court. However, lawmakers must have been concerned about rural overcrowding, which led to the fragmentation of parcels. By adjusting patterns of landholding for the rural population, local officials could consolidate parcels and make room for new grantees.

The origins of rural overcrowding are visible even in 702. Consider the plight of the Hanyū villagers. This community was located in a small basin surrounded by mountains in Gifu prefecture. Iyanaga Teizō has reconstructed the landscape of Hanyū and determined that about 120 *chō* (360 acres) of land could be converted to rice agriculture.[56] Yet, according to the law codes, the residents of Hanyū village should have been allocated more than 150 *chō* of land. The shortage of land would have become more acute as Hanyū grew. At a growth rate of 1 percent per year, more realistic than the inflated figures calculated for either Hanyū males or females, the population of Hanyū would have increased by more than one-third in just thirty years. Peasants must have resorted to forms of subsistence other than rice farming, but these, too, had their limits. The population boom of the early eighth century could not continue indefinitely.

CHAPTER TWO

Population Trends and Epidemic Disease

In *Plagues and Peoples,* William McNeill has stated that, in Japan's early age, "epidemics . . . coming approximately a generation apart must have cut repeatedly and heavily into Japanese population, and held back the economic and cultural development of the islands in a drastic fashion."[1] McNeill's assertion contradicts the assumptions of many specialists, who devote little attention to disease and think population growth was constant and rapid throughout the eighth and ninth centuries.[2] Here I propose to test the validity of McNeill's model by exploring the role of epidemics in *ritsuryō* Japan.

McNeill has indicated that mankind has passed through several stages in its relation to viruses.[3] In the initial phase, settlements of hunters and gatherers were so sparsely inhabited that few viruses or parasites could survive to affect the size of the population. In the second stage, as agriculture became the dominant form of food production and the size of the human community grew, killer diseases which had first afflicted domesticated animals spread to the new human host. The infestation of mankind with microparasites, as McNeill calls the viruses, commenced in the densely settled cradles of civilization. The Mediterranean, Egyptian, Mesopotamian, Indian, and Chinese populations each developed a unique pool of viruses and immunities.

The third phase, lasting from 500 B.C. to A.D. 1200, was the first step in the microbial unification of the world. During this era, the cradles of civilization expanded into new areas, either encountering the differing disease pool of another culture or bringing a disease into a land where people had no immunity. The confluence of diseases resulted in demographic debacles throughout Europe and Asia. Bubonic plague decimated the population of Justinian's Europe and smallpox arrived in China for the first time in this period. Later, as agricultural innovations took place, the population in most regions grew and the exposure to viruses became more frequent. Resistance rose until infectious diseases retreated to endemic status, signified by their evolution into the afflictions of childhood, like measles and chicken pox today.

McNeill has presented evidence to show that Japan's geographical position resulted in a unique relationship to the disease pools of other civilizations in the third stage. Specifically, he has suggested that Japan's isolation cut two ways. First, it protected the Japanese population from continental epidemics. Free from the constant threat of infection, peasant settlements grew relatively dense.

Second, Japan's geographical seclusion also meant that no immunities were created. When a disease entered the islands from another culture, it swept the population quickly and virulently. As immunity levels receded after the epidemic, Japan's isolation guaranteed that another encounter with the same disease would have equally disastrous results. Isolation lengthened the time Japan required to come abreast of continental disease patterns. For England, whose seclusion mirrored that of Japan in Europe, no significant population growth took place until the fifteenth century, by which time repeated exposure to continental diseases had raised the general level of immunity.[4]

How well does McNeill's thesis apply to *ritsuryō* Japan? Rates derived from the Mino and Kyushu household registers, as well as laws issued at court, indicate that the population was probably expanding in Japan after 702. Was this growth temporary, as McNeill would suggest, or was it constant and long-term, as conventionally assumed? An examination of the frequency and effects of epidemics in early Japan will provide an answer.

THE NATURE OF THE EVIDENCE

References to pestilence between 645 and 900 are plentiful (see Appendix Table B). Court histories, the major source for information on epidemics in the early period, list plagues in seventy-one years, more than a quarter of the *ritsuryō* age. The abundance of documentation can be ascribed largely to the thorough adoption of the Chinese system for monitoring disease.

Provincial and capital officials were charged with the duty of reporting pestilence immediately. An article in the Statutes on State Documents and Forms (*Kushiki-ryō*) specifies the actions required of government workers:

In cases where there are great omens, military hostilities, natural disasters, epidemics, or unusual events in a province, send a messenger by emergency post and report to the Council of State. [5]

One legal scholar defined epidemics (*ekishitsu*). The commentator, known only by the single character Ato, explained that an infectious outbreak was to be considered epidemic when the number of patients exceeded the total stricken in a normal year. [6]

Plagues of infectious disease, which could wipe out the taxpaying peasantry, were weighty matters for local and capital officials. An epidemic was deemed so serious that the codes gave the highest priority to messengers announcing an outbreak. According to another article in the same chapter on the system of state transportation, the fastest messengers could travel up to 300 *ri* (about 168 kilometers) in one day. [7]

When notified of an epidemic, the court had several options. It might choose to apply medical remedies concocted by specialists trained in Chinese theory in the Bureau of Medicine (*ten'yaku-ryō*) at the capital, and administered by regional doctors with access to provincial medicines. Capital officials might also resort to economic relief, such as grain doles, tax remission, or rice loans. If concrete countermeasures failed, government leaders tried to soothe the feelings of the gods thought to be responsible for the plague. Political gestures like a grant of amnesty or the cancellation of court ceremonies might be made. Sutra-chanting and religious festivals were more direct appeals to the angry spirits.

When annalists compiled the court histories in the eighth and ninth centuries, reports of epidemics and records of the countermeasures adopted by the court were normally included in edited form. For example, the *Shoku Nihongi*, the court history of the eighth century, noted for the 3rd day of the 3rd month of 698 that "Echigo province reported an epidemic. We granted medicine and succored the populace." All entries use the accepted legal term for epidemic (*eki*), as defined by the jurist Ato.

The terse entries in the court histories leave three essential questions unanswered. First, chroniclers often do not reveal the geographical extent of plagues; references to "many provinces" or "the whole nation" are common. Without specific information on the regions affected by the pestilence, it is not possible to trace the origin or progress of the infection.

Second, the disease is rarely identified. Normally historians simply state that the infection is an epidemic and do not describe the symptoms or use Chinese medical terminology. Even when available, Chinese nomenclature is difficult to translate into modern Western medical terms. Entries probably include afflictions ranging from mild influenza to smallpox or cholera. Because infectious diseases vary greatly in virulence, it is difficult to measure the true impact on population trends and economic activities.

Third, mortality in an epidemic is often a matter of guesswork. As a rule, historical accounts do not quantify deaths. Phrases like "almost half" or "the great majority" are employed only during severe outbreaks and are neither reliable nor precise. Elaborate government policies may actually exaggerate the impression of fatality. Uncertainty about the origin, nature, and deadliness of the epidemics is a major weakness of McNeill's hypothesis on the drastic influence of foreign-borne infections on Japanese population.

But one epidemic described in the court histories is unique. Numerous entries in the *Shoku Nihongi* and other eighth-century materials contrast with the usual laconic reports. As McNeill has argued, the disease was imported from Asia and its spread within Japan can be traced. The infection is clearly identifiable as smallpox, and documents preserved in the Treasure House of Tōdaiji give detailed information on regional death tolls. The Great Smallpox Epidemic of 735 to 737 brought an abrupt end to the population boom of the early eighth century.

THE ARRIVAL AND INITIAL RAVAGES OF THE DISEASE

The Great Smallpox Epidemic of the Tempyō era (729–749) had a modest beginning which belied its eventual terror. A fragment from a medical text compiled about seventy years after the outbreak records that a Japanese fisherman who ran afoul of an infected "barbarian" was responsible for the introduction of the disease to the islands.[8] A late Heian history differs only slightly, stating that a "barbarian ship" infested with the disease transmitted the virus.[9]

Medieval historians were convinced that the smallpox epidemic had a foreign source. The author of a thirteenth-century compilation identified the barbarians as men of Silla.[10] According to this source, a fisherman from Kyushu became lost at sea and ran aground on the Korean peninsula where he became infected with the disease. A later medieval history agrees that Korea was responsible for the plague.[11]

The credibility of these accounts is open to question. It is unclear how well the fragments of the medical text that remain extant today match the text of the ninth century, and the medieval sources are not reliable. Caution is advised when a Japanese historian attributes an evil to Korea, since Silla was the traditional scapegoat throughout the early period. The lack of trustworthy contemporary records makes locating the precise origin of the epidemic a difficult task.

Chinese and Korean sources do not note any epidemics for the 730s, and thus shed no direct light on the introduction of the disease. The lack of documentation in other Asian histories may be the result of faulty record-keeping, but it is more likely that there were in fact no epidemics in Tang and Silla at this time. Yet, an absence of epidemics need not be interpreted as an absence of disease. Smallpox had ravaged the Chinese population since at least the fourth century, while Korea, by the mid-eighth century, had probably known the infection for two hundred years.[12] Smallpox could easily have afflicted a few individuals without meriting attention in a court history. Random contact between an infected foreigner and a Japanese trader or traveler is not hard to imagine.

Whoever was responsible for the entry of the disease into Japan, the port of Dazaifu was the first to feel its effects. Beginning on the 12th day of the 8th month in 735, reports filtered in from Japan's military outpost in Kyushu that a killer disease was on the rampage. On that day, the superintendents of all Kyushu announced formally to the court that an unusual number of peasants had died from an infectious disease. Resistance of the Kyushu populace was probably low in 735, since crops had failed in 732 and 733. Peasants were to suffer from famine once more in the year of the outbreak.[13]

The response of officials at the capital in Nara was a predictable mixture of prescriptions and prayers. Authorities sent medicine to combat the pestilence, as had been the custom earlier in the eighth century. The court also ordered prayers to appease the local Kyushu deities. Provincial governors in western Honshu were commanded to perform purification rites to pacify the gods and prevent the spread of the infection. The Nara government also had Buddhist monks in Dazaifu and the provincial headquarters under Dazaifu's jurisdiction read sutras to succor the people. The court's heavy reliance on religion may mean that medical remedies were proving ineffective against the killer infection.

An unprecedented policy worked out by court bureaucrats was more indicative of the deadliness of the new infection. The Household Statutes had originally provided grain relief only to those suffering from famine.[14] In 726, just after his accession to the throne, the Emperor Shōmu (r. 724–749) made grants of grain to disease victims, but the wording of the edict makes it clear that his action was extralegal.[15] The 8th month of 735 marked the first time that provincial officials were ordered by the court to dole out grain from local storehouses to the victims of an epidemic. The imperial edict used the word *shingō* (to succor) which had previously appeared only in orders for famine relief. The legalization of grain allotments to assist epidemic victims implies that the crisis facing the government was grave.

The emergency at Dazaifu did not abate. Eleven days after the first report, on the 23rd of the 8th month, the military government of Kyushu submitted the following petition to the court:

A pestilence characterized by swellings has spread widely in the provinces under our jurisdiction. The whole populace is bedridden. We request exemption from the local products tax [*chō*] for this year.

Authorities in the capital granted the request.

Additional evidence suggests that the smallpox epidemic had spread beyond Kyushu by the end of 735. In the intercalary 11th month, Shōmu issued an amnesty to all in his realm, citing the plague as a major reason for his action. The amnesty was a favorite palliative of Confucian rulers facing a domestic crisis; Shōmu's action pointed to the growing impact of the disease on the country-side.[16]

The final entry in the *Shoku Nihongi* for 735 provides a grim summary of the major event of that year:

In this year, the harvest failed completely and from summer to winter the whole realm suffered from smallpox [*entōsō*]. Colloquially this disease is called *mogasa*. Those who died were many.

Four points are notable in this entry: first, the epidemic was accompanied by a failure of the harvest; second, the outbreak of the disease predates the initial Dazaifu report by four months; third, the infection is described as affecting all Japan; and, fourth, the disease is clearly identified as smallpox.

Two entries in the *Shoku Nihongi* suggest that the smallpox epidemic was still raging in 736. First, in the 7th month, an order was issued to give medicine and grain to all commoners, monks, and nuns who were ill. Second, a report from Dazaifu dated the 22nd day of the 10th month states that "all males and females" were afflicted by the pestilence, and that, as a result, Kyushu peasants were abandoning their fields. Harvests were so poor that the military governor requested and received exemption from the land tax for 736 "to keep the populace alive."

By the winter of 736, the people of Kyushu had been suffering from the dread disease for more than a year. And the epidemic appeared to be spreading. Soon not even the aristocracy would be safe from the grim killer.

THE EPIDEMIC AT ITS HEIGHT

In the 2nd month of 736, the Emperor Shōmu appointed his third mission to Silla. Headed by Abe no Ason Tsugumaro, the party planned to effect a change in Japanese-Korean relations, which had soured earlier in Shōmu's reign. Only six years earlier, in 730, a Korean source notes that Silla forces had routed a Japanese invasion force of 300 junks.[17] In 731, the Koreans requested a decrease in the symbolic tribute they paid to the Nara court. Although the Japanese accepted the revision, tense relations continued, as shown by a mobilization order handed down for all Japan immediately thereafter. When, early in 735, a Silla emissary named Kim Sang-jŏng demanded that the Japanese court stop referring to his country in derogatory terms, Nara officials rejected his plea and threw the Silla party out of the country.

Abe no Ason left the capital in the 4th month of 736. Following the coastline along the Inland Sea, the emissaries made their way to Dazaifu in preparation for the short voyage to Korea (see Map 4). As many official travelers did in the eighth century, Abe no Ason and his party composed poetry along their journey.

The chief emissary thought of his home:

> We are our Sovereign's envoys
> We know this well.
> Yet after our long journey
> How we yearn for home! [18]

Abe was never to return home. When the party reached the small island of Iki just off the Kyushu coast, misfortune struck:

On the death of Yuki no Muraji Yakamaro from a sudden attack of pestilence upon his arrival at Iki

> O you, who were voyaging to the land of Korea
> As our Sovereign's deputy—
> Since you told your mother who suckled you
> "I shall return when autumn comes,"
> Weary months have passed.
> And your family waits and longs,
> "He may be home today,
> He will surely come tomorrow."
> But, have your kinsmen failed
> In their rites of purification?
> Have you failed in your duties?
> Before you reached the distant land,
> And far away from Yamato,
> You lie forever here
> On this isle of rugged rocks. [19]

Abe no Ason Tsugumaro contracted smallpox and died when the group made port in Tsushima. His mission never reached Silla's capital. Ōtomo no Sukune Minaka, Abe's second-in-command, also fell ill and was forced to remain outside Nara while an advance party notified the court of the fate of the emissaries. [20] As the party struggled home, they carried the disease with them along the Inland Sea.

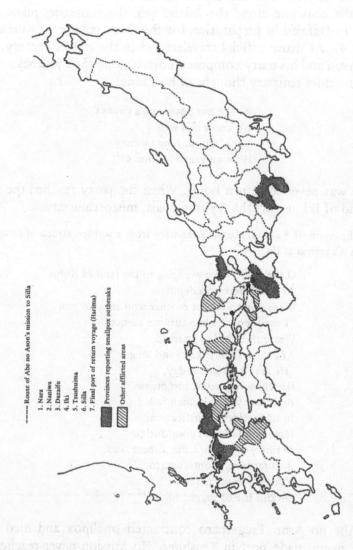

Map 4. The Great Smallpox Epidemic in 737

------- Route of Abe no Ason's mission to Silla

1. Nara
2. Naniwa
3. Dazaifu
4. Iki
5. Tsushima
6. Silla
7. Final port of return voyage (Harima)

▓ Provinces reporting smallpox outbreaks

▨ Other afflicted areas

Sources: The map is found in Aoki Kazuo, *Nihon no rekishi 3 Nara no miyako*, appendix. By permission of Chūō kōron sha. For the route of Abe no Ason's mission, see NKBT, *Man'yōshū* 4, #3578–#3722, 54/95. Areas afflicted with pestilence are noted in the text except for Suō (*DNK* 2/137), Bitchū (*DNK* 2/247–252), Tajima (*DNK* 2/58), Awaji (*DNK* 2/104), Izumo (*DNK* 2/201–247), and Kawachi (*DNK* 24/59–60).

Evidence on the epidemic in this year is abundant. Two amnesties declared in 737 mention the epidemic outbreak as an important factor in the formulation of government policies. The *Shoku Nihongi* repeatedly records orders for the chanting of sutras and prayers to Shintō deities. In the midst of these actions, a long laudatory account of a successful expedition against barbarians in the north reads suspiciously like an attempt to distract attention from domestic troubles.

Smallpox wracked the entire population of Japan in 737 (see Map 4). On the 19th day of the 4th month, Dazaifu announced continued distress from the epidemic. As in 735, the court reacted with prayers, medicine, and grain relief. In the 7th month, Yamoto, Izu, and Wakasa reported outbreaks as required by law; later in the same month, Iga, Suruga, and Nagato followed suit. In each case, courtiers permitted grain stored at provincial offices to be allocated to the sick. The nationwide scope of the disease is reflected in tax exemptions granted for all Japan in the 8th month of 737.

The farming populace was not the only level of society riddled by the epidemic. Many high-ranking officials also died in that year. Although the cause of death is never listed, the high mortality rate among the ruling elite was undoubtedly a result of the epidemic. In the 6th month, court business was postponed because of the great number of courtiers suffering from the infection. About two weeks later, Prince Nagata of imperial blood died. The most famous victims of the plague were the four Fujiwara brothers: Fusasaki, Umakai, Maro, and Muchimaro. The demise of all four Fujiwaras in 737 left control of the government to their bitter rival, Tachibana no Moroe.

The final summary in the *Shoku Nihongi* gives an apt description of the epidemic's toll:

In the spring of this year, an epidemic disease characterized by swellings raged widely. It came first from Tsukushi [Kyushu]. Through the summer and fall, people in the realm from aristocrats on down died one after another in countless numbers. In recent times, there has been nothing like this.

GOVERNMENT MEDICAL POLICY AND
IDENTIFICATION OF THE DISEASE

The final entry for the year 735 in the *Shoku Nihongi* identifies the infection as smallpox. But the annal does not name the disease that resulted in the crisis of 737. Because smallpox is similar to many other illnesses, such as measles, more information is required to identify the infection with certainty. In Europe, smallpox was often confused with other viruses.

A fuller description of the disease and its treatment survives. This fascinating order was issued by the Council of State:

The Council of State issues an order to the provincial offices of the Tōkaidō, Tōsandō, Hokurikudō, San'indō, San'yōdō, and Nankaidō.

In toto seven articles on personal care and dietary restrictions for those bedridden from the epidemic.

One: This infection is called "red swellings" [*sekihansō*]. When it first begins, it is similar to autumnal fevers. Suffering in bed lasts for three or four days in some cases, five or six in others, before the blotches appear. For three or four days as the swellings appear, the limbs and internal organs become hot as if on fire. At this time, the victim will want to drink cold water. (Firmly restrain him and do not let him drink.) When the swellings have gone down and the patient is about to recover, at last the fever will let up. Then diarrhea will start. If it is not brought under control quickly, the end result will be bloody stools. (The period when the diarrhea starts is not established.) Distresses which occur along with the infection are of four types. In some cases there are coughs [*shiwabuki*], in some vomiting [*tamahi*], in others the regurgitation of blood, and yet others nosebleeds. Of all secondary illnesses, diarrhea is the worst. Be aware of this, and strive diligently in personal care.

Two: Wrap the victim's abdomen and hips thoroughly in hemp cloth or floss silk. Without fail, keep the patient warm. Never let him become chilled.

Three: When there is no floor, do not lie directly on the earth. Spread a straw mat on the ground and lie down to rest.

Four: We recommend the drinking of rice gruel, either thick or thin, and broth made from boiled rice or millet. But do not eat raw fish or fresh fruits and vegetables. Also do not drink water or suck ice. Strictly restrain the patient. If diarrhea should develop, boil onions and scallions well and eat many. If the bowel movement turns bloody or white diarrhea occurs, mix in eight or nine parts of glutinous rice flour, boil, and drink while warm. Repeat this procedure two or three times. Also, eat either dried glutinous or non-glutinous rice as a thick gruel. If the diarrhea still does not stop, repeat this prescription five or six times. Do not be negligent. (In pounding dried rice, do not leave it coarse.)

Five: In general, people with this illness have no appetite. Force the patient to eat. From the moment the illness begins, put seaweed or salt in the victim's mouth from time to time. Even though the mouth and tongue fester, it is still wise to use these items.

Six: For twenty days after the illness passes do not carelessly eat raw fish or fresh fruit or vegetables; do not drink water, take a bath, have sex, force yourself to do anything, or walk in wind and rain. If you overdo it, a relapse will begin immediately. Diarrhea will start again. The condition of relapse is called "the quakes" [convulsions]. (An illness which begins again is named "the quakes.") How could even Yu Fu or Bian Zhuo put a stop to a relapse of the infection! After twenty days, if you want to eat fish, first boil or broil it well. Foods like dried abalone or bonito are fine whether boiled or not. (Dried fish is also acceptable.) Be careful not to eat mackerel or saurel even though dried. (Do not eat sweetfish under any circumstances.) Milk products, honey, and soya bean paste [*miso*] do not fall within the twenty-day dietary resrictions.

Seven: In general, if you want to bring this illness under control, do not use pills or powders. If a fever arises, take only a little ginseng boiled in water.

Concerning the above, since the 4th month all in the capital and Kinai have been bedridden with this disease. Many have died. We are also aware that people in the provinces have been afflicted with this distress. So we have written up this set of instructions. Each provincial governor should send it along to his neighbor. When it arrives, make a copy and designate one official at the district office [*gunji*] who holds the position of secretary [*shuchō*] or higher to act as the messenger. The messenger should go quickly to the next place without delaying. The provincial office shall make a tour of its jurisdiction and announce these instructions to the people. If they have no rice for gruel, the province shall make an estimate, grant grain relief from government stores, and report to the Council. When the order arrives, carry it out.

Ki no Ason, Great Liaison of the Right [*udaiben*], senior 4th rank, lower grade.

Mibu Tsukai no Nushi, Great Secretary of the Right [*udaishi*], junior 6th rank, lower grade and 11th merit rank.

Tempyō 1/6/26 [737] [21]

The opening paragraph directs the order to six of seven circuits in Japan. Only Kyushu was omitted, either because a prior policy was in effect, or because the disease had already run its course there. In 737, the government was facing a nationwide crisis.

The authors of the guidelines were anxious to see them implemented. According to the law codes, all orders dispatched to the provinces were to bear the imperial seal.[22] The *Ordinances of Engi* required an imperial seal for instructions to open provincial storehouses.[23] But no imperial seal was applied to the 737 order. In their haste to succor the populace, lawgivers used only the stamp of the Council of State. The procedure adopted for relaying the instructions strengthens the impression of official urgency.

The detailed instructions on personal care and diet during and after the illness are interesting. Chinese theory formed the basis for early Japanese medicine, and is reflected throughout the order, even to the reference to classical figures like Yu Fu and Bian Zhuo.[24] The practical recommendations of the Japanese court contrast sharply with the European reaction to the epidemic of bubonic plague in the fourteenth century. Western experts attributed the malady to earthquakes and the triple conjunction of Saturn, Jupiter, and Mars in the fortieth degree of Aquarius.[25]

Yet, one point is disturbing. Authors of the order identify the disease as *sekihansō*, "red pox." This term is neither the one used by the compilers of the *Shoku Nihongi* in 735 to mean smallpox (*mogasa, entōsō*) nor the accepted Chinese word for the disease (*hōsō*), but is the classical word for measles.[26] Some historians have suggested that the symptoms noted in the first article correspond more closely to measles than smallpox.[27] Scholars who contend that the Council's order refers to measles argue that two different infections caused the epidemics of 735 and 737.

A set of recommendations from the Bureau of Medicine resolves the debate:

The Bureau of Medicine investigates and reports on the treatment of smallpox [*hōsō*].

One: Dietary restrictions after the onset of the fever.
Do note drink water. (You will do harm to your heart, your palms will burn, and you will be unable to sleep.)
Eating and drinking a lot after falling ill will cause death.
Do not eat fatty or oily fish, whether cooked or raw. Do not consume carp, tuna, shrimp, mussels, mackerel, saurel, sweetfish, or sea bass. Eating them will cause diarrhea and you will be beyond help.
If you eat the five hot vegetables, your vision will become blurred. This is also true for fresh fruits and vegetables. (Heat them on your hearth.) If you do eat raw fish, do not drink rice wine. The resulting diarrhea is difficult to

treat. Distress arising from the consumption of oily and fatty foods is hard to control. Eating raw fish together with garlic will cause great harm. If you eat water oats with raw fish after the onset of the illness, diarrhea will begin.
If you drink rice wine and suffer a relapse, you will die right away. If you eat uncooked medicinal herbs and suffer a relapse, you will die. After recovery, abstain from all activities.
Stuffing yourself and drinking rice wine will lead to drunkenness and you will drink water. (If you begin to perspire do not clean yourself.)

Two: Treatment of the fever and the pox.
When the illness begins, and you become aware of it and wish to take some remedy, boil 5 ounces [*ryō*] of rhubarb and take some of it. Or put 2 ounces of birthwort root in 3 measures [*shō*] of water, boil it down to 1 measure and apply it to the swellings all over your body. Or boil 3 ounces of coptis root in 2 measures of water and, obtaining 0.8 of a measure, drink it down.
Or mix flour made from red beans with the white of a chicken egg and apply the paste to the pox.
Or mix a woman's menstrual flow with water and bathe in it.
Or wrap a small infant in a woman's menstrual cloth.

Three: Eliminating smallpox [*entōsō*] scars.
Cover pockmarks with yellow ocher powder.
Or mix powdered falcon feathers with lard and apply the mixture to the affected areas.
Or put white lead on them.
Or apply powdered silkworm cocoons.
Or put honey on them.

Concerning the above, we investigate and report in compliance with the imperial order.

Tempyō 9/6 [737] [28]   Director

The investigation of the Bureau of Medicine repeats many points in the Council's recommendations. Dietary restrictions and warnings about diarrhea correspond closely to the discussion in the Council instructions. The exact relationship between the two records is unclear, but medical officials probably first made a study of the pertinent Chinese texts. Advice from the specialists within the Bureau of Medicine then formed the nucleus for the command of the Council.

The Bureau's findings make clear the identity of the 737 disease. In contrast to the Council's instructions, the report of the Bureau employs the accepted Chinese terminology for smallpox (*entōsō*, *bōsō*). It is possible to state without doubt that the infection which took so many lives in the 730s was smallpox.

MORTALITY IN THE GREAT EPIDEMIC

Court records agree that many people died during the smallpox epidemic of 735 to 737. The *Shoku Nihongi* gives a strong impression of high mortality from the disease, especially once the infection reached the capital. The set of instructions issued by the Council of State attests to the national scope of the epidemic. Yet, neither source permits quantification of the plague's effect on population.

A more exact measure is available, however. The Shōsōin contains twenty-five provincial fiscal reports (*shōzei chō*) dating from 730 to the 760s. Although these ledgers are not in perfect condition, a careful analysis of local budgets can reveal in more precise terms the impact of the Tempyō pestilence on population.

The fiscal report served as the annual financial statement of a province to the central government. It described the current condition of provincial assets, including granaries and their holdings in rice, millet, and salt. Scribes also made entries on the health of the province's horses and the upkeep of postal and military equipment. The budget reads just like any ledger, with revenues listed first, followed by expenditures and the balance. The legal format of the budget is specified in detail in the *Ordinances of Engi.* [29]

Despite its importance in provincial finance, little is known about this document. The law codes do not explain the procedure for its compilation. The form and contents of the provincial fiscal report were not dictated by the Order of 717, as was the case for the tax register. [30] Local financial records were probably first compiled at the district level and then passed on to provincial officers, who completed the ledger near the end of the fiscal year. A low-ranking provincial worker (*shōzei chō shi*) was charged with the reponsibility of conveying the document to the capital. [31] The fiscal report underwent careful scrutiny at the Bureau of Taxation (*shuzei-ryō*) in the Population Ministry. [32]

By far the most important of all the province's assets were its stores of rice. [33] Holdings fell into two categories. First, the rice tax (*denso*) was collected each fall and stored as unhulled kernels in bins located throughout the province. The grain in these store-houses was then further classified as "unmovable" or "movable grain" according to use. "Unmovable grain" (*fudō goku*) was dispensed only in case of a national emergency. Stockpiles were begun in 708 and had grown to enormous proportions by the early 730s. As a symbol of the tight control over "unmovable grain," the keys to these granaries were kept in the capital. "Movable grain" (*dōyō goku*) was allotted regularly to the indigent.

The second major source of revenue, and the most important for quantification of mortality in the epidemic, was the interest that accrued from provincial rice loans. Based on the custom of communal sharing of seed rice, rice loans began to take on the character of a tax as early as the sixth century.[34] By the late 600s, a system of state-run rice loans had evolved as an integral part of government finance.[35] According to the system as it had developed by 735, provincial and district officers lent rice sheaves stored in granaries to local peasants for the spring planting. In the fall after the harvest, the principal came due with 50 percent interest.

Peasants could not always repay the loans they received from provincial bureaucrats. The provincial fiscal report listed two categories of defaults on provincial loans. First was the death of the borrower. In this case the borrower's family was relieved of any responsibility either to return the principal or pay the interest. A document from Bitchū (Okayama prefecture) shows that provincial headquarters made separate lists of peasants who defaulted for this reason.[36] Second, "uncollected rice" was a catch-all category which included defaults that had occurred for other reasons, such as illness or migration. Unpaid loans from previous years were also considered to be "uncollected rice."[37] Under normal circumstances, non-payment in both categories totaled about 10 percent.[38]

Table 15 shows the default percentages for five areas where provincial fiscal reports are extant for the epidemic years. The five provinces averaged about 33 percent non-payment on provincial loans, more than three times higher than normal. Almost a quarter of the defaults can be traced directly to the death of the borrower. The mean percentage of defaults due to the death of the borrower in the three hard-hit provinces of Bungo, Izumi, and Suruga is a startling 35 percent for the year 737 alone. If it can be assumed that the default percentages were an accurate indication of death tolls for the epidemic, then total mortality for the three

Table 15. Defaults on Provincial Rice Loans[a]

Province, District	Amount Loaned[b]	Defaults due to Death	%	Uncollected Rice	%	Total %
Satsuma, Takagi	10,100	135	1	0	0	1
Bungo, Kuzu	6,212	1,850	29	1,630	26	55
Bungo, Nahori	4,536	1,420	31	1,314	29	60
Nagato, Toyoura[c]	6,338	595	9	3,973.7	63	72
Nagato, (all)[c]	96,442	11,231	12	15,193.7	16	28
Izumi, Hine	8,000	1,810	23	1,646	21	44
Izumi, (all)	30,000	13,060	44	2,012	7	51
Suruga, unclear	27,900	9,456	33	0	0	33
Suruga, unclear	37,400	11,082	29	0	0	29
Total	212,590	48,234	23	20,149.7	10	33

Notes: a. Figures from Satsuma are for the year 736, while information for other provinces reflects non-payment in 737.

b. All calculations are in sheaves of rice.

c. In 737 no interest was charged on rice loans in Nagato province, and some rice was loaned out as grain. In drawing up this table, it was assumed that each stalk of rice yielded 0.05 *koku* of rice (about 1.2 liters), the standard rate of conversion throughout the eighth century.

years from 735 to 737 must have exceeded 60 or 70 percent in some areas, and could easily have ranged from 25 to 35 percent for all Japan.[39]

The estimation of national mortality from the smallpox epidemic was based on the following reasoning.[40] Surviving documents suggest that the epidemic attacked all Japan's major population centers and riddled several areas, like northern Kyushu and western Honshu, for two or three years. It by-passed only sparsely settled regions like southern Kyushu and northeastern Japan (see Map 4). When the high mortality in populous western and central Japan is averaged with the low death rates in the epidemic-free, sparsely inhabited parts of the country, the result would probably be similar to a one-year epidemic ranging over all Japan, or 25 to 35 percent. Given the lethal effects of smallpox in other cultures, most remarkably on the Incas and Aztecs, a death toll of 25 to 35 percent may actually be somewhat conservative.[41]

Statistics alone do not convey the full impact of the smallpox epidemic. According to an early-ninth-century law, the usual bor-

rowers of provincial rice loans were adult males.[42] The large percentage of defaults due to death, and thus the high mortality,
among adult borrowers indicates that the Tempyō outbreak was
the first encounter with smallpox for most Japanese.[43] Only the
elderly, who may have been exposed to the smallpox virus at some
earlier time, and children, whose immune systems were flexible
enough to rebound from the shock of an unknown infection,
would have fared better. After 737, many parts of Japan would
have been left with only a few productive young and middle-aged
adults, precisely when the other, more dependent, age groups
needed them most.

Three years of heavy mortality from the infection counterbalanced population gains made during the early part of the
century. If the 1 percent rate of increase posited in Chapter 1
continued from 702 to 735, losses of 25 to 35 percent from the
smallpox epidemic would have negated the growth. Fatalities
from the smallpox infection undoubtedly showed regional variation. In Mino province, some net growth may have remained
after the ravages of smallpox; lack of figures for Mino during
the epidemic makes any conclusion difficult to sustain. The plague
hit Kyushu first and hardest, and the effects on population there
were disastrous. The Tempyō epidemic may have triggered the
island's eventual decline to backwater status by the medieval era.

A population debacle of this magnitude is always accompanied
by changes in society. Four far-reaching government reforms were
enacted in the decade following the outbreak and must be interpreted in the context of depopulation from the epidemic. First, in
739, lawgivers rescinded the 715 Ordinance, which had established
numerous new households and administrative villages. Just as the
creation of new villages and households was to some extent a result
of the population boom of the early eighth century, repeal of the
715 Ordinance must be linked to the demographic contraction of
the 730s. It is instructive to recall that the decade-long plague in
fourteenth-century Europe was accompanied by the disintegration
of entire villages.[44]

Second, government leaders reorganized the system of provincial
loans in 745. According to provincial ledgers, granaries were full
before the plague. But the smallpox outbreak sharply reduced
revenues from the system of rice loans. Losses in 737 alone
amounted to more than 20 percent of all provincial stores in rice

sheaves. In addition, constant grain relief wiped out the reserves of rice grain.[45] Even rice listed as "unmovable grain" was in use not long after the onset of the crisis.[46] Depletion of provincial financial reserves required a new policy to replenish the lost holdings.

The new law announced in 745 established a system of tax-farming.[47] Each province was expected to derive its income from the loaning of rice sheaves; official quotas were set by the central government. Because governors received their salaries from the interest accruing to the rice loans, they had a stake in collecting as much as possible. The new system of tax-farming relied heavily on the honesty of the provincial elite, and eventually allowed local officials to build private fortunes by siphoning off the agricultural surplus which would normally have gone to the central government.

Third, the Great Smallpox Epidemic affected government policy toward Buddhism. The Emperor Shōmu was educated as a good Confucian ruler. He dispatched emissaries to the continent who returned with the latest in Tang musical instruments, weapons, and scholarship. When his nation was wracked by starvation and ravaged by infection, he felt personally reponsible. In 732, Emperor Shōmu accepted the blame:

Since the spring there has been drought, and into the summer there has been no rain. The rivers are dry and the five grains have been damaged. This situation has come about because of Our lack of virtue.[48]

Shōmu was even more contrite when the plague hit:

Recently untoward events have occurred one after the other. Bad omens are still to be seen. I fear the responsibility is all mine.[49]

Other edicts in Shōmu's reign show his deep-seated feelings of guilt over the plight of his country.

Shōmu buried such feelings in a growing devotion to Buddhism. His piety set the tone for Japanese culture during the Tempyō era and led to the construction of Tōdaiji and the Great Buddha housed therein. His growing attachment to Buddhism was also the moving force behind the order to build branch temples (kokubunji) all over Japan. The shift in state policy from strict control of Buddhism to generous financial support of the religion set an example later followed by Shōmu's daughter, the Empress Shōtoku, and her ally, the monk Dōkyō, and contributed to the bankruptcy of ritsuryō financial institutions.

Fourth, the smallpox epidemic was directly responsible for the most significant reversal of land policy in the *ritsuryō* era. In 743, peasants and aristocrats were given the right to hold in perpetuity all rice paddies they had cleared with their own capital. This law has been interpreted in both Japanese and English works as an act of greedy officials eager to increase their private landholdings.[50]

Other more powerful forces, however, were also at work. Recall the effects of the plague on rice revenues. Provincial budgets show that loans remained uncollected not just because of death, but owing to illness, migration, and other causes as well. The entry in the *Shoku Nihongi* that reads, "All men and women are in distress, agriculture has been forsaken, and the harvest has failed" states succinctly the impact of the epidemic on agriculture. In 736, law-givers tried to reverse peasant flight from their homes by altering laws on residence and vagrancy.[51] The 743 law permitting private possession of newly opened rice paddies was another attempt to compensate for the abandonment of fields and stabilize the rural economy.[52]

The Great Smallpox Epidemic was not solely responsible for these four major changes. Formulation of government policy is always a complex process. For instance, Kishi Toshio has implied that the political shift away from the Fujiwara after the deaths of Maro, Umakai, Fusasaki, and Muchimaro in 737 and the rise of the Tachibana clan were key elements in the institutional changes that took place in the following decades. But Kishi, too, emphasized the role of the epidemic.[53] Built on the population boom of the early 700s, *ritsuryō* institutions were rocked by the demographic crisis of the 730s.

OTHER EPIDEMICS IN THE RITSURYŌ PERIOD

The Great Smallpox Epidemic of 735 to 737 fits the pattern suggested by William McNeill almost perfectly. Although the precise origin of the infection is unclear, there is little doubt that it came from abroad. The killer took a heavy toll of the populace, especially among adults. Heavy mortality among the adult population meant that Japanese of the Tempyō era probably had never been exposed to smallpox before. After the pestilence had run its course, population density must have dropped to pre-702 levels in many areas.

McNeill's thesis in *Plagues and Peoples* calls for not just a single foreign-borne epidemic of high mortality, but for repeated ravages which could act as a damper on long-term population growth. Smallpox is pathologically well-suited to McNeill's interpretation. It is communicable only by humans who have contracted the disease. Animals do not carry the virus, as is the case for bubonic plague, nor is there chronic asymptomatic carriage of the disease. Smallpox is not a smouldering disease like tuberculosis, which kills the victim slowly over a period of years, but is quick-acting. Those who recover from the infection obtain life-long immunity but, most important, resistance cannot be passed along to the next generation. In a population where smallpox has not yet reached endemic status (signified by the infection's becoming a childhood disease), foreign-borne epidemics of heavy mortality could be repeated every generation.[54]

The historical record for smallpox in Japan also lends credence to McNeill's view. A ninth-century chronicler wrote in 853 that, "in the 2nd month, residents of the capital and outside the Kinai suffered from smallpox [bōsō]. Many have died. In 737 and 814, this disease appeared and this year again we have not been relieved of it."[55] A document written in the late eleventh century states that smallpox did indeed strike Japan about every generation well into the Heian period. Until 1061, smallpox plagues swept Japan at an average interval of thirty years.[56]

The 814 plague of smallpox shows a pattern similar to the 737 epidemic. Sources are fragmentary and a full account is difficult to obtain, but there is evidence that this infection also entered Japan from the continent. The initial report of pestilence came from the port of Dazaifu.[57] The disease spread slowly up the Inland Sea, eventually reaching the Eastern Mountain Route (Tōsandō). Fatalities amounted to "almost half" the population. The Kyushu peasantry was particularly harshly afflicted; the ravages of smallpox coupled with famine resulted in the formulation of a remedial agricultural policy for Kyushu.[58]

The origin and extent of other smallpox epidemics are unclear. Yet, what evidence there is hints at foreign origin and high death tolls. For example, a wave of smallpox swept Japan in 790, afflicting all persons in the capital aged 30 or less.[59] The disease also struck the countryside. Unlike the 737 outbreak, the 790 pestilence can be linked to a series of epidemics in several Chinese seaports regularly frequented by Japanese traders.[60]

Unfortunately, the record for most diseases is not as complete as it is for smallpox. Historical documentation, so rich for the Tempyō infection, is disappointingly fragmentary and cryptic for other epidemics. In most cases, neither the disease nor the death toll is clear. Many plagues were probably "seasonal fevers" (influenza) which spread among peasants during unusually harsh weather. Without more information, any interpretation of the record of Japanese epidemics remains subjective to some degree.

Yet, even when the infection and its extent are unknown, certain features do suggest the McNeill pattern. For instance, in 763, a plague struck the small island of Iki off the coast of Kyushu. Later the same year, Settsu and Yamashiro in the Kinai reported epidemics. By the eighth month of the following year, most provinces along the Inland Sea had announced similar outbreaks. The timing of the provincial reports implies that the pestilence entered Kyushu from the continent, and was carried up the Inland Sea by infected travelers and traders.

The record of epidemics in Tang China and Silla lends further credence to McNeill's position on plagues in Japan (see Appendix Table B). An almost point-to-point correspondence existed between plagues sweeping Europe and the Middle East and pestilence in China, Korea, and eventually Japan.[61] Until about 750, epidemics were transmitted by Turkish caravans following the Silk Route into China. After 750, sea voyagers from the Persian Gulf carried infections to the mouth of the Yangtze River, where Koreans and Japanese visiting the Middle Kingdom acquired the new viruses. China suffered especially severe losses from foreign-borne plagues. Populations throughout East Asia were gradually coming under the influence of a worldwide pool of killer parasites.

The Great Smallpox Epidemic of the Tempyō period was a classic example of the devastating, foreign-borne pestilence McNeill describes in *Plagues and Peoples*. Solid, although incomplete, evidence for similar epidemic outbreaks throughout the eighth and ninth centuries in Japan is also available. Disease patterns in the rest of East Asia corroborate the conclusions drawn from the Japanese evidence. Thus, the McNeill thesis which postulates recurrent epidemics of heavy mortality in the early period merits acceptance, and sustained, substantial population increase for *ritsuryō* Japan is out of the question.

A pattern of alternating growth and epidemics characterized the eighth and ninth centuries. Did this cycle also operate during the seventh century? There is little indication that any infection affected Japan for more than one hundred years prior to 702. The only outbreaks listed in Japan's first history, the *Nihon shoki*, are concurrent with the arrival of Buddhism to Japan. In 587, the *Nihon shoki* records:

Again the land was filled with those who were attacked with sores and died thereof. Persons thus afflicted with sores said:—"Our bodies are as if they were burnt, as if they were beaten, as if they were broken," and, so lamenting, they died. Old and young said privately to one another, "Is this a punishment for burning the Image of Buddha?"[62]

The 587 disease has sometimes been identified as smallpox, but the entry must be regarded with skepticism.[63] The pro-Buddhist faction at court may have invented the pestilence to discredit enemies responsible for the burning of the Buddha's image.

The long stretch without recorded epidemics can be viewed in two ways. First, the era can be seen as a period free from epidemic outbreak. If no plagues struck Japan, the seventh century must have witnessed unprecedented expansion. Continuous increase would have formed a demographic basis for the adoption of Chinese institutions in the mid-seventh century.

A second and more reasonable answer is that the epidemics of the seventh century and earlier went unrecorded. The seventh century is a particularly poorly documented period and the *Nihon shoki* is notoriously unreliable. A system for reporting and treating disease was not established until at least 689 and the implementation of the Kiyomihara Codes.

Evidence of heavy traffic between Japan and the continent deals a further blow to the idea that the seventh century was infection-free. Eleven groups of Japanese emissaries went to China in the 600s, while seven Chinese ambassadors visited Japan. If the *Nihon shoki* is to be believed, the sixth and seventh centuries saw about eighty missions to and from Korea. Unofficial trade and migration must have been even more frequent between Japan and the continent. Many lethal viruses had been known in China since early times, and with such frequent contact Japan could not possibly have escaped all bouts with plagues in the seventh century.

When did the plagues begin to recede? The eventual taming of

Japan's lethal epidemics is a topic beyond the scope of this book. But, according to Fujikawa Yū, neither smallpox nor measles seems to have reached endemic status until the thirteenth century. [64] By the 1200s, both diseases had become chronic in the Japanese population as infections of childhood; adults no longer commonly died from either disease. The decline of smallpox and measles plagues by the early medieval period is probably associated with a rise in population density and a sizeable increase in agricultural productivity.

CHAPTER THREE

Land Clearance

The most common argument for sustained population growth in early Japan is based on evidence of continuous land clearance. Support for this interpretation appears in the 723 law cited in Chapter 1:

The Council of State remonstrates: Recently population has gradually increased and farmland has become congested. We [the Council] request that the Empress [Genshō] encourage the people of the realm to open more lands.

The court repeatedly exhorted peasants to bring more land into cultivation in the eighth and ninth centuries. Although other orders do not mention population, it is generally believed that each law was enacted to relieve rural overcrowding.

Many historians have eagerly espoused the idea that land clearance was synonomous with the growth of early Japanese population. The words of Abe Takeshi reflect this assumption:

Flourishing activity in land clearance in the Nara and Heian periods is especially noteworthy. . . . In an economy based on land, a contradiction will appear when population increases on a fixed area. The only way to resolve the contradiction is to expand the land under cultivation. [1]

This argument originated in prewar times and has been widely accepted in the best Japanese and Western academic circles. [2]

The discussion of epidemics in Chapter 2 raised doubts about the conventional view of population growth in the *ritsuryō* period. Instead of constant expansion, I have argued that the eighth and ninth centuries were characterized by a pattern of repeated demographic boom and bust. In this chapter, I will question the widely held assumption that land clearance in *ritsuryō* Japan resulted in an overall increase in the acreage under cultivation.

LAND CLEARANCE IN THE LAW CODES

The law codes contain only one article on land clearance:

In cases where state or private land has gone out of cultivation for three years or more, and there is a person who is able to rent and farm the land, refer the matter to the proper government officials and hand down a decision to rent the parcel. Even though the land is far away from the person's residence, allow him to rent. In the case of private land, after three years return the parcel to the original cultivator. In the case of state land, after six years restore the field to the government. On the day when the time limit is reached, if the renter's land grant [*kubunden*] is less than the legal standard, in the case of state land only, immediately permit the assignment of such land to the renter's land grant. Do not allow this in the case of private lands.

If an official has wilderness [*kūkanchi*] within his jurisdiction and wants to cultivate the land, allow him to farm it as he pleases. On the day when he is dismissed or rotated to a new position, return the land to the state.[3]

Lawgivers attached much greater importance to renovating deserted fields (*kōhaiden*) than opening wilderness. In the first paragraph, the law sets a time limit for application to farm another's fields and establishes correct procedures for the rental of abandoned lands. It distinguishes between private and state parcels and makes provisions for the eventual restoration of rejuvenated fields to the control of the original cultivator. The second paragraph refers only in general terms to an official's right to clear wilderness while in office.

Japanese law strongly favored returning a cultivator to his abandoned parcels. The Taihō Codes stipulated that officials should "expend every effort on behalf of the original farmer" of deserted fields. Authors of the Yōrō Statutes deleted the passage in 717, but retained a mandatory three-year grace period during which the absent tiller could reclaim his land. In contrast, Tang law prescribed a mere two years before forfeiture of rights. The greater emphasis on the original cultivator's title in Japanese law may imply that there was enough land to go around: the court would have lost valuable revenues holding fields for an absent tiller if others needed the land. The longer grace period for Japanese cultivators may also be a recognition of the need to let deserted fields lie fallow for a time before resuming cultivation.

The codes also provide a clue to the cause of land abandonment. A Taihō commentator, whose work is known as "The Old Record" (*Koki*), explains: "When dikes are destroyed and cannot be repaired, and someone can fix them and cultivate the land, allow him to farm the parcel." This scholar, a man noted for his realism, emphasized poor technology as a major reason for desertion of once-productive fields.

The second part of the article is a brief treatment of the clearance of new lands (*kūkanchi*). According to the state-authorized interpretation of the early 800s, only provincial officials were given the right to clear wilderness. Because governors were the court's representatives outside the capital, they were a logical choice to play a major role in local agriculture. Many Japanese scholars believe that lawmakers actually intended to restrict the powers of the provincial elite by granting the right to open new lands only to incumbents. Other officials residing in the provinces and capital were legally prohibited from exploiting wilderness. Peasants were probably also permitted to open small plots of previously uncultivated land as long as they used their own resources.[4]

The statute on land clearance has two themes. First, it emphasizes the problem caused to the government by field abandonment. Maintenance of farmland was difficult and much effort was expended reopening deserted parcels. Second, developing new paddies from wilderness was a job essentially reserved to incumbent provincial officials. Other aristocrats were prohibited from engaging in the activity by the government and cultivators were limited to the land they could clear on their own.

SUBSEQUENT LEGISLATION

Lawgivers reformed the Taihō statute in 711:

We Ourselves proclaim an edict: Aristocrats ranked as imperial prince and below, and rich and powerful houses are enclosing wilderness and interfering with peasants' livelihoods. Henceforth, strictly ban this activity. In cases where wilderness is to be converted to fields, file an application with the provincial office and thereafter heed the decision of the Council of State.[5]

The 711 edict does not condemn nobles for converting their enclosures into rice fields. Rather, the privileged were criticized for preventing peasants from gathering food and fuel by partitioning off territory and failing to develop it.[6]

The court had denounced similar illegal practices in the past:

Recently aristocrats have enclosed many mountains and swamps, but make no effort to cultivate. They strive against each other in their covetousness and emptily hinder the use of the land. If peasants try to collect grasses, aristocrats rob them of their tools and cause them great hardship.[7]

Plans for land clearance were often a subterfuge for other activities. The object of much of the courtiers' greed was more land, not more rice paddies.

The 711 edict established a mechanism to control land hunger: a courtier desiring to occupy an area with the intent of opening new fields was ordered to file with the proper provincial office. As in the codes, governors were expected to take the lead in such projects. Each application undoubtedly contained descriptions of the area and location planned for development. Once the provincial governor consented to the scheme, he sent it to the Council of State, where final approval was given.

In 722, the Council of State formulated the first of many policies to increase the amount of land under cultivation:

. . . We request the encouragement of agriculture and stockpiling of grain as a precaution against flood and drought. Thus we will charge officials to conscript laborers and open a million *chō* of high-grade fields. They should limit labor to ten days per worker, grant food and provisions, and lend government goods to make implements. After the harvest, have them make more tools for the next year.

If provincial or district officials act fraudulently and let their projects stagnate, and do not permit the opening of lands, dismiss them. Even if there is an imperial amnesty, do not pardon them.

If the people of the region apply their efforts to wilderness and harvest 3,000 *koku* or more of any grain, bestow the 6th merit rank on them. If they harvest 1,000 *koku* or more, do not conscript them for corvée for the rest of their lives. If they already hold the 8th court rank or higher, promote them one level in merit. If, after being rewarded, people become lazy and do not farm, then confiscate their certificate of court rank and return each person to his original status.[8]

Eighteen months earlier, in 720, rebellious natives of Mutsu (northeastern Japan) had murdered Kamitsukenu no Ason Hirohito, an official of the north. The court had then commissioned

Shimotsukenu no Ason Iwashiro to serve as the leader of a punitive expedition. The order to open wilderness lands should be seen as a step in bringing Mutsu under firmer imperial control.[9]

The Mutsu scheme was not realistic. Even in the medieval era, all Japan did not possess a million *chō* (about 3 million acres) of high-grade fields. Conscripting enough laborers and making sufficient tools to clear such a large expanse would have been a herculean task, especially in a hostile region like Mutsu. Awards of court and merit rank were aimed at gaining the cooperation of local notables, but sources do not record any instances of such rewards actually being granted during the time the law remained in effect. The 722 order should be viewed as a general exhortation, not a concrete plan.

The authors of the Mutsu plan did not specify the grain to be planted, implying that dry-cropping may actually have been intended. Severe drought had afflicted Japan in 721, and a steady supply of water for irrigation of paddy rice was probably difficult to secure.[10] Inadequate irrigation was once again recognized by lawgivers as a problem, just as in the Taihō statute on land clearance.

The 722 scheme refers to the abandonment of new fields. "Lazy" people cleared new lands, received awards of court rank, and then stopped cropping their parcels. Cultivators may have seemed indolent to the court, but their behavior can also be seen as a product of concrete factors like technology, climate, and soil conditions.

A year later, in 723, another step was taken to invite the creation of more paddy land:

The Council of State remonstrates: Recently population has gradually increased and farmland has become congested. We request that the Empress [Genshō] encourage the people of the realm to open more lands.

If a person builds new ditches and ponds and clears new lands, grant him the lands without regard to area and make them heritable for three generations. If he follows old ditches and ponds, allot him the land for his lifetime.[11]

Additional mouths to feed had placed an even greater strain on peasant communities where fields often did not stay in continuous production. The government offered long-term tenure to developers to solve the problem posed by growing population.

According to Tokinoya Shigeru, a precise relationship existed

between the 723 law and the Taihō statute on land clearance.[12]
The provision in the 723 law which granted lifetime tenure for the
opening of paddies where irrigation works were intact probably
referred to the reopening of abandoned lands. A person who reno-
vated a deserted field could now expect to hold the parcel for his
lifetime, instead of the three to six years specified in the 702 code.
The clause concerning the construction of new ditches and ponds
applied only to the clearance of wilderness. A pioneer who opened
paddies in the wilderness could keep the land in his family for
three generations.

In 743, twenty years after the edict of 723, lawgivers promul-
gated the most famous land law in premodern Japanese history.
The most complete text appears in the *Shoku Nihongi:*

We Ourselves issue an edict: Thus it has been heard: "According to a Yōrō
7 [723] regulation, newly opened fields should be confiscated in the manner prescribed by law after the time limit on tenure has been reached. Because of this, peasants are lazy, clear land, and then abandon it. Hereafter
let land be a private possession freely without reference to a lifetime or three
generations. Never let anyone be dispossessed.

"Grant imperial princes of the 1st degree and those holding the 1st court rank
the right to open 500 *chō.* Bestow on princes of the 2nd degree, and courtiers
of the 2nd rank the rights to 400 *chō.* Assign those with the 3rd and 4th imperial ranks or the 3rd court rank 300 *chō,* the 4th court rank 200 *chō,* the
5th 100 *chō,* the 6th through the 8th 50 *chō,* and to those of the initial rank
down to the undistinguished grant rights to 10 *chō.* Permit greater and lesser
magistrates [*tairyō; shōryō*] 30 *chō,* and the administrative officer [*shusei*]
and secretary [*shuchō*] 10 *chō.* [All are district officials.] If there are cases in
which a person was allotted land previously and his holdings exceed these
limits, confiscate excessive lands according to convenience. Fraud and decep-
tion will be punished according to law."

Provincial officers should obey the previous regulations on newly opened
lands as long as they hold their posts.[13]

Another source adds this provision:

But when a person occupies land with the intent of clearing fields, first let
him go to the provincial office and make an application. Thereafter let him
open the land. Let no one in this way occupy and apply for land in a way
that interferes with people. If, after receiving the rights to land, the developer
does not open fields in three years, allow another person to develop the land.

Tempyō 15/5/27   [743][14]

Peasant indolence is once again the chief culprit in official eyes. By 743, lawgivers suspected that a defect in the 723 regulation was responsible for cultivators' behavior: peasants left fields they had cleared because they were not guaranteed permanent possession. The proposed remedy to the problem was the abolition of the time restrictions established in 723.

The Great Smallpox Epidemic of 735 to 737 was a major factor in the decision to eliminate time restrictions on the tenure of fields. Even in pestilence-free years, a Japanese who survived infancy could expect to live only about 40 years. If the parallel of medieval Europe is at all applicable, life expectancy during the epidemic may have dropped by as much as half. Granting land to a peasant for his lifetime, as lawgivers did in the 723 law, would be little reward to the family of a person who died in young adulthood. A peasant would seek greater security such as the right to keep new fields within his family. Repealing the time limits was a natural response to the high mortality inflicted by the deadly smallpox virus.

The 743 law did not authorize unlimited land clearance, but established new restraints.[15] In place of the time restrictions devised in 723, legislators made the amount of land a person might clear dependent upon his social status. Allowances for each rank were based on an article in the Chinese codes, and these limitations were enforced vigorously. Unlimited land clearance was forbidden until the Heian period, when area restrictions were probably rescinded.

The 743 law placed constraints on the area a person might plan to clear. The new allowances should not be confused with actual fields. At a time when land could not be kept under cultivation reliably, and when designs for new fields exceeded their realization, bureaucrats found it simpler to control the amount of land enclosed rather than the actual area under cultivation. To understand the 743 law, land abandonment, as well as land clearance, must be taken into consideration.

The new legislation on land clearance ensured that plans for converting wasteland into rice paddies were realistic. All projects had to be completed within three years of approval. If a peasant failed to open lands to which he had title, the law permitted another person to apply for the right to open the area. The chief function of the three-year restriction was to prevent court aristocrats and local notables from enclosing land without opening new fields, a problem noted in the 711 edict.

Three years seems like ample time to convert wilderness into productive fields, but usually it was not long enough. According to an 896 order of the Council of State, most people could manage to clear only 30 or 40 percent of their stake within the prescribed three years.[16] Others, presumably aristocrats, then argued that the peasant developer had failed to meet the provisions of the 743 law, and requested the right to cultivate the land. Provincial and district officers had no choice but to act in the plaintiff's favor. To correct this defect, the Council ordered that the opening of only 20 percent of one's claim within three years was sufficient to prevent reassignment of the land.

The 711, 722, 723, and 743 laws all have a common purpose— to encourage the extension of cultivated land. But exhortation should not be confused with accomplishment. The necessity to repeat pronouncements actually indicates the failure of government policies to expand the amount of land producing crops and yielding taxes.

Different conditions required dissimilar means to the same end: the opening of new lands. Population pressure was a factor on only one occasion, in 723. In 711, the aim of policy was to prevent aristocratic obstruction of peasant activities and to make land hunger profitable by ensuring that developers actually opened the lands they enclosed. In 722, settlement of the northern frontier spurred issuance of a new law. In 743, the government acted to return stability to rural areas depopulated in the Great Smallpox Epidemic of 735 to 737.

The major problem faced by officials was maintaining fields in continuous production. Making room for more peasants occasionally made their work even more difficult. Yet the long-range problem was not too many people for too little land, but too few farmers sporadically cultivating wide-open spaces.

EARLY EXAMPLES OF LAND CLEARANCE

Few records depict farming conditions in more detail than a 740 report from Hamana district in Tōtōmi province.[17] The Tōtōmi document is a register of land tax receipts (yuso chō) and describes the effects of one of the typhoons that frequently ravaged the

area. In submitting the account, local officials sought to gain remission of the land tax in accordance with the codes. The information necessary to receive such authorization included the
amount of farmland, its legal status, and a list of those peasants
whose crops were ruined by the typhoon.

Of the slightly less than 1,100 *chō* in the area, about 230 *chō*,
or nearly 21 percent, were no longer under cultivation (see Table
16). All 16 *chō* recently opened by residents of Hamana had been
abandoned. These lands had not been deserted because of the
typhoon, as its toll was calculated only for land sown in the
spring. Fields listed as abandoned in the report had not been
planted at all in 740.

Hamana peasants deserted certain kinds of fields more frequently
than others. Almost half (49 percent) of the surplus land was not
farmed. Surplus fields (*jōden*) were paddies that remained after
the allocation of land grants and entailed payment of four to seven
times the tax owed for the land grant. Thus, tax evasion probably
stimulated some land abandonment.

Agricultural technology was also a factor in the miserable farming conditions at Hamana. Fields were located at the mouth of
Lake Hamana in modern Shizuoka prefecture. Most of the land
was swampy and low-lying, and local peasants suffered frequently
from flooding.[18] They could not protect themselves from changes
in the lake's water level, nor did they possess engineering technology adequate to raise water and flood paddies far from the
lake. The only form of irrigation employed by peasants in Hamana
was probably the seasonal fluctuation in the region's water table,
as practiced by their Yayoi forebears.

A document issued by Gufukuji (Kawaradera) describes the
state of farmlands in the Kinai in a similar fashion.[19] Gufukuji was
one of the most powerful temples of the eighth century. Its farmland was located in Kuze district in Yamashiro (west of the modern
city of Uji on the Asuka plain), where many other temples administered lands in the early period.

Desertion of fields was a serious problem even for Gufukuji
(see Table 17). Abandoned land accounted for about 40 percent
of all parcels under Gufukuji's control. This percentage remains
constant even for high-grade lands; several large, high-grade parcels
were almost totally deserted. Because the temple was located in

Table 16. Farming Conditions in Hamana District, Tōtōmi Province, 740

Land Category	Area[a]	Abandoned Fields	Percent
Land grants	880.4.276	127.0.060	14
Surplus lands	170.3.220	83.7.135	49
Newly opened fields	16.6.236	16.6.236	100
Office lands	15.6.000	—	—
Other	3.0.133	—	—
Total	1086.1.145	227.4.071	21

Note: a. Areas are given in *chō.tan.bu.* One *chō* = about 3 acres or 1.2 hectares, and is composed of 10 *tan.* One *tan* = 360 *bu.*

Table 17. Rice Farming in Yamashiro Province, 743

A. High-Grade Fields

No.	Area[a]	Abandoned
1	0.2.072	—
2	0.1.216	—
3	0.9.243	0.8.315
4	0.4.000	0.4.000
5	0.0.095	—
6	1.0.000	0.9.144
7	0.5.140	0.0.284
8	1.0.000	0.1.000
9	0.9.288	0.8.144
10	0.4.167	0.4.123
11	0.1.216	0.1.016
12	0.0.324	—
13	0.8.044	—
14	0.1.072	—
15	0.0.259	—
16	0.5.136	—
17	0.8.000	—
18	0.8.108	0.0.007
	9.1.220	3.7.313
	(41% abandoned)	

B. Low-Grade Fields

No.	Area[a]	Abandoned
19	0.0.144	—
20	0.1.317	0.0.101
21	0.1.029	0.0.317
22	0.3.127	0.2.127
23	0.1.048	0.0.048
24	0.1.073	0.0.145
	0.9.018	0.4.018
	(44% abandoned)	

	Area	Abandoned
A + B:	10.0.238	4.1.331
	(42% abandoned)	

Source: Torao Toshiya, *Handen shūju hō no kenkyū,* p. 469. By permission of Yoshikawa Kōbunkan.

Note: a. Area is listed in *chō.tan.bu.*

Asuka near these fields, the abbots were undoubtedly aware of the problem in managing the Kuze lands.

Gufukuji had held these lands since at least 709.[20] Could some of its holdings have been abandoned because of soil exhaustion? Under optimal circumstances in the modern world, soil exhaustion does not occur in wet-rice agriculture.[21] However, in an era when irrigation was unreliable and fertilizer was not widely used, depletion of soil minerals was probably frequent and widespread.

EARLY SHŌEN

In 743, six months after issuance of the edict permitting permanent private possession of newly cleared fields, the Emperor Shōmu ordered the construction of a great statue of the Buddha and a temple to house it.[22] At the time, Shōmu's court resided at Shigaraki, southeast of Lake Biwa in Ōmi province, and initial work began there on Tōdaiji, the most famous temple of the *ritsuryō* era. In 745, when the government returned to Nara, the construction shifted sites. In the 8th month of the same year, Shōmu and his consort Kōmyō participated in a groundbreaking ceremony for the statue.[23]

In 749, when the statue was nearing completion, Emperor Shōmu and his entourage made another pilgrimage to the construction site.[24] Shōmu's purpose was to announce the discovery of gold in Mutsu and to reward officials responsible for the find. In a proclamation (*semmyō*) issued during the ceremony, Shōmu announced plans to grant several Buddhist temples the right to develop rice paddies throughout Japan. Later in 749, court bureaucrats set a limit of 4,000 *chō* for Tōdaiji's projects. Produce from the new fields was to finance the building of pagodas and halls, which continued for the rest of the century.

Officials established a special agency called the Office for the Construction of Tōdaiji (*zō Tōdaiji shi*) to oversee the activities of the new temple. The new commission was organized in four tiers (*yontō kan*) like many other government offices. In 748, it began collecting building materials, mobilizing and provisioning laborers, and financing construction.[25] The Office also managed a bureau where sutras were copied for the faithful. By the end of the 700s, the Office for the Construction of Tōdaiji was as large as any ministry in the central government.

The Office served as a liaison between temple officers and

regional bureaucrats. For instance, when the monk Heiei went to Echizen (Fukui prefecture) in 749 to enclose wilderness for one of Tōdaiji's most important projects, he was accompanied by an official of the Construction Office, Ikue no Omi Azumabito. Azumabito was an Echizen native and provided contacts with local bureaucrats like Tsukimoto no Oyu, a district secretary, and Mutobe no Azumabito, a provincial worker. Later, when the clearance of land commenced, Azumabito moved back to his home in the Asuwa district of Echizen, where he succeeded his relative Yasumaro to the hereditary post of Asuwa magistrate and acted as foreman of Tōdaiji's first *shōen*. The pattern of cooperation between central and local authorities was repeated in other areas, and shows that Tōdaiji drew upon the great knowledge and resources of both local and capital elites.

Only a few cases permit more than a glimpse of agricultural conditions at Tōdaiji's projects. First is Kuwabara *shōen* in Sakai district, Echizen province (north central Fukui), where some land had already been opened under Ōtomo no Sukune Maro, a court aristocrat. He sold the rights to 100 *chō* of land to Tōdaiji in 755.[26] Maro received 180 strings of copper cash for the land, and was raised to the 4th court rank.[27]

The bill of sale indicates that Tōdaiji still had a great deal of work to do on the *shōen:* only 32 *chō* had been cleared. A report issued under Azumabito's authority in the spring of 755 states that Maro had opened only 9 *chō* before the sale.[28] Azumabito takes credit for developing the remaining 23 *chō* in 755.

Annual reports from Azumabito and other officials present detailed information on the operations at Kuwabara during its early years.[29] The 757 account relates that the land originally farmed by Maro went out of cultivation. Seven *tan* (2.1 acres) of land cleared by Azumabito in 755 are also listed as abandoned. The desertion of these fields negated the efforts of Azumabito, who had developed 10 more *chō* earlier in 757. Azumabito had about 5 *chō* cleared in 758, but Maro's lands remained unproductive.

A later record bearing Azumabito's signature describes the problem with Maro's lands:

The messengers of Echizen province report on conduits and ditches which the office at Kuwabara should open.

Altogether three places:

Productive land that will be ruined: 1.8 *chō* (All of this is land granted to peasants.)

Expenditures: 2,700 sheaves of rice.

Manpower: 1,500 units paid 1,500 sheaves of rice (1 sheaf per unit).

Provisions: 600 sheaves of rice (0.4 sheaves per unit).

One: A ditch 1,230 *jō* long, 1.2 *jō* wide, and 5 *shaku* deep.
Manpower: 1,230 units.

Two: A ditch 300 *jō* long, 6 *shaku* wide, and 4 *shaku* deep.
Manpower: 200 units.

Three: Repair of Udemi ditch, 210 *jō* long, 5 *shaku* wide, and 3.5 *shaku* deep.
Manpower: 70 units.

24 conduits: 6 conduits 5 *jō* long,
                3 *shaku* wide;
             6 conduits 2.5 *jō* long,
                3 *shaku* wide;
            12 conduits 1.5 *jō* long,
                3 *shaku* wide.

Thirteen conduits were here from the beginning (3 were damaged, 10 in working condition).

Fourteen conduits to be dug now at a total cost of 670 sheaves of rice.

Six conduits 5.3 *jō* long, 3 *shaku* wide.

Cost 420 sheaves (70 sheaves per conduit).

Six conduits 2.5 *jō* long, 3 *shaku* wide.

Cost 210 sheaves (35 sheaves per conduit).

Two conduits 1.5 *shaku* long, 3 *shaku* wide.

Cost 40 sheaves (20 sheaves per conduit).

Concerning the above, there was a ditch here from before which reached Ōtomo's lands. But the ditch was low and the fields were high, and thus the land has gone out of cultivation. Even though all this land was opened previously, we could not rent it to peasants. If we dig the above-noted ditches, the fields already cleared ought to be good land and the remaining wilds can be opened in a year or two. When we consider these points, the losses from ruined peasant fields are small and our profits are great. We request that the temple issue a report [*chō*] to the provincial office. If the office does not permit the reopening of these once-productive fields, we request an exchange of temple lands for land now under cultivation.

Thus we note fully conditions here, entrust this document to Awata no Hitomaro and appeal for your disposal of this matter. Hereby we report.

Tempyō Hōji 1/11/12 [757]

Temporary assistant [*sanji*] of Sakai,

Ato no Sō
Chief magistrate of Asuwa district,
Ikue no Omi Azumabito
Provincial clerk [*shishō*],
Ato no Sukune Otari[30]

The report specifies that Maro's fields were abandoned because
of poor engineering. Udemi ditch, which had been dug by Maro,
was not adequate to supply water to the new fields Azumabito
had opened. According to Hara Hidesaburō, the ditch was probably
not efficient enough to irrigate continuously even Maro's 9 *chō*
of paddies.[31]

Kuwabara peasants were left with two options to restore Maro's
land to productivity. First, they could rely on the natural fluctuation of the water table, a practice followed by the farmers at
Hamana. Some fields were probably situated on low-lying, swampy
terrain which was well suited for such a cultivation technique.
Cultivators working the soil in this way relied heavily on receiving
adequate amounts of rain and sun at the right times; even in good
times productivity was low.

Second, Kuwabara engineers could dig more ditches to draw
water from the Takeda River, which curved in a wide arc to the
east of their fields. The length of the ditches specified in the report was adequate to this task.[32] The expensive plan to dig more
ditches and build conduits applied the highest technology of the
eighth century and was available only to aristocrats and rich institutions like Tōdaiji.

Cultivators seeking to tap the flow of the Takeda River would
have had to channel water over the river's natural embankment.
Today, farmers use electric pumps to raise water from the river to
their paddies, but the Kuwabara peasants lacked even a simple
water wheel to perform this function. Because access to the
Takeda was so difficult, Maro's 9 *chō* may have remained barren
even with a sizeable investment in new ditches and conduits.

Tapping the Takeda River also carried a social cost. Officers
of Tōdaiji were forced to wreck nearly 2 *chō* of peasant fields to
build sluices and conduits. The high-handed act required the
acquiescence of the Echizen provincial office, but the permission
of local officials would hardly have assuaged the feelings of Echizen cultivators. Peasant hostility against Tōdaiji occasionally boiled
over, and resistance took the form of sabotage against the temple's

projects. In Enuma district (southwestern Ishikawa prefecture) the filling of ditches caused 13 *chō* to go out of cultivation.[33] A social factor must not be discounted in explaining land abandonment.

Takaba *shōen* in Takakusa district, Inaba province (west of modern Tottori City) was another of Tōdaiji's projects. Although established in a manner similar to Kuwabara and at about the same time, Takaba developed along different lines.[34] In 756, Heiei and a group of district and provincial officials surveyed about 68 *chō* of wilderness. Nine years later, in 765, Tōdaiji purchased an additional 6 *chō* from a member of the Takakusa elite named Kuni no Miyatsuko Katsuiwa.[35]

Tōdaiji's fortunes in Inaba province changed in 801 when the monks of the great temple sold about 55 *chō* to Fujiwara no Ason Tsunanushi. The reason for the sale is of special interest: "I [Fujiwara no Ason] have heard that the land you have selected is of no profit to the temple. If it is for sale, I would like to buy it for 4,000 sheaves of rice."[36] Two years later, all land remaining from the 756 enclosure was sold to the governor of Inaba province, Fujiwara no Ason Fujitsugu. Development of the original Takaba lands still proceeded slowly and fitfully, despite the change in ownership.

Tōdaiji retained the 6 *chō* it had bought from Katsuiwa. An 843 record reveals that only about a third of the remaining fields at Takaba was farmed in 842 (see Table 18). Reasons for desertion varied. One small parcel was ruined when a river suddenly altered its course, and almost 3 *chō* were abandoned because of repeated drought or flood. All the abandoned parcels were located on soft, marshy terrain.[37] The high incidence of burnt and flooded fields at Takaba suggests that inadequate irrigation was a major problem afflicting cultivators trying to open and farm new fields.

Tōdaiji also laid claim to lands in Etchū province (central Toyama). The *shōen* in Etchū were established in 749, at about the same time as those in Echizen. Like Echizen, land clearance in Etchū drew support from both provincial and district officials. When Heiei traveled to Etchū to enclose new lands, his host was the Provincial Governor, a famous poet, Ōtomo no Sukune Yakamochi. At a farewell banquet in 749, Yakamochi proposed a toast to his cleric guest:

> Send more guards
> To Tonami Pass
> Starting tomorrow!
> Let us keep you here![38]

Yakamochi continued to assist Tōdaiji into the next year.

Heiei and his party received more local support from Tonami no Omi Shirushi, the Chief Magistrate of Tonami district in Etchū. Their relationship was of long standing. In 747, two years before Heiei's expedition to Etchū, Shirushi had contributed 3,000 _koku_ of rice toward the construction of the Great Buddha. Tonami was also rewarded with advancement to the 5th court rank in recognition of his gift of 100 _chō_ of wilderness to the temple in 767.[39]

Table 18. Agriculture in Inaba Province, 842

Parcel	Area[a]	Percent of Total
Productive fields	1.9.324	34
Abandoned land	0.3.216	7
River erosion	0.1.000	2
Drought/flood	2.8.080	47
Other ruined lands	0.6.272	12
Total	5.9.172[b]	

Notes: a. Area is given in _chō.tan.bu_.
      b. The document lists total area as 5.8.216.

Three reports and fourteen maps depict the state of agriculture in Etchū (see Appendix Table C).[40] Because the figures in two reports, compiled within six months of each other in 767, do not match, these records cannot be considered completely reliable. Several explanations for the discrepancies have been advanced, but none has yet been widely accepted.[41] The maps also contain many errors and often contradict one another. Thus, care is necessary in using these materials.[42]

Land clearance proceeded slowly in Etchū. According to the more reliable of the two 759 reports, only about 26 percent of the wilderness had been converted to farmland ten years after Heiei's trip. Expanding the land under cultivation was difficult, even with close cooperation from local notables. By 767, the documents lead one to believe that officials had managed to increase the productive acreage to more than 400 _chō_, which would have been about half the temple's holdings in Etchū. But workers were unable to expand Tōdaiji's fields beyond 400 *chō*.

By 767, written documents and maps both indicate that land abandonment had become a significant factor in Etchū. Between 19 and 24 percent of Tōdaiji's fields were no longer under cultivation by this time. In a few cases, field desertion had become unmanageable. At Kinabiru, 48 percent of the fields had been abandoned. At Suka, almost two-thirds of all parcels were not in cultivation in 767. Fields in Etchū were difficult to open and, once opened, required hard work to maintain.

The causes for land abandonment in Etchū were the same as those noted earlier. Historians and geographers agree that the Etchū *shōen* were established in low-lying, swampy areas, and that irrigation was poor.[43] Social conflict also played a role in field desertion. Etchū records show that peasants resisted intrusions by Tōdaiji officials by filling in irrigation ditches and destroying dikes.[44]

Kuwabara, Takaba, and Etchū were not the only examples of land clearance in the early period. Records are extant for other *shōen* in Ōmi, Awa, and Mino, although they do not depict farming conditions in the detail of the Echizen and Etchū reports. But most of Tōdaiji's early *shōen*, which commanded so much attention in the eighth century, share one common feature: by the middle of the Heian period, nearly all the land had gone out of cultivation. In 951, Tōdaiji officials described 3 Echizen *shōen* as follows: "Even though the outlines of the fields [*jōri*] still exist, the area is all wilds and swamps, and the cultivators are gone."[45] A Tōdaiji report on the Echizen *shōen* dated 998 reads: "Most land has gone out of cultivation. Only a little is productive."[46] Projects in Etchū, Echigo, Harima, Inaba, Sūo, Awa, Iyo, Kii, Mino, and Kaga also suffered the same fate.

By the middle of the Heian era, both Tōdaiji and the central government which had supported it had entered a period of decline. The loss of political clout is partially responsible for the collapse of so many of the temple's *shōen*. Elaborate institutional arrangements had been instrumental in the formation of the *shōen*; when the institutions waned, Tōdaiji's economic enterprises also suffered. But, in most cases, other individuals or institutions did not undertake farming these once-productive lands when Tōdaiji left. The decline of Tōdaiji's *shōen* is testimony to the constant care necessary to maintain its far-flung rice paddies, and raises doubts about the view that *ritsuryō* land clearance resulted in substantial permanent expansion of Japan's farmland.[47]

LAND CLEARANCE IN THE EARLY AND MIDDLE HEIAN PERIOD

In 824, the Council of State again addressed the problem of field abandonment:

The Council of State orders: People should be made to farm deserted fields [*jōkōden*] in the provinces.

Concerning the above, the remonstrance of Kiyowara no Mabito Natsuno, Governor of Shimōsa, General of the Left Imperial Guard, and Advisor [*sangi*] with the rank of lower 4th senior grade, says: "In addition to land that cannot be cultivated [*fukanden den*], there is also land that is permanently out of cultivation [*jōkōden*]. As long as people are farming a parcel, provincial officials collect the land tax. People fear this burden and customarily avoid cultivation. I request that [the Emperor Junna] allow the farming of land permanently out of cultivation for a whole lifetime. Only after six years collect the land tax as in the law codes."

The Minister of the Right [*udaijin*] announced: "I have received an imperial edict. 'Comply with the remonstrance. But do not permit peasants to use water from ponds, ditches, and sluices built with state-conscripted labor. Let the powerful not cultivate these lands.'"

Tenchō 1/8/20 [824][48]

Legislators distinguished between two types of abandoned fields: "those which cannot bear cultivation" (*fukanden den*), and "parcels permanently deserted" (*jōkōden*). Historians have debated the meaning of these terms.[49] Some believe that fields in the former category were farmed intermittently, while permanently deserted parcels were so barren that the government had no hope of enticing tillers to return. Sakamoto Shōzō has argued that the distinction was a matter of institutional convenience and was unrelated to a field's fertility. But all scholars agree that field abandonment was a constant problem in the ninth and tenth centuries.

The first half of the ninth century was a period of repeated epidemics and drought in Japan. Fatalities and flight from the land induced by these calamities were major factors in the unstable character of farming in the early Heian era. An 841 regulation makes the connection between disease and field desertion explicit:

... People know of this law [the 824 regulation] and begin cultivation. But, after only a few years, they succumb to an early death. Thereupon their labors in land clearance are wasted, and peasants cannot secure a harvest in consecutive autumns. In this way, they become fearful and have no heart for opening new lands.[50]

The pattern of clearance, desertion, and reopening of fields continued well into the Heian period. Consider the *shōen* of the Buddhist temple Eizanji in Yamato.[51] Eizanji was located in Uchi district (west central Nara prefecture), and was one of the most powerful temples of the mid-Heian era. Its lands were adjacent to the temple grounds along the Yoshino River.

A large cache of documents records variations in the amount of land cropped in each of 35 1-*chō* units. According to the fifteen surveys covering the period from 990 to 1059, cultivation of almost half Eizanji's domain (17 *chō*) fluctuated dramatically. In some years, fields were extensively farmed, in others they were not. Thirteen *chō* were planted somewhat more regularly. Only 4 *chō* under Eizanji's control were listed as being fully cropped in each of the records. According to Toda Yoshimi, who first analyzed the Eizanji documents, variation in the area under cultivation was haphazard rather than regular, as in a fallow system.[52] Toda attributes the unstable farming regime in Eizanji's *shōen* to an inability to secure a steady supply of water.

Agrarian historian Furushima Toshio was one of the first scholars to analyze land clearance in early Japan.[53] He noted that an encyclopedia of the mid-tenth century called the *Wamyō shō* listed Japan's arable land at 862,000 *chō*, while a compilation of the mid-1300s, the *Shūgai shō*, tallied only 946,000 *chō*. Furushima interpreted these figures to mean that most land had already been brought into cultivation during the *ritsuryō* age, and that the opening of new fields had stagnated during the medieval era. His argument received additional support from laws such as the imperial edict of 723, which exhorted the peasantry to clear more fields.

But the two tallies of farmland should not be accepted as having the same weight.[54] As a close examination of the law codes, court policies, and land documents shows, any number said to represent Japan's total arable land in the mid-tenth century or earlier must include not just permanent rice paddies, but also fields that had been abandoned or perhaps even permitted to lie fallow. Did cultivators usually open and plant 80 percent of their lands, as in Hamana? Or was the 60 percent of Kuze peasants closer to the norm? Or were most regions like Eizanji's domain, where only 11 percent of potential farmland was sown completely?

Because the area under cultivation fluctuated from year to year, it is difficult to determine how much permanent new farmland had actually been created by the 900s. Quantitative data on land use is scarce even for the usually rich *ritsuryō* era; for the following centuries, the historian is permitted at most brief glimpses of a particular region or village. But, if these examples are combined with the trend evinced in the laws relating to land, the pattern of land abandonment and official attempts to stem it would appear to argue for a more pessimistic view of cultivation during the Nara and early Heian periods. The conversion of wilderness to productive fields was not a linear progression yielding a constant increase of food, but rather a continuing cycle of clearance, abandonment, and then, in time, clearance again.[55]

The figure from the *Shūgai shō* is a different matter.[56] To the extent that it is accurate, it probably enumerated land actually under cultivation. By the fourteenth century, land was cropped much more intensively. *Shōen* records suggest that peasants in the Kinai had settled down to exploit land much more thoroughly by the twelfth century.[57] The Kinai farmers tilled the earth more like early modern cultivators, and were the forerunners of a dramatic transformation that might even be called an agricultural revolution.

CHAPTER FOUR

Land Use and Agricultural Technology

Farming technology in Japan has frequently been depicted as static and uniform. Historians have assumed that wet-rice cultivation predominated almost from its introduction in the Yayoi era and that it remained relatively unchanged throughout the premodern period.[1] As a result, descriptions of the eighth-century countryside often read much like portrayals of rural Japan in the 1700s.

Evidence presented in Chapter 3 suggests a somewhat different interpretation. *Ritsuryō* peasants continually opened new fields only to have them become barren within a few years; irrigation problems seem to have been an important factor in this cycle. The instability of wet-rice farming and the crucial role of technology in the *ritsuryō* age would seem to raise doubts about the conventional assumptions of historians. How did *ritsuryō* farmers irrigate their fields? Was wet-rice cultivation the only form of agriculture? How did land use relate to the system of tenure? The examination of archaeological, geographical, and written testimony can help answer these questions.

ARTIFICIALLY IRRIGATED RICE FARMING

Most wet-rice paddies in the world today are irrigated by man-made devices. Ditches and ponds first dampen fields in the spring just prior to planting, and continue to water the parcels through the hot summer. When the crop is harvested, the same man-made system permits the complete drainage of fields for the winter. The cycle of inundation and dessication is essential to maintain soil fertility, and results in the high annual yields for which rice farming is so well known.

The engineering expertise necessary to build man-made irrigation facilities began to spread to Japan from Asia in the fourth century. The moats that surround the tombs of fourth-century rulers testify to the advent of the new technology. The *Nihon shoki* provides a clue to the origin of these skills:

Men of Koryŏ, men of Paekche, men of Mimana, men of Silla all together attended court. Orders were then given to Takechi no Sukune to take these various men of Han and make them dig a pond. Therefore the pond was given a name, and was called the Pond of the Men of Han.[2]

As artificial watering techniques were adopted, iron tools also appeared. From about the year 500, peasants in many regions began to forge iron tips for hoes and spades and iron blades for sickles.[3] Plows with iron shares were devised.

Iron tools and artificial irrigation enabled cultivators to plant rice in thicker soils and at higher elevations. Tools with iron parts could bite more deeply into fertile earth. To conserve water, farmers employed the technique of transplanting (*taue*). Rice seed was sprouted in seedbeds, and seedlings were then moved to the fields in bundles for the growing season. Raising rice plants from bundles of seedlings meant that the crop was most easily harvested at the root (*negari*), a task for which the iron sickle was well suited.

Yields were high under optimal conditions. A 729 fiscal report from Yamato discloses that only 20 sheaves of seed rice were needed to sow 1 *chō* in Soenokami and Hirose districts.[4] The *Ordinances of Kōnin (Kōnin shiki)*, a ninth-century legal source, lists the harvest from a middle-grade paddy at 400 sheaves per *chō*, or an amazing 20-fold return on the initial investment. A bad harvest of only 150 sheaves per *chō* still netted a 7.5-fold return. Productivity in early Japanese rice farming compares favorably to eighth-century European yields, which were frequently lower than twice the amount of seed used in planting.[5]

But few paddies produced steadily at such a high rate. The major problem confronting farmers cropping parcels on higher ground was the inability to secure a continuous water supply. Some sophisticated engineering skills may have been available as early as the fourth century, but peasants often lacked either the ability or the will to apply them. In 800, the Council of State described the difficulty:

A rich nation and a peaceful people are blessings conferred by good fields. Opening high-grade lands is really founded on the construction of sluices and ponds. Yet We have heard that ditches and ponds are left unrepaired and paddies have become wasteland. We should establish a special regulation to correct this violation of the law.[6]

The Council repeated its ruling just twenty-four years later in 824:

This action [the 800 ruling] was merely a case of officials establishing another regulation for the provinces. It did not really call peasants to account. In present conditions, the houses that use water do not expend efforts to construct irrigation works. ... The scorching of rice crops can only be due to their neglect. We request that provincial officials be allowed to punish offenders with eighty strokes of heavy bamboo without reference to status.[7]

The early ninth century was a time of drought and repeated epidemics, conditions which upset the regular repair and maintenance of ditches and ponds.

A recent survey of the Nara basin has uncovered the most telling evidence of poor technology.[8] The rice paddies in this region are presently watered by about 15,000 ponds, which may be separated into two categories. The first type (*tani ike*) is constructed by damning up one end of a valley to catch the run-off and remains full for the whole year. Such ponds are often small and fairly easy to build. Some pools constructed in this fashion predate the eighth century.

Most of the ponds found today in the Nara basin are not *tani ike*. They are called "saucer ponds" (*sara ike*), and are usually located on relatively high portions of the basin. These ponds hold water for only part of the year, and their sole function is to keep rice paddies sufficiently watered during the growing season. Irrigated rice agriculture would be impossible in much of the basin without these ponds.

Kinda Akihiro has attempted to date the construction of the ponds in the Nara basin. His dating technique is based on the system of land division (*jōri sei*) widely believed to have been implemented in the Kinai during the eighth century. According to this system, arable land was arranged into blocks (*ri*) measuring 6 *chō* (about 642 meters) to a side and covering 108 acres (43.2 hectares). These large blocks of land were further subdivided into 1-*chō* units called *tsubo* which might be enumerated or given a name (see Figure 6).[9]

Kinda discovered that the ponds in the Nara basin fell into four groups. If the names of a pond and a *tsubo* coincided, Kinda assumed that the pond had been built when the land was first surveyed in the early period. When the name of a pond and a *tsubo* differed, the pool was presumed to postdate the *ritsuryō* era. If the name of the pond included the word "new," Kinda concluded that the pool was of still more recent origin. A fourth group included the few cases which were unclear.

Kinda's work showed that only one saucer-shaped pond predated the Kamakura era (1185–1333). Most trace their origins back only as far as the Edo period (or Tokugawa, 1600–1868). According to Kinda, a large portion of the Nara basin would therefore have been insufficiently watered for rice farming in the Nara and Heian periods. Because the Nara basin was the home of the aristocracy and the most advanced area in early Japan, other regions must also have suffered from the same inadequacy.

Most ponds in the Nara and Heian periods were located in valleys along the edge of the basin (*tani ike*). The center of the Nara basin, where saucer-shaped ponds irrigate rice fields today, was without watering facilities. Securing water to cultivate higher ground was so difficult that peasants preferred to farm in narrow valleys, where steep mountains guaranteed that run-off would be sufficient to fill ponds.

In the fourteenth century, peasants overcame some irrigation problems by building water wheels. Water wheels commonly appeared in Muromachi (1333–1573) literature.[10] A Korean emissary to the Muromachi court noticed these devices everywhere, and commended the Japanese peasant for his ingenuity.[11]

In the early ninth century, the Council of State had attempted to import this valuable instrument from China:

The Council of State orders: Water wheels ought to be built.

Concerning the above, we have received an announcement from Yoshimine no Ason Yasuyo, General of the Right Imperial Guard and Councillor [*dainagon*], holding the upper 3rd court rank: "The advantage of farming lies in rice

Figure 6. System of Land Division (jōri sei)

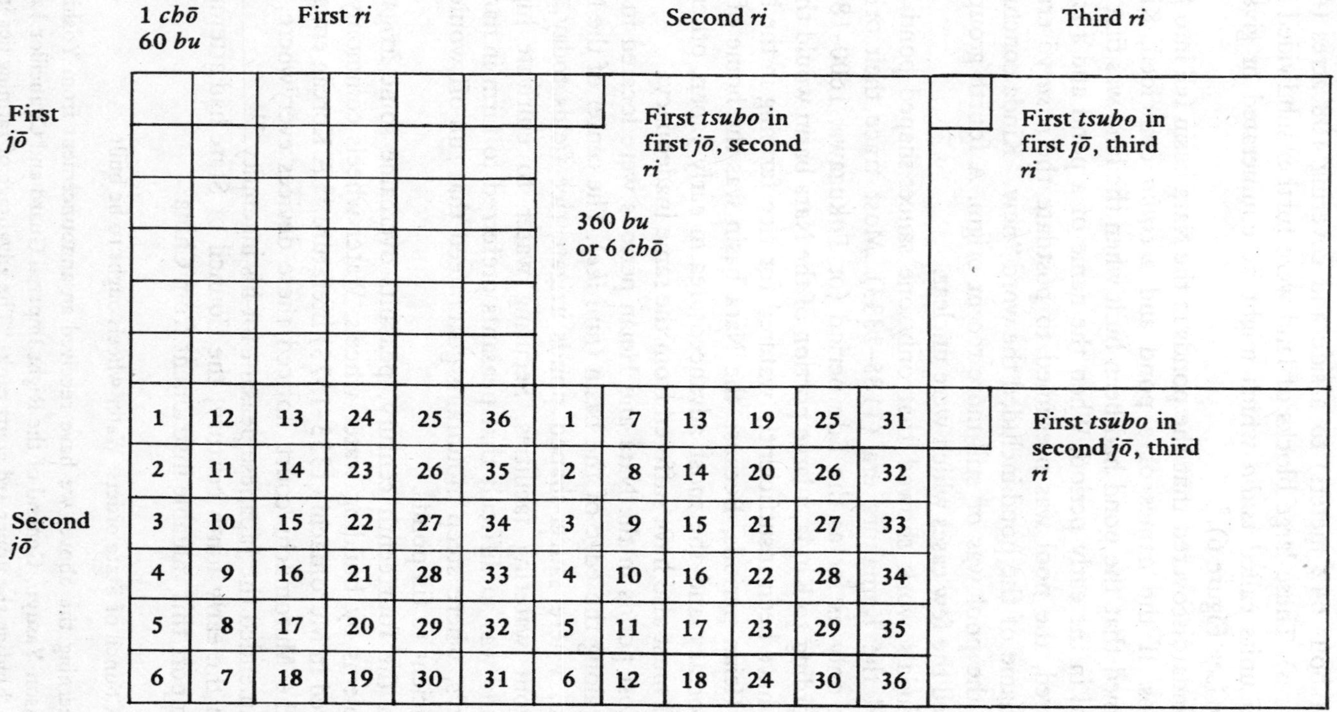

First ri   Second ri   Third ri

1 chō
60 bu

First tsubo in first jō, third ri

First tsubo in second jō, third ri

First tsubo in first jō, second ri

360 bu
or 6 chō

First jō

Second jō

	12	13	24	25	36		1	7	13	19	25	31
1	11	14	23	26	35		2	8	14	20	26	32
2	10	15	22	27	34		3	9	15	21	27	33
3	9	16	21	28	33		4	10	16	22	28	34
4	8	17	20	29	32		5	11	17	23	29	35
5	7	18	19	30	31		6	12	18	24	30	36
6												

Chidori enumeration of tsubo.   Parallel enumeration of tsubo.

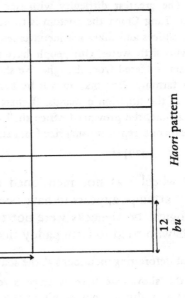

one tan

Haori pattern

12 bu

30 bu

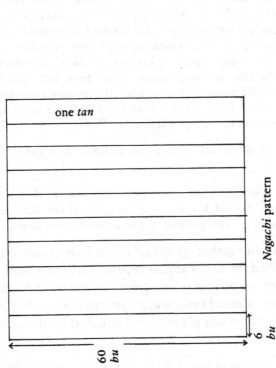

one tan

Nagachi pattern

6 bu

60 bu

Figure 6 (continued)
Divisions of one *tsubo*.

Source: Aoki Kazuo, *Nibon no rekishi 3 Nara no miyako*, p. 211. By permission of Chūō kōran sha.

cultivation. The greatest difficulty with rice agriculture is drought. I have heard that in Tang China the custom is to build numerous water wheels in places where sluices and dikes are inconvenient. One can thus take advantage of regions with little water. Our people have no knowledge of this machine and have often suffered from drought. We should order them to build it to improve our farming. One may turn it by hand, rotate it by foot, or run it using cattle, as the situation demands. If there are poor peasants who cannot build the machine, the provincial office shall construct and supply it. When the wheel wears out, repair it using rice from emergency funds [*kyūkyū tō*]."

Tenchō 6/5/27   [829] [12]

The water wheel was not mentioned again in *ritsuryō* records. Yoshimine's attempt appears to have been a failure.

Technological bottlenecks were not the only source of trouble for peasants who tried to farm paddy rice at higher elevations:

Prohibition of deforesting mountains at the source of rivers:

Concerning the above, we have received a report from Yamato province: "The work of agriculture is not simply in building dikes and ponds. The fundamental principle for securing water is found in the combination of rivers and trees. The vegetation on mountains should always be lush. The reason for this is that, while the origin of great rivers is always near thickly vegetated mountains, the flow of small streams comes from bald hills. We know the amount of run-off depends on mountains. If a mountain produces clouds and rain, rivers will be full for 9 *ri* [about 5 miles]. If the mountain is stripped bald, the streams in the valleys will dry up." [13]

The effect of deforestation was described in the Council's decision:

Peasants . . . strip groves on mountains near rivers as they please. When a drought comes, run-off is scarce and the crops wither. Damage to fields results. We request . . . that peasants not be allowed to cut forests freely.

Logging and the gathering of fuel could have caused the deforestation described in the Yamato report. Slash-and-burn agriculture was an object of official proscription for the same reason.

The destruction of some water systems occurred by accident. In other cases, havoc was planned and wreaked by the peasants themselves:

The Council of State orders: Fishing in irrigation ponds should be prohibited throughout the provinces in the Seven Circuits and the Kinai.

Concerning the above, we have received an announcement of the Minister of the Right: "I have received an imperial decree: 'The way to enrich the nation is to encourage agriculture. Irrigation ponds are built for the purpose of watering fields. But greedy people like to fish by breaking down ponds. Foolish officials permit this activity and apprehend no one. In the fall and winter, the ponds are empty and the water is gone for spring and summer. The abandonment of fields can be the only result. Hereafter we ought to ban this behavior strictly. If there is a violation, punish the offender according to the severity of the crime. If he holds high rank, incarcerate him and send him to the Council. If provincial and district officers do not correct this situation, inflict heavy punishment.'"

Enryaku 19/2/3 [800] [14]

Inadequate irrigation was the chief difficulty for peasants who tried to grow paddy rice at higher elevations. Unable to secure sufficient water in continuous supply, cultivators chose other livelihoods that granted them a steadier, although less bountiful, return. Only when farming technology improved markedly in the medieval era could artificially irrigated rice become the predominant crop in the Japanese countryside.

NATURALLY IRRIGATED RICE FARMING

Man-made devices are not the only means to water a rice paddy. Note these eighth-century poems from the *Man'yōshū*:

> On Suminoe's bank
> I cleared a field.
> Until I reap the rice sown [*makishi*] there,
> I shall not see you! [15]

> The ears of early rice
> Have ripened where I sowed [*makeru*].
> Look at the garland I made
> And remember me, my love! [16]

The words chosen by the poets to describe planting (*makishi, makeru*) indicate that a more primitive form of rice cultivation commonly practiced in the Yayoi period could still be found in the eighth century. [17]

These poems allude to a planting technique that relied on seasonal fluctuations in the water table to provide moisture for fields. Farmers constructed only the crudest ditches to distribute water. This method could be employed in low-lying regions, such as marshes; the setting of the first poem, the banks of Suminoe, suggests the water-logged character of the poet's paddies. Drainage of these lands was poor, and, because the paddy was inundated for the entire year, the soil was not very fertile. Yields were markedly lower than under systems in which man-made devices regulated the water level.

The elevation of fields determined how a crop was planted. When ditches and ponds controlled the water supply, cultivators first allowed rice seeds to sprout in a specially prepared bed (*nawashiro*) and then transplanted the seedlings to paddies in bundles for the growing season. Peasants who farmed naturally irrigated lands scattered seeds directly onto the ground (*jikimaki*), and preparation before planting was minimal.

Each method of planting was associated with a different style of harvesting. Rice which had been arranged in bundles and then transplanted was reaped at the roots with a sickle (*negari*). Conversion of rice on the stalk to food then required two operations—separating the grain from the stalk and hulling the kernels. When seeds were broadcast, the crop was not harvested at the root. The ear was removed with a knife and part of the stalk was left standing in the field. Although this method (*hokubi gari*) was time-consuming during the initial stage of the harvest, the rice ears could be easily stored as sheaves and quickly transformed into edible kernels by pounding in a mortar.

Each farming system employed distinct tools. Tillers of artificially irrigated lands preferred iron tools in their work. Cultivators in areas where paddies were naturally watered often used wooden hoes and spades, since little preparation of the fields was necessary. They harvested with a knife which was held in the palm of the hand.[18]

The extent of naturally irrigated rice farming in the eighth century is not clear. The *Man'yōshū* contains references to both methods of planting rice.[19] Evidence on harvesting techniques is also evenly divided. The authors of the Taihō and Yōrō Codes did not specify farming practices in the Land Statutes (*Den-ryō*), and commentators did not address this question in detail.[20]

Administrative records of the eighth century seem to indicate that naturally irrigated rice farming was widespread. Provincial financial reports (*shōzei chō*) use the rice sheaf as the chief unit of taxation in most areas. The more primitive Yayoi style of rice

*Table 19. Iron Remains Uncovered from
Peasant Settlements, 350–900*

Date	(Period)	No. of Sites	No. of Sites Yielding Iron	%
350–450	(Goryō)	225	5	2.2
450–500	(Izumi)[a]	118	10	8.5
500–650	(Onitaka)	223	35	15.7
650–800	(Mama)	135	25	18.5
800–900	(Kokubun)	206	78	37.9

Source: Harashima Reiji, *Nihon kodai shakai no kiso kōzō*, pp. 25–31, 315–317. By permission of Mirai sha.

Note: a. I have included Harashima's Yaguradai period with the Izumi era.

agriculture must have been common for the rice sheaf to predominate in provincial operations. Regional storehouses also contained a large volume of rice grain, but these stores could have been obtained from sheaf rice.

Archaeological evidence lends a new perspective to the debate over early rice farming (see Table 19). This evidence has two limitations. First, sites are not evenly distributed over Japan, but are concentrated in the Kantō. Excavations of the Tōhoku (northeastern Japan) were excluded from the survey by the compiler, and only about 3 percent of the settlements dated from 500 to 900 were located in the Kansai region (Kyoto-Osaka). Second, the sites vary greatly in size. In many cases, archaeologists could uncover only a portion of a village because the owner of the land adjoining the excavation would not give consent to further digging.

Harashima Reiji, the historian who compiled Table 19, has argued that his data greatly underrepresented the percentage of peasants possessing iron tools.[21] Many iron implements had undoubtedly rusted away, or had been salvaged by other needy cultivators. To adjust for these factors, Harashima has proposed multiplying the percentage of peasant settlements yielding iron remains by 2.5. In Harashima's view, almost all peasants in the Kantō region possessed iron tools by the year 900.

Harashima's work has been strongly criticized by archaeologists.[22] His greatest mistake was the inclusion of many non-agricultural iron remains in the data on farm implements. When Kitō Kiyoaki, a historian employed by the Nara National Institute of Cultural Properties, reexamined Harashima's evidence for iron blades from hoes, spades, and sickles, he found none before the year 500. A mere 2.5 percent of the excavations dated from 500 to 800 contained metal agricultural implements. Iron farming tools were present in only 5 percent of the ninth-century sites. Even if Harashima's multiplier is applied, cultivators in only 12.5 percent of settlements employed metal implements in 900.

Of course, the low percentages of iron tools may be explained in many ways. Iron was a valuable commodity in the *ritsuryō* period, and peasants may have carried off many metal tools when they vacated a settlement. The dependence on other livelihoods, like hunting and fishing, could also explain the dearth of iron farming tools. Rust may have destroyed more hoes and spades than accounted for by Harashima's multiplier. But if the villagers represented in Harashima's sample raised paddy rice, the absence of iron tools may also indicate that natural irrigation and wooden tools were predominant.

Several examples of naturally irrigated rice farming were presented in the discussions of Hamana district and the Tōdaiji domains in Chapter 3. Fields in these areas were not necessarily farmed annually, but were cropped according to the amount of rainfall:

> Water was plentiful,
> And we planted the higher ground.
> Just as the millet is weeded out,
> So am I left to sleep alone! [23]

Sufficient water permitted the natural irrigation of higher terrain, but, when rainfall was scarce, or did not fall at the proper time, paddies watered by a rise in the water table were often barren.

Reliance on rainfall for the irrigation of paddies was made even more chancy by a climate that was both hotter and drier than it is today. Numerous laws and entries in the court histories testify to the impact of frequent drought on rice agriculture. Court diaries show that cherry blossoms opened earlier in the Nara and Heian eras. [24] An archaeologist who has conducted a pollen analysis near modern Sendai found the weather to have been hotter and drier during the *ritsuryō* period. [25] The hotter, drier weather in early Japan was part of a worldwide trend that has been labeled the "Little Climatic Optimum." [26]

Naturally irrigated rice farming, as practiced at Tōdaiji's *shōen*, was highly dependent on the amount of rainfall. Fields cultivated in this way were unproductive in times of drought, while in wetter years rice could be planted on previously barren, high lands. Even artificially irrigated fields, as in the Nara basin, were vulnerable to changing weather conditions. The deficient irrigation technology resulted in shifting patterns of land use in the early period; land clearance was not permanent, nor did wet-rice cultivation always yield an annual crop. Conventional assumptions about the stability of rice farming and the minor role of technology do not seem to hold true for *ritsuryō* Japan.

DRY FIELDS

Even a casual visitor is struck by the peculiar scenery near Ichinomiya City in Aichi prefecture. The landscape resembles an intricate maze, with dry fields and rice paddies interspersed at random. Closer investigation reveals that all parcels are not on the same plane, but that the dry fields are located on mounds a foot or so higher than the paddies. Despite the appearance of irregularity, each parcel generally measures about 1 *chō* in area and fits neatly into the local grid pattern.

The landscape around Ichinomiya is not natural, but man-made. Each cultivator divided his parcel into two sections and lowered one side by digging down a few inches. He then piled soil from the pit on top of the other portion. The raised area became a dry field while the lowered one made an easily flooded rice paddy.

This farming technique created reliably productive rice paddies in areas with poor access to water. An area which once grew rice only when rainfall was plentiful could now produce both rice and a dry crop like wheat, soya beans, or barley. The conversion of higher terrain to non-irrigated fields meant that dry cropping had developed sufficiently to occupy an important place in farming. If dry fields were not productive, a peasant would not have wasted his time remodeling half his holding into a non-irrigated parcel.

Historical geographers once believed that these raised fields, known as *shimabata* or *takabata,* were created at the same time as the system of land division, the *jōri sei.* [27] But the topography at Ichinomiya suggests that the separation of the land into rice paddies and dry fields occurred long after the area was arranged into regular squares. [28] Cultivators have applied the same efficient technique throughout the Kinai and central Honshū, but never before the early medieval period.[29]

The role of dry farming in early agriculture is not clear. The state land system (*handen sei*) charged each peasant to plant rice unless otherwise specified; lawgivers made few provisions for dry farming in the law codes. Initially, the land tax was payable in rice alone.

Cultivation maps, court histories, and bills of sale give some clues to the extent and productivity of dry-cropping in early Japan. An eighth-century map shows how the temple Gakuanji in Nara farmed over 12.5 *chō* of land (37.5 acres or 15 hectares).[30] Dry fields occupied over 2 *chō*, or nearly 20 percent, of Gakuanji's farmland. This proportion is considerably higher than that shown in Meiji (1868–1912) maps of land use. Gakuanji's domain contained many hills and plateaus, terrain not easily irrigated in the eighth century. Kinda Akihiro has examined several maps of the Kinai from the early period, and concluded that dry farming was more extensive at that time than at present.[31]

From time to time, aristocrats ordered peasants to plant dry crops:

The Council of State orders: Everyone in the Kinai and Seven Circuits should plant wheat and barley.

Concerning the above, wheat and barley are most important for man. They are unexcelled as sustenance during periods of starvation. For this reason, We allocated government resources and had them planted throughout the realm in the reign of the Empress Jitō. Since that time, we have failed altogether to cultivate the grains and have been afflicted by starvation. Suffering grows greater and greater. This condition is not just a result of the people's laziness, but is really the fault of provincial and district officials. Hereafter encourage people not to miss the season for growing these crops. Every year note fully the area planted in wheat and barley and the harvest. Entrust the record to the messengers who carry the tax registers to the capital and report to the Council.

Yōrō 7/8/28   [723][32]

Similar laws appeared in 693, 715, 820, 839, and 840.[33]

These instructions are perplexing. Two were issued in the spring, but the others were circulated in late summer and fall. Did lawmakers intend peasants to sow these crops immediately, or were they to wait until the following year? The laws often berated cultivators for being unfamiliar with non-irrigated farming. Does this criticism mean that dry cropping was unknown? Or were the courtiers just blaming their own troubles on the ignorance of their subjects?

A closer reading of the court histories suggests a possible solution. Each appeal to raise wheat, barley, and other dry crops was formulated during a severe drought.[34] Officials may have been exhorting peasants to employ a system of crop rotation based on the amount of rainfall. When rainfall was plentiful, farmers planted high-yielding rice; during times of drought, peasants converted their paddies to dry crops. Alternation between rice and other grains was a common practice in the Heian period.[35]

Faced with the lower productivity of non-irrigated farming, cultivators planted rice even when conditions were not ideal. A map of Gufukuji's holdings in Sanuki (Kagawa prefecture) documents the low yield of dry fields (see Table 20 and Map 5). Dry fields in Sanuki were only one-fourth to one-third as productive as neighboring rice paddies. Even a poor rice paddy (1B) yielded about 33 percent more grain than a dry field.

Land prices also reflect the relatively poor output of a wheat or

Table 20. *Farming Conditions in Sanuki Province, 735*

Parcel	Type of Field	Area	Yield	Relative Productivity
1A	New rice paddy	50 *shiro*	1.5 *koku*	
1B	Old rice paddy	110 *shiro*	1.1 *koku*	33% of 1A
1C	Dry field	240 *shiro*	1.75 *koku*	24% of 1A
2A	Rice paddy	70 *shiro*	1.3 *koku*	
2B	Dry field	100 *shiro*	0.5 *koku*	27% of 2A
3A	Rice paddy	250 *shiro*	3.5 *koku*	
3B	Dry field	30 *shiro*	0.1 *koku*	24% of 3A
4A	Rice paddy	450 *shiro*	4.7 *koku*	
4B	Dry field	50 *shiro*	0.15 *koku*	29% of 4A
5A	Rice paddy	400 *shiro*	4.6 *koku*	
5B	Dry field	100 *shiro*	0.3 *koku*	26% of 5A
6A	Rice paddy	450 *shiro*	5.0 *koku*	
6B	Dry field	50 *shiro*	0.2 *koku*	36% of 6A

Source: DNK, 7 44–50. A *shiro*, a pre-645 land measurement = about 23 square meters. 500 *shiro* = 1 *chō*.

Map 5. Farming Conditions in Sanuki Province, 735

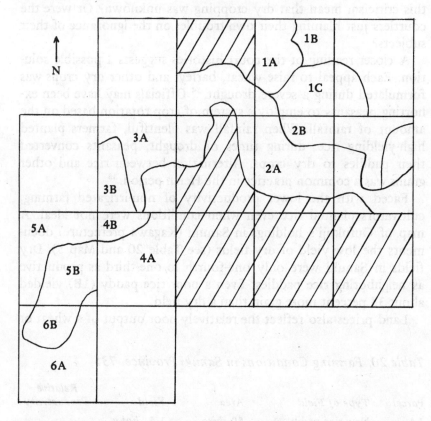

Each four-sided figure is a *tsubo*. Shaded areas indicate peasant dwellings and fields.

Source: See Table 20. Map slightly modified.

barley field. According to Kikuchi Yasuaki, dry fields sold for only a fraction of the price of rice paddies throughout the Nara and early Heian periods.[36] In the tenth century, the price of a dry field began to rise, and, by the early eleventh century, its market value equaled the sale price of some rice paddies. The rise in the value of dry fields corresponded to a jump in productivity and was a condition for the development of the *shimabata*.

Surviving documentary and geographical testimony indicates two points about dry farming in early Japan. First, non-irrigated fields were fairly extensive. They probably covered large areas that could not be successfully irrigated for rice farming. Second, yields in dry agriculture were a distant second to rice harvests. Government officials recognized this difference in output and generally encouraged rice over all other crops.

SLASH-AND-BURN AGRICULTURE

As ancients did in China and the West, the compilers of Japan's first history, the *Nihon shoki*, created a myth to explain the origin of agriculture in their country:

The next child of Izanagi no Mikoto and Izanami no Mikoto [the progenitor and progenitrix of Japan] was Kagu-tsuchi, the God of Fire. Izanami no Mikoto was burnt by Kagu-tsuchi, so that she died. When she was lying down to die, she gave birth to the Earth Goddess, Hani-yama-hime, and the Water Goddess, Mizu-ha-no-me. Kagu-tsuchi took to wife Hani-yama-hime and they had a child named Waka-musubi [lit., Young Growth]. On the crown of this Deity's head were produced the silkworm and the mulberry tree, and in her navel the five kinds of grain.[37]

Farming is described as being the marriage of fire and earth, symbolized by the gods Kagu-tsuchi and Hani-yama-hime respectively.

The combination of fire and earth recalls a primitive form of agriculture, slash-and-burn cropping (*yakibata*). Swidden farming is usually practiced in mountainous regions and is characterized by a minimal investment of labor and the inefficient use of the soil. Cultivators use an ax to clear away forest and underbrush, and then burn the remaining vegetation to produce ash for fertilizer. The land is sown in beans, potatoes, millet, or some other dry crop for the few years the soil is productive, and then abandoned. Records from the Tokugawa period indicate that shifting agriculture was popular in some regions among peasants seeking to avoid rice farming and taxation.[38] Surveys of modern Japan show that slash-and-burn farming is still practiced in the highlands of Shikoku and Kyushu.[39]

Written sources from the early period occasionally refer to this regime:

In cases where beacon fires have been mistakenly started, the place which originally started the fire should report the unauthorized beacon immediately to the provincial office. If, after an investigation, the office finds the report to be true, the province should send a messenger by emergency post and report to the Council.[40]

Kiyowara no Mabito Natsuno, a legal scholar of the early 800s, noted that one source of confusion arose when peasants burned off forest on a mountainside and soldiers mistook their fires for warnings of attack. Kiyowara was surely referring to swidden agriculture.

Another article also implies that slash-and-burn farming was prevalent. The compilers of the penal codes permitted the firing of fields and wilderness (no) between the 3rd and 11th months only.[41] Offenders were punished with fifty lashes of light bamboo. Since the law also includes fields in its purview, authors were not necessarily referring exclusively to swidden cropping. Cultivators also used fire to clear land before conversion to rice paddies.

The poets of the Man'yōshū were fond of comparing passion to fire:

> He who burns sere weeds
> On the open plain [no] in early spring—
> Is it not enough?
> Must he burn my heart, too?[42]

Lyricists also alluded to slash-and-burn cropping in descriptions of war:

> War horns blew, as tigers roar,
> Confronting the enemy,
> Until all men were shaken with terror.
> Banners, hoisted aloft, swayed
> As sway in the wind the flames that burn
> On every moorland [no] far and near
> When spring comes after winter's imprisonment.[43]

> Warriors go forth
> With birchwood bows in their hands
> And hunting arrows under their arms—
> On the hill slope of Takamado;
> There flamed up fires
> That seemed like moorland [no] fires
> Burning in spring. [44]

Each poet employed a word (no) which means previously un-cropped land, leaving little doubt that shifting agriculture is intended.

Place-names sometimes suggest slash-and-burn farming. For example, Suhata no Eji Michitari, a manual worker (shichō), resided in an administrative village called Hida, or "Fire-field."[45] Lands in Echizen were named "Burn-Off-and-Sow-Field."[46] The allusion to swidden farming is unmistakable. Slash-and-burn agriculture offers a tempting explanation for the shifting cultivation patterns in Echizen and Etchū.

Like Tokugawa officials, Nara and Heian lawmakers sought to discourage swidden agriculture. Its ephemeral character made it hard to control, and productivity did not compare with wet-rice cropping. In 676, Emperor Temmu reissued a longstanding ban on shifting agriculture:

In the course of this month [the 5th] the Emperor forbade the cutting of grass or firewood on Mount Hosokawa. Indiscriminate burning and cutting were forbidden on all mountains and plains in the Home Provinces, as to which a prohibition had always existed. [47]

Nearly two hundred years later, in 867, another prohibition was declared:

Today We Ourselves barred the people of Yamato province from setting fire to sacred Mount Isogami to plant barley or beans. [48]

The crops tilled by Yamato farmers were the same as those sown by modern cultivators, and may have been rotated to replenish nutrients in the soil.[49] Even in the Kinai, the seat of government and the most economically advanced area in early Japan, slash-and-burn agriculture was practiced.

Written sources offer little hope of establishing how many people lived by swidden farming. But a comparative perspective indicates that it was a common livelihood. Social scientists who study shifting cultivation throughout the world have noted that it is associated with low population density. Harold Conklin, in studies of farming in the Philippines, has found that the maximum density in areas where shifting cropping is common is 50 persons per square kilometer. In Sarawak in Indonesia, the ceiling is 25 persons per square kilometer.[50]

Map 6 shows population distribution in Japan in about 900. This model is based on the work of Sawada Goichi, who believed that early Japan contained about 5.5 million people.[51] His estimate is the highest proposed by any demographer.

Population density in a large area of Japan was appropriate for swidden cropping. Even if the lower Indonesian estimate is used, only north central Kyushu, the eastern Inland Sea and the Kinai, and the eastern Kantō are safely above the limit for shifting agriculture. Unrecorded because of government emphasis on paddy rice, slash-and-burn farming must have been an important means of subsistence for many *ritsuryō* peasants.

THE EARLY LANDSCAPE

Many different agricultural regimes were common in early Japan. Why has attention focused so exclusively on rice farming? A major reason is the assumption that the system of land division was enforced throughout the nation beginning in the seventh and eighth centuries. Because most scholars have believed that all land within the grid pattern was cropped annually in rice, the early and complete implementation of the *jōri sei* seemed to signify Japan's total conversion to wet-rice cultivation.

The first article of the Land Statutes written in 702 specifies the dimensions of fields:

Land of 30 *bu* ["paces"] in length and 12 in width shall be a *tan* [0.3 acres]. Ten *tan* shall be a *chō*.[32]

One-*tan* fields measuring 30 by 12 *bu* correspond to the *haori* pattern of the *jōri sei* (see Figure 6). The land statute seems to sustain the conclusion that district and provincial officials mapped out the checkerboard field system during the early eighth century.

Some historians went even farther. They cited the third article of the Taika Reform Edict, which also included the same order for

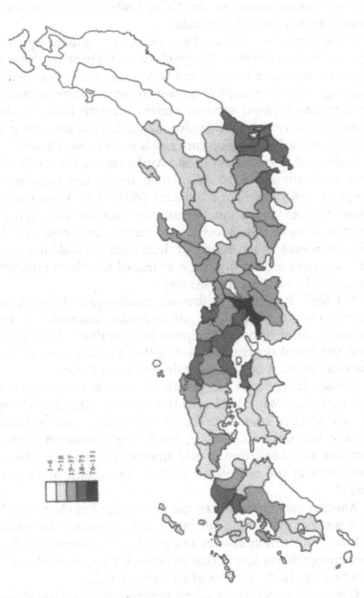

Map 6. *The Population Density of Japan in the Early Tenth Century (persons per km²)*

1–6
7–18
19–37
38–75
76–151

Source: Aoki, *Nara no miyako*, p. 18. By permission of Chūō kōron sha.

uniform fields, as proof that the origin of the grid pattern lay in the early seventh century. The invention of the field system predated Japan's all-out effort to centralize the state under the Emperors Tenji and Temmu.[53] The inclusion of the same stipulation for land measurement in the Taihō Codes would therefore have merely spelled out existing reality.

Some Japanese scholars have recently begun to appraise the *jōri sei* more critically. Geographers and historians have joined forces to determine how old and widespread the system really was. Although a more complete answer to these questions must await detailed geographical surveys, present research indicates that the conventional view which divided all arable land into the grid pattern by the early eighth century needs to be reconsidered.

Kishi Toshio has surveyed the Asuka region, the cradle of Japanese civilization.[54] After calculating the precise location of the Empress Jitō's capital of Fujiwara (694–710), Kishi found that some temples and stone monuments outside the capital were erected at regular distances of 106 meters, or almost exactly one *chō*, from each other. Based on these findings, Kishi has conceded that a system of land division may indeed have been established in Japan by the early seventh century.

Yet Kishi is cautious in drawing conclusions. He never uses the term *jōri sei* to describe the grid in Asuka, and makes no attempt to relate the division of the plain to agriculture. Kishi prefers to view the initial system for dividing land as being closely related to the establishment of Chinese-style capitals in Japan.

A map dating from 735 reveals land use at Gufukuji's holdings in Sanuki (see Map 5). The fields were not arranged by the system of field division commanded in the law codes. Land in Gufukuji's domain was only 5 *chō* wide, not 6 as was standard in the Land Statutes. Local variation in field arrangement must have been common even in the mid-eighth century, the zenith of the *ritsuryō* period.

Another map charts the region just north of modern Nara.[55] The area was neatly marked off into squares covering the mandatory 108 acres; irrigation ditches and ponds were entered on the map. The cartographers stated that their work was compiled in 772 and 808 as a step in the process of allocating paddies.

Comparison with the modern topography near Nara shows that bureaucrats divided the land into the checkerboard design regardless of terrain. The field system was drawn over mountains and rivers, lands which have never been farmed. No trace of field partitioning was visible in the modern landscape. In a region just north of the capital, the *jōri sei* was probably a bureaucratic fiction.[56]

A final verdict on the field system still hangs in the balance. Contributions from other disciplines, particularly archaeology, have yet to be weighed. But scholars have so far determined three points. First, the *jōri sei* may have originated in the early seventh century in Asuka, but initially the institution was probably unrelated to farming. Second, local variation in field patterns was common. Although evidence is scanty, there is no reason to assume that Japan's farmland was uniformly sectioned in the eighth century. The field system was probably not enforced in some areas until Heian or even medieval times. Third, division of an area did not mean that the land was continuously cultivated, or even farmed at all.

LAND USE AND LAND TENURE

Rice agriculture in early Japan was beset by a fatal flaw: inadequate technology. Bottlenecks especially hampered peasants who cultivated rice by artificial irrigation. Large ponds which would have guaranteed a steady supply of water and safety from drought were few, even in the advanced Kinai. Iron tools which would have aided in planting and harvesting may have been held by a mere 15 percent of all peasants. The water wheel probably never progressed beyond the planning stage. The poor distribution of techniques and tools made artificially irrigated rice cultivation an unreliable regime.

Peasants compensated for technological shortcomings in various ways. One option was to plant paddy rice in low-lying regions where the high water table or a little rainfall could irrigate the fields. Yet this technique yielded smaller harvests than rice grown using artificial irrigation, and a stand of rice could still be ruined by drought or flood. Raising non-irrigated grains like wheat or barley meant that the farmer could be less concerned with the water supply, but these crops were relatively unproductive. Swidden agriculture required minimal labor and technological inputs, and may have been widely practiced in mountainous regions.

A *ritsuryō* legislator described the constantly changing farming conditions:

The location of productive fields and wasteland varies every year; irrigated paddies and dry fields change daily.[57]

An analysis of the state system of landholding further emphasizes the ever-changing nature of early agriculture. According to the law codes, the government was supposed to allocate productive rice paddies to all individuals 6 years of age or older, giving males 2 *tan* and females two-thirds that amount.[58] Each peasant held his or her parcel for life, and was prohibited from permanently transferring or passing it along to an heir. Every six years, the state adjusted holdings by distributing land to new grantees and confiscating parcels from households that had lost members.

Japanese courtiers had borrowed the idea of state land allocation from China, where several different versions of the system had developed.[59] The rulers of the Han dynasty (206 B.C.–A.D. 220) first applied the land institution on the northern frontier, where farming was difficult and population unsettled because of frequent barbarian attacks. After the collapse of the Han dynasty, China entered a period of political decentralization and demographic instability. The kingdoms of North China were harshly affected by these conditions, and adopted the Han land system to enforce continued cultivation and tax payment. The Northern Wei dynasty (A.D. 386–535), which specified a minimum holding of 40 *mou* (about 5 acres) for peasants, is an instructive example.

The Northern Qi dynasty (550–579) altered the land institution significantly. The amount granted to an adult male was raised to 80 *mou*, and a peasant was no longer required to farm this area. Instead, the new figure represented the maximum area a person was allowed to hold. The ceiling on landholding varied according to social status, and the principle aim of lawmakers was to discourage the excessive accumulation of farmland by wealthy peasants or aristocrats. The Sui (589–617) and Tang (617–906) dynasties accepted the reform of the Northern Qi rulers and emphasized the maintenance of the social hierarchy.

When Japan's leaders copied the Chinese-style land system in the late seventh century, they adapted it to fit the demographic and agricultural conditions in their own country. Rather than copy the Tang institution, which set forth a maximum on land holdings to keep the social hierarchy intact, Japanese legal experts chose as their model the system of the Northern Wei, which proposed only a minimum. The 2-*tan* grant made to all males 6 years of age and older was the smallest area each person was permitted to farm.

The adoption of the Wei model suggests that Japanese lawgivers saw a parallel between early Japan and fifth-century China. In China, constant warfare depleted population and drove peasants from their fields; in Japan, repeated epidemics and inadequate irrigation technology produced the same effects. Both the Northern Wei and the Nara governments compensated for unsettled farming conditions by establishing a land system which required continuous cultivation of a fixed area.

CHAPTER FIVE

Rural Settlement

Assumptions about the reliability and predominance of wet-rice agriculture in early Japan have given rise to a widely accepted view of rural settlement.[1] *Ritsuryō* peasants are usually portrayed as living in densely populated, compact villages, much like the settlements of the early modern period. Once established, a settlement was permanent, and migration would have been rare.

The picture of *ritsuryō* population and agriculture offered in earlier chapters would seem to call this view into question. How common was rural migration in early Japan? What was the prevalent settlement pattern? How did migration and settlement relate to other factors, such as agriculture, epidemics, or institutional life?

MIGRATION IN THE LAW CODES

The authors of the Taihō and Yōrō Codes strongly opposed migration. The official policy is expressed in the following article:

If a household lives in a congested region and wants to move to an unrestricted area without leaving the province, make an application to move at the district office where the household register is kept, and have the provincial officials dispose of the matter.

If a household wants to move outside the provincial boundaries, then file an application with the Council of State and await a reply.

Provincial and district officials shall take them away during the slack months in the farming calendar.

After officials at the new residence have escorted persons to their new residence, officials in the provinces where the old and new residences are located shall report to the Council.[2]

The only legal ground recognized for leaving one's residence was overpopulation. Other reasons for moving, such as economic opportunity or natural disaster, were ignored. Furthermore, only an entire household was permitted to migrate; the official commentator on the Yōrō Codes, Kiyowara no Mabito Natsuno, argued that individuals were not allowed to change their residences under any circumstances. Even when an entire household was given permission to move, district and provincial officials were expected to supervise movers closely by escorting the household from the old to the new home and reporting the move to the Council of State.

Lawgivers proposed sanctions to deter unauthorized migration, and delineated the responsibilities of those who remained behind at the original home:

If a household absconds, have the remaining four families in the unit of mutual responsibility [goho] search after it. If they do not find the household after three years, remove the names of members of the household from the tax register [keichō] and confiscate their land.

In the period before the land is confiscated, have the remaining members of the unit of mutual responsibility and relatives of the third degree of kinship and closer divide up the land and farm it. These persons shall also pay the land [denso] and local products [chō] taxes in place of those who have fled. (Relatives of the third degree and closer refers only to those living in the same administrative village.)

If a member of a household runs away, his household shall pay his taxes in his place. If he is still absent after six years, remove his name from the tax register. Dispose of his land as described previously.[3]

This law indicates the importance attached to keeping peasants in one village all their lives. Relatives and neighbors of illegal migrants were required to search for runaways, to pay their taxes, and to farm their land.

The authors of the codes also designed a statute to deal with the unlawful movers:

When vagrants and runaways let their registration lapse, servants [kenin] or slaves [nuhi] are freed to become commoners, or if servants or slaves sue for commoner status and are manumitted, in all cases register these persons where they are found. If the persons wish to return to their original place of registration, permit them to do so.[4]

The epithets "vagrant" and "runaway" expressed the court's opposition to rural migration.

This article seems to contain an escape clause permitting mobility. Upon discovery of peasants who left their homes, local officials were empowered to enter the peasants' names in the household registers for the village of current residence. Movers were apparently allowed, but not required, to return to their previous homes. Nagayama Yasutaka has concluded that lawmakers did not aim to restrict mobility, but demanded only the registration of peasants wherever they went.[5] In Nagayama's view, the government's major concern was collecting taxes, not prohibiting peasant migration.

Nagayama's interpretation assumes that the government could maintain contact with migrants easily, and is therefore somewhat naive. In Chapter 1, analysis of household and tax registers showed that officials frequently misrecorded the age or gender of peasants who had resided in one administrative village for twenty or thirty years. The age structures of the Mino and Kyushu registers further suggested that some adults, presumably lifelong residents of the area, were never enrolled at all. If cultivators were allowed to move freely, they probably would not be re-registered until at least the next census, which could occur as much as six years later. Obtaining accurate information from migrants in new surroundings would have been even more difficult for officials. The systems of registration and taxation functioned best when peasants remained in one village all their lives; thus, the law codes did not countenance freedom of movement.

According to Kamata Motokazu, the clause permitting the registration of illegal movers where they were found referred only to a few special cases.[6] When a peasant was absent from his former home for a long time, neighborhood ties were broken and he could no longer make a living there. In 720, the *Shoku Nihongi* described the plight of these migrants: ". . . their [former] family enterprise has been lost, and they have no means of subsistence." The court could hardly expect these people to pay taxes at their former village, and therefore preferred to register them where they had been found. But, if there was any chance that illegal migrants could be escorted home and be productive, the codes obliged them to return as part of a general policy outlawing mobility.

GOVERNMENT ATTEMPTS TO ENFORCE THE CODES

Government attempts to curtail migration predate the compilation of the Taihō Codes in 702. The first nationwide census in the year 670 was implemented partly to put an end to unrestricted peasant mobility.[7] In 689, the Empress Jitō ordered a second nationwide census:

This winter, registers of population are to be made. Not later than the 9th month, let vagabonds [furō] be sought out and arrested.[8]

The use of the epithet "vagabond" to describe movers emphasizes court disapproval of rural migration.

Immediately after the proclamation of the Taihō Codes, the problem of "vagrancy" cropped up again. In 709, the court conducted a search for runaway laborers (shichō) in the Kinai and Ōmi:

We enact a prohibition: People of the Kinai and Ōmi province lack respect for the law and conceal vagrants and runaway laborers [shichō] in order to put them to work privately. For this reason, workmen are numerous in those places and do not return to their former villages or households. This problem is not due solely to the people's disregard for the law. Provincial officials also are at fault for not meting out punishments. Injury to state and private interests could not be greater than this.

Hereafter let this not be so. Serve notice to these provinces that they are to conduct a search until the 30th of the 11th month and then report to the Council. Within five days of the arrival of this order, have both runaways and those who have hidden them come forth. If they do not appear within the allotted time, punish them according to penal law. If someone knows of this ban and yet hides workers, punish him as if he were a runaway himself. Do not permit the guilty to resign their court ranks or make payments to expiate their crimes. If the provincial office does not punish offenders, penalize officials according to the law.[9]

The laborers mentioned in the 709 law were probably employed in heavy construction at the new palace in Nara, which was occupied by the imperial family only four months after this enactment. Unnamed private persons were encouraging manual workers to flee work at Nara for labor at unspecified projects; the runaway peasants then often failed to return to their homes. This command implies that demand for laborers in the Kinai considerably outran supply, and that restrictions on migration were necessary to maintain adequate tax revenues and a pool of corvée laborers.

The 709 law was aimed at a specific area and group of peasants. In 715, the government made its first general statement of policy on unhindered rural migration:

We Ourselves proclaim an edict to the provincial messengers who assemble at court [chōshū shi]: Many people of the realm have turned their backs on their places of registration and fled to another area to avoid taxation. If vagrants stay in one place for three months or more, have them pay local-products [chō] and corvée-exemption [yō] taxes there. Record their names and note their former district and province, entrust the document to the messengers who deliver local-products tax [chō shi], and send the record to us.[10]

Lawmakers charged roaming persons with absconding to avoid taxation. The court's assessment of motive is accurate as far as it goes: when persons moved without official consent, the result was a loss of local revenues. But the avoidance of taxation was only one cause for peasant wanderings. Unauthorized migration could arise for other reasons, such as local famine or disease, or a search for more productive lands.

The 715 law strictly applied the intent of the Taihō Codes. Runaways who stopped in one place for three months or more were forced to pay taxes in that area, thereby fulfilling the government's desire for regular taxation. Migrants also were obligated to furnish information on their former residences to the authorities, who then sent the addresses to the capital. Hayakawa Shōhachi has argued that the purpose of this provision was to tax roaming peasants at both their old and new homes.[11] Such a policy was intended to encourage migrants to return to their former homes, where they would owe taxes only once. Hayakawa's interpretation is supported by the wording of a 677 law in which a similar posture was adopted.[12]

Five years later, in 720, lawgivers again expressed their disapproval of rural migration:

The Council of State remonstrates: . . . The ignorant people are unaccustomed to the law and avoid corvée labor. There are many cases of runaway peasants. They go to another region [gō] and forget about their former homes after a few years. Even though there are some who realize their error and want to return to their original place of registration, their [former] family enterprise has been lost and they have no means of subsistence.

We request that those who have run away from their former homes for six years or more, and who regret their mistake and want to return, be granted a one-year exemption from taxation so that they can resume their livelihoods.[13]

The 720 measure continued previous government policy. The assumed motive, avoidance of taxation, was the same as in the 715 order. The reaction of courtiers was still to try to return wanderers to their former residences.

In the next year, 721, the court reversed its stand. The edict has not been preserved intact, but included these provisions:

... If you catch a vagrant and find out his former residence, and he regrets his error and wishes to return home, escort him back to his original place of registration by relays. ...

... Otherwise, if no information on his former home is available, enter his name in the register for the place where he is living.[14]

The 721 regulation records an important shift in government policy toward migration. Lawmakers no longer charged local officials with escorting movers home at all costs, as they had in the codes and in previous enactments. After making a diligent effort to discover the peasant's former home, a provincial or district official might simply register the person in his own jurisdiction. This procedure reduced the responsibilities of governors by reinterpreting the intent of the law codes, which specified that all migrants be sent back home.[15]

One factor in the more permissive attitude toward population mobility was political. Barely five months after the enactment of the 720 law, which had granted a remission of taxes to runaways who returned home, the advocate of that policy, Fujiwara no Fubito, died. As author of the Yōrō Codes, he had tried to implement the law codes as written. Fubito's successor, Prince Nagaya of imperial lineage, was not so scrupulous. In the first month of 721, Nagaya became Minister of the Right, a post held by Fubito at his death. One of Nagaya's first actions was to issue a new law which nullified the stand of his rival, Fubito.

The edict of 721 was a compromise policy. It did not adhere to the provisions of the law codes as strictly as previous laws had, but it aimed at returning as many peasants as possible to their former homes and then registering the remaining migrants where they were, so that they might be granted land and pay taxes. A compromise between the strict enforcement of the principles enunciated in the law codes and the abandonment of those tenets marked most policies of Prince Nagaya. The 723 law on land clearance, discussed in Chapter 3, was another compromise fashioned by Nagaya.

Another reason for the shift in government policy was the bankruptcy of earlier efforts. The 721 order suggests the problems that arose when the government sought to escort some migrants back to their former homes. Discovering a runaway's original place of registration was not always easy. Reluctant peasants lied about the location of their original residences, and in some cases may even have forgotten the official name of their old village. Even when local officials discovered the truth about a person's origin, it was difficult to force the migrant to return. In 721, lawmakers instituted a system of forced return by relay, but this arrangement must have been burdensome for local bureaucrats. By permitting the registration of migrants at the new residence, the court cut red tape and allowed provincial and district officials to increase local revenues and the labor supply.

Prince Nagaya's attempt to stem the tide of illegal movers was superseded in 736 by another command:

We Ourselves proclaim an edict: The regulation of Yōrō 5/4/27[721] says: "If you catch a vagrant and find out his former residence, and he regrets his error and wishes to return home, escort him back to his original place of registration by relays." Yet the vagrant is afflicted still more on the road home. If he wants to go home, give him the proper papers and send him off.

It also says: "Otherwise, if no information on his former home is available, enter his name in the register for the place where he is living." Stop this practice and record his name directly in a special register. Have him pay taxes and put him to work at the place to which he has fled.

Tempyō 8/2/25 [736][16]

Once again the court, this time under the Emperor Shōmu and the Fujiwara, revised its thinking. The 736 law completely abandoned the forced escorts authorized in the 721 decision, and permitted migrants to pay taxes in the district where they took up residence. Yet, peasants whose names were inscribed in the special register mentioned in the 736 order became second-class citizens.

The special register was probably the prototype of the Vagrant Rolls (*furōnin chō*) of the early ninth century, and forced the hapless persons whose names were entered therein to pay taxes without a state land grant.[17] The 736 order was similar to the 715 law in establishing a means of controlling mobility. Shōmu and his court had revived the original intent of the codes.[18]

A major smallpox epidemic was sweeping Japan in 736, and the infection was a factor in the new formulation in two ways. First, it played a role in the decision to abandon the forced escort of persons returning home. One problem movers and their official escorts would have encountered on the way home was contact with infected persons. Lawmakers chose to let the peasant return on his own with identifying papers. Many persons must have ignored the commands of local officials to go home and wandered off in a new direction.

Second, the disease had an important effect on the policy that denied state land grants to runaways. According to the Land Statutes, only productive fields were suitable for allocation. With the onset of the epidemic, large tracts of land went out of cultivation. As rice paddies were abandoned, local bureaucrats were faced with a shortage of fields. One way to solve this problem was to encourage the opening of wilderness; this policy was adopted in the 743 law on land clearance treated in Chapter 3. Another way to deal with the dearth of productive land was to deny paddies to certain persons. The victims were migrants.

The 736 edict is usually cited as a turning point in government policy toward migration, partly because it established a separate status for the vagrant, and partly because early Heian legislators followed it. However, it was not the last measure aimed at restricting mobility. In 780, the court rescinded Shōmu's edict; the Vagrant Rolls were discarded, and new members of the community were treated like lifelong residents.[19] In 781, the government supplemented its ruling of the previous year, but only four years later lawmakers reverted to the 736 enactment.[20]

Government policy toward rural migration vacillated constantly. When officials tried to follow the intent of the codes and return migrants to their former settlements, they had trouble discovering their homes and relocating them. When lawmakers allowed peasants to register wherever they went, governors were sorely tempted to use them as a private labor pool, and demands on local land

resources often could not be met. The edicts and orders that describe government policy in early Japan are similar to laws enacted
in Europe after the Black Death:

Enterprising peasants . . . found little difficulty in evading statutes, since it
was in the direct interest of the powerful to aid them in subverting the law. . . .
Flight from the land became common despite all efforts to prevent it; laws
were multiplied and reiterated but to no avail. In 1406, almost 60 years after
the first great plague, statutes were still being enacted to stem the exodus of
peasants from the soil. Their chief effect was to document the failure of
earlier legislation to prevent disaster. [21]

MIGRANTS AND THEIR MOTIVES

Prewar historians took the descriptions of migrants in the law codes
at face value:

Unable to bear up under the harsh requirements of corvée, these peasants
wandered on foot over the countryside, even to the point of severing bonds
of kinship. They disappeared into the great houses of some stranger and became laborers. [22]

Four tax registers from the Kinai suggest that a majority of
movers were not poor, lonely refugees from venal officials. [23] Most
of the persons listed as "runaways" in these records were not men,
but women, who were not taxed (see Table 21). Many males in
Table 21 were also untaxed because they were not yet 17, the
youngest assessable age.

The migrant was not a lonely wanderer. Eighty-eight percent of
the 83 persons leaving the Kinai traveled in groups of 2 persons or
more, and 71 percent, or 59 people, moved from their original
residences in groups of 3 or more people. In some cases, an entire
household left its former home. For instance, Izumo no Omi Omimaro was listed in 726 as the 34-year-old head of a family of 5
registered in Lower Izumo in Yamashiro, even though he and his
relatives had long since departed the region. [24] In 709, Omimaro,
his mother, and a young woman named Tojime departed for Urahara district in Echigo (east of Niigata). Three years later, in 712,
the other two members of Omimaro's household, Izumo no Omi
Hanime and her daughter Kasugabe no Suguri Mayame, left for
Kurita in Ōmi province (southeast of Lake Biwa in Shiga). It is not
clear why Omimaro's family went in different directions. But
much land clearance took place in Echigo after 750; Omimaro

Table 21. Male and Female Vagrants in Four Tax Registers

Area	Male (A)	Female (B)	% Female (B/A + B)
Upper Izumo	7	12	63
Lower Izumo	4	27	87
Ukyō, 3-3	1	5	83
Atago	16	11	41
Total	28	55	66

All persons listed in the sample are free.

Source: DNK 1 333–380, 481–490, 493–494, 501, 505–549.

may have migrated to participate in the opening of a new frontier.

The household of Nishikibe no Atai Nemaro moved to Echizen, a frontier province which also probably presented numerous economic opportunities for Nemaro and his family.[25] Six members of Nemaro's family traveled to Echizen, but they did not all migrate at once. His son and two daughters were the first to move, in 712. Once the younger members of his household had established a foothold in Echizen, the elder Nemaro and his wife followed.

Izumo no Omi Matari was the head of a household boasting a membership of 32 persons in Upper Izumo.[26] Ten of Matari's relatives, including his mother, his eldest son, his only daughter, and 7 nieces and nephews, left Yamashiro to go to Kyushu. Many relatives were too young to travel alone, and could not have supported themselves in Kyushu once they arrived there. Matari possessed court rank, and may have taken his family with him after appointment to office at Dazaifu.

Many "vagrants" whose names appear in the Kinai registers were not poor, as the conventional view implies. Izumo no Omi Matari of Upper Izumo was a court official holding the junior 8th rank, lower grade and merit rank, yet members of his household were listed as vagrants. The household of Izumo no Omi Ōshima, a possessor of the 6th court rank, also contained many runaways.[27]

Low-ranking bureaucrats and other moderately wealthy persons may have moved even more frequently than victims of poverty. Audits of household registers (*kanjaku*) trace the movements of nine officials from 721 to 750.[28] The low-ranking bureaucrats for whom these records were compiled were officials in Tōdaiji's

Office of Sutra Transcription (*shakyō sho*) and lived in Kii (modern Wakayama) and Kawachi (modern Osaka) provinces in the Kinai. Four of the nine officials changed their residences from one village to another in the 30-year span. Three bureaucrats had three or more homes in that time. Because the moves took place over some distance, there is little chance that the address changes were due to the revision of boundaries.

Migration was not just a revolt against taxation but an integral part of early Japanese society. At least four factors fostered population mobility: the low level of wet-rice technology, the demand for labor, the abundance of livelihoods, and marital practices. Inadequate farming technology resulted in shifting patterns of cultivation. Tax registers of the 720s and 730s describe several examples of migration from the Kinai to the frontier in Echizen and Etchū, where new lands were being opened. Twenty-one migrants listed in the registers, just over 25 percent of all runaways, journeyed to Echizen, Etchū, or Echigo. The establishment of Tōdaiji's *shōen* in the 760s in these provinces must have also proved attractive to migrants from other regions. Yet, as Tōdaiji's *shōen* went to ruin in the tenth century, the cultivators were then forced to migrate to other areas. The same pattern was repeated as farmers opened new paddies and then abandoned them when they were no longer productive.

Second, migration was also encouraged by a shortage of labor. Several laws earlier analyzed suggested the scarcity of workers; this command from 790 implies a similar condition:

The Council of State orders: Dispensing fish and rice wine to field hands should be prohibited.

Concerning the above, we have received an announcement from the Minister of the Right: "I have been given an imperial decree. 'We have banned the dispensing of fish and rice wine to workers repeatedly in the past. But it has been heard: Recently, provincial officials in the Kinai have not followed the intent of these regulations and issue no prohibitions. Because of their leniency, the wealthy store up great quantities of rice wine and fish and delight in the easy completion of their tasks. The poor can prepare only vegetables and suffer hardship in planting their crops. The rich and poor vie with each other in exhausting their family resources to feed field hands. No greater harm can be done than this.

" 'We consider these conditions unjust. Order the concerned chief officials to apprehend all offenders, and have an official charged especially with this duty

go directly to villages and investigate in detail. If there is a violation, punish the criminal according to the severity of the offense, even in the case of court officials. Let this remain a precedent forever. Do not be lenient.'"
Enryaku 9/4/16 [790][29]

The year 790 saw a virulent outbreak of smallpox in the capital region; finding sufficient laborers for planting and harvesting in that year must have been difficult. Healthy workers were in a position to bargain for the best payment they could get.

A recently discovered wooden tablet shows that people traveled outside their native province to find seasonal employment:

I humbly petition the Barrier Office:

Cultivators by the permission of Aki no Suguri Tariiwa of the greater initial court rank, senior grade, from Aki administrative village in Urao district, Ōmi province [on the east bank of Lake Biwa in Shiga prefecture].

The same Itokomaro and Ōyakeme. The aforementioned two persons are members of the household of Kasa no Ason Yasu of the greater initial court rank, senior grade, of the Oharida section of the eastern half of Fujiwara [southern Nara prefecture].

The aforementioned two persons are being sent back to the capital.

[They ride] a brown, 7-year-old stallion.

Administrative Village Headman, Owari no Tsurugi[30]

The wooden tablet was uncovered near the remains of an official road on the Yamashiro-Yamato border.

The construction of imperial capitals and temples also required large inputs of skilled and unskilled labor. The building of Ishi-yamadera in Ōmi (just south of Lake Biwa) in the 760s provides an excellent example of the labor problems on large projects. The erection of this Buddhist temple was supervised by the Office for the Construction of Tōdaiji. Records show that maintaining a sufficient supply of workers was a nagging problem. In the 3rd month of 764, the problem reached a critical stage:

We respectfully communicate recent news....

... *Point Three:* The workers we have hired to construct the temple have been laboring both at the construction site and in the mountains. Every day we must employ from 60 to 100 people. But we have used up all the cash, rice, and vegetables we received before from the Office. We have asked for more and sent our messages by way of Hata no Tarihito to your [Tōdaiji's] office at Nara. If you do not allocate these items to us, the workers will quit.

Moreover, it is difficult to buy vegetables for the workmen. We cannot get salt or seaweed. If you give us only a little of these items, conditions here will be intolerable. If you do not grant the items requested previously and the workmen here scatter, we fear they will be difficult to rehire.

Respectfully reported,
Tempyō Hōji 6/3/13 [764] Secretary [sakan]
Ato no Otari[31]

Workers who were inadequately recompensed for their labors migrated to other jobs where the payment was more to their liking.

Third, many livelihoods entailed frequent relocation. Swidden agriculture was an important way of life for a large sector of the populace, and required high mobility. Many peasants survived by gathering, another mobile occupation. Groups specializing in fishing were such a prominent part of the population that, when the Emperor Shōmu died in 752 and a one-year moratorium on the killing of all animal life was announced in accordance with his Buddhist beliefs, fishing specialists (ama) were excluded from the ban.[32] These fishermen did not live in one place, but were constantly on the move.[33]

Fourth, kinship and marriage patterns promoted mobility. Most historians now believe that kinship was bilateral and marriage duolocal in the early period.[34] Descent could follow either the mother's or the father's line; newlyweds could choose to live on their own, or with either spouse's parents. The flexible character of kinship made changes in residence relatively simple. According to Robin Fox, a well-known anthropologist, bilateral kinship "makes for mobility and easy distribution of population among farming units."[35]

Of course, institutional and class factors sometimes provided motives for true vagrancy:

Hata no Otogimi	100 copper coins
Tsuki no Otomaro	100 copper coins
Kura no Komaro	80 copper coins
Kusakabe no Hirohito	60 copper coins
Hata no Tachihito	100 copper coins
Ōtomo no Morohito	40 copper coins
Miwahito no Hiromaro	100 copper coins
Tsuki no Tamatari	100 copper coins

The above-mentioned men received cash as a monthly loan [from the Office of Sutra Transcription of Tōdaiji] on the 27th of the 12th month in 761, and absconded without repaying the loans.

They adopted aliases and, when we heard that they were serving at Ishiyamadera, we petitioned Lord Yoshinari. If these men are in the vicinity, subtract the amounts listed in this record from their pay, and reimburse us. We humbly report.

Communication of Totori no Kunimaro.
Tempyō Hōji 6/3/21 [761] [36]

Pressure exerted by government agents provided the immediate impetus for flight, but, without the labor opportunities at Ishiyamadera, these eight men would have resisted the authorities in a different manner.

Population mobility was high in early Japan. Migration was stimulated by the shifting character of rice farming, the shortage of laborers, the diversity of livelihoods, and kinship patterns. The frequency of rural migration was intimately related to the pattern of settlement, in which both landscape and residents were constantly changing.

RURAL SETTLEMENT PATTERNS

In 761, a dispute arose between the governor of Echizen and functionaries of the Office for the Construction of Tōdaiji. The crux of the conflict was that some of Tōdaiji's estates included within their boundaries recipients of state land grants who had settled in Echizen before 749, the year the temple acquired rights to clear lands for its *shōen*. The officers of Tōdaiji sought the removal of peasants who farmed land in its *shōen*; the Echizen governor wanted to retain authority over the peasants and fields which had been assigned as state lands according to law.

The central government in Nara finally settled the argument in 766, sustaining Tōdaiji in its claims. The court ordered the sale or exchange of all peasant land that fell within the estate limits: fields that had been occupied before 749 became part of Tōdaiji's domain. Land grants outside the *shōen* boundaries were distributed to the displaced cultivators.

To document the complex process of adjustment, the Provincial governor of Echizen submitted a report to Nara. The record noted the size of each peasant's holding, his official place of residence, and the location of his parcel before and after resettlement. The *shōen* document provided this information for 48 peasants.

Peasants who held lands where Tōdaiji eventually established Komi and Tamiya *shōen* came from all over the Fukui plain (see Map 7).[37] Cultivators' official residences were often a great distance from their parcels; 18 of the 48 farmers lived 8 or more kilometers from their rice paddies. A peasant would probably not travel 16 kilometers every day to plant and harvest his rice paddies. How did these state land grantees manage to crop their fields?

One solution may have been for the grantees to rent their lands to local cultivators to avoid the nuisance of constant travel between home and field. Rental was a common practice when peasants lived a great distance from their fields in both Nara Japan and Tang China.[38] Yet another option was open to unfortunate peasants registered far from their allotments: to build homes near their parcels. This practice is alluded to in several *Man'yōshū* lyrics:

> Though I have yet to topple
> The makeshift hut [*kari ho*] where I reap,
> The cry of the goose is chilling
> Just like the first frost.[39]

> Amidst the fields where the spring mist trails,
> I raised a hut [*iho*].
> Until the autumn's reaping,
> I can only long for her![40]

A regulation from the early ninth century also speaks of cultivators who "leave their villages and go to their fields to live."[41]

The *Man'yōshū* poems imply that the dwellings farmers erected near their fields were temporary, but the temptation to make them into permanent residences was great. Maintaining two homes meant division of the family and increased upkeep costs. If one abode was left unoccupied, thieves could pillage the deserted dwelling with impunity. Many peasants at Komi and Tamiya undoubtedly lived near their fields permanently, without regard for their official residences. If this interpretation is correct, settlement in Echizen would not have been compact, but dispersed. The landscape of the Fukui plain must have consisted of a few houses scattered about in rice paddies and wasteland.

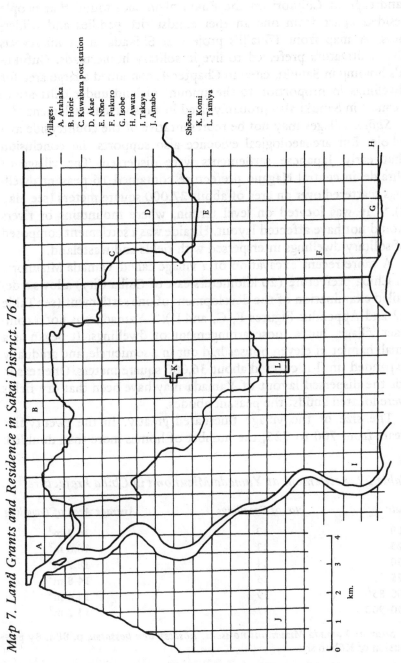

Map 7. Land Grants and Residence in Sakai District. 761

Villages:
A. Arahaka
B. Horie
C. Kuwabara post station
D. Akae
E. Nōne
F. Fukuro
G. Isobe
H. Awata
I. Takaya
J. Amabe

Shōen:
K. Komi
L. Tamiya

Source: Kishi, Sekichō, pp. 390–391 (insert).

Other *shōen* records also suggest a dispersed pattern of settlement. Two historical geographers have reconstructed the early landscape at Chimori on the Fukui plain, and found that people resided apart from one another amidst rice paddies and wilderness. A map from Tōdaiji's project at Shikada in Etchū reveals that cultivators preferred to live in solitary homesteads. Gufuku-ji's holding in Sanuki, cited in Chapter 4, contained a large area for dwellings in proportion to the amount of land under cultivation; farmers in Sanuki also probably lived in a dispersed settlement. [42]

Shōen villages may not be representative of the countryside as a whole. But archaeological evidence also supports the conclusion that early Japanese settlements were dispersed. The village of Hiraide in central Nagano prefecture contained 16 peasant dwellings scattered over an area of about 27,000 square meters (see Map 8). [43] It was located on level terrain, where mountains or rivers would not have affected layout. Hiraide was a settlement composed of solitary dwellings interspersed with fields and wasteland.

A more recent excavation of a village called Yamada Mizunomi in Chiba prefecture (20 kilometers east of Chiba City) allows a detailed examination of the development of one settlement (see Table 22 and Appendix Figures F, G, and H). [44] Yamada was not a compact village, but a loose arrangement of dwellings. It began as a small hamlet of eleven houses laid out in a semicircle, and gradually expanded until it covered about 36,000 square meters. One reason for the dispersed layout of Yamada may have been that dry fields were located amidst the peasant abodes.

The size of the village fluctuated greatly. In the twenty-five years from 700 to 725, the number of homes more than doubled.

Table 22. Settlement at Yamada Mizunomi in Chiba Prefecture

Date	No. of Dwellings	Average Area of Dwelling
700	10	16.3 m^2
725	23	16.6 m^2
750	24	18.7 m^2
775	26	14.8 m^2
800–850	19	14.4 m^2
850–900	17	13.2 m^2

Source: Yamada Mizunomi no iseki: kōsatsu hen bessatsu, p. 886. By permission of Kōbun sha.

Map 8. Hiraide in the Eighth Century

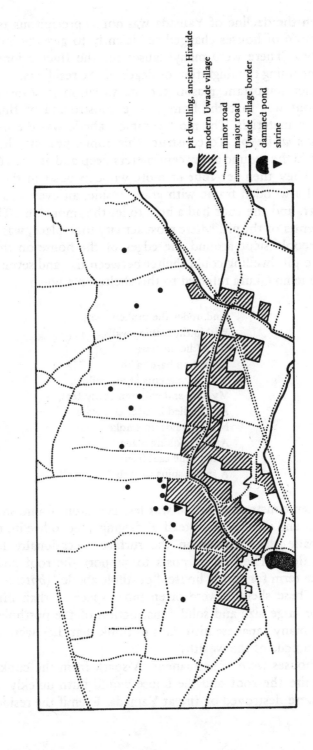

● pit dwelling, ancient Hiraide
▨ modern Uwade village
⋯⋯ minor road
⫶⫶⫶ major road
⋯⋯ Uwade village border
◖ dammed pond
▲ shrine

Source: Kinda, "Sonraku keitai," p. 85. By permission of Shirin.

Although the decline of Yamada was not so precipitous as its rise, the location of houses changed sufficiently to give the impression of fluidity. There were many causes for the fluctuations at Yamada, including the migration or death of the residents.

Another important reason for the variation in Yamada's size and layout was that the homes were constructed of flimsy and perishable materials. The most common abode was the pit dwelling (*tate ana jūkyo*). To construct this home, peasants dug a shallow hole in the ground a few centimeters deep and about 16 meters square. They then set four or more wooden posts in the pit and thatched a wooden frame with grass. Inside, an oven was molded from dirt, and the roof had a hole to let the smoke out. The earth in the center of the pit, where most activity took place, was tamped down. People slept around the edges of the house on the softer dirt. One pit dwelling could shelter between five and seven people. Yamanoue no Okura referred to this shelter in a poem:

> And under the sunken roof,
> Within the leaning walls,
> Here I lie on straw
> Spread on bare earth.
> With my parents at my pillow,
> My wife and children at my feet,
> All huddled in grief and tears.
> No fire sends up smoke
> At the cooking place,
> And in the cauldron
> A spider spins its web.[45]

Another construction style was less common, found mostly in the Kinai and vicinity.[46] Instead of digging a pit to live in, the residents made their homes on the surface, occasionally laying a wooden floor. They raised posts to support the roof and walls, hence the term for such a house, "posthole abode" (*hottate bashira jūkyo*). These shelters were often more spacious than pit dwellings. The large size and solid construction of the posthole abode have led many Japanese historians to think that they were the preferred domicile of the wealthy.

Both houses were impermanent. A spark from the cooking fire could ignite the roof and the house would burn quickly. Several abodes were destroyed by fire at Yamada. Even if the resident was lucky enough to escape such hazards, he would still be confronted with the slow deterioration of the grass and wood used to build his home. The average length of occupancy at Yamada has been estimated at a mere fifteen years. One is reminded of the ritual rebuilding of Ise shrine every twenty years.

Hiraide, Yamada, and the Tōdaiji *shōen* are not the only places where *ritsuryō* villages can be reconstructed. Kinda Akihiro, who has studied settlement patterns in detail, has analyzed more than twenty examples of village layouts drawn from land titles, *shōen* documents, and the archaeological record. Although the study found considerable variation in size and landscape, Kinda could not find a single instance of the densely populated, compact settlement most historians had assumed characterized the countryside in the *ritsuryō* era.[47] Objections can be raised to Kinda's findings due to scanty or unreliable documentation; the study of settlement patterns is still in its infancy in Japan. But, until a clear example of a compact village is uncovered, Kinda's interpretation should be judged the most convincing.

In addition, written evidence supports Kinda's view.[48] Five gazetteers (*fudoki*) from Izumo, Hizen, Harima, Bungo, and Hitachi are basic sources for analyzing village patterns. The gazetteers usually describe village landscapes as encompassing wasteland, mountains, and rivers. In the gazetteer from Harima, Ise moor and Mt. Asauchi (western Hyōgo prefecture) are depicted as areas where people lived in scattered dwellings.[49]

Three factors were crucial in determining settlement patterns. First, the low level of agricultural technology was important.[50] Irrigation technology was primitive in many parts of early Japan; fields periodically went out of cultivation. The unreliable nature of farming methods was reflected in the fluid and dispersed nature of settlement.

Second, typography was a significant determinant of settlement type. Most of Japan is mountainous. In this respect, Japan resembles medieval Scotland, where settlements also tended to be small and dispersed, rather than the English Midlands, with their classic compact villages.[51]

Third, the lack of outside threat in most parts of Japan played a role in settlement layout. Except for northern Honshu and southern Kyushu, Japan was free from the constant warfare that was to plague it during the medieval era. Peasants living in most of Japan had little need to band together to ward off external threats. Only in the Tōhoku (northern Honshū), where natives threatened the colonists sent by the court, could hostilities have provided the impetus for official, walled settlements.

SETTLEMENT PATTERNS AND LOCAL GOVERNMENT

The early village has been portrayed as follows:

Geographically isolated from all but a few neighbors, farming communities since prehistoric times have been compact settlements whose families ... were huddled together physically. [52]

While future discoveries may produce evidence that makes this description more appropriate, the present work of historians, geographers, and archaeologists suggests that this interpretation may need rethinking. Rather, *ritsuryō* settlements were characteristically small; peasants lived in solitary homesteads or hamlets; and their huts were strewn over the landscape amidst mountains, valleys, and fields. The predominance of these small and dispersed settlements resulted from the mountainous terrain, the lack of outside threats, and the shifting patterns of cultivation.

Ritsuryō peasants were on the move constantly, as verified by examination of the laws on vagrancy and tax documents. Although tax evasion was undoubtedly an important spur to migration, the very nature of early Japanese society also encouraged mobility. Men and women moved to take advantage of opportunities in an economy short of labor. Marital patterns, agricultural technology, and the variety of livelihoods also resulted in a mobile populace. Even the poor quality of building materials contributed to this trend. Faced with a mobile population which settled in a dispersed fashion, lawmakers encountered difficulties in taxing and conscripting their subjects.

The court's mechanisms of local control must be viewed against the backdrop of the dispersed and fluid character of settlement in early Japan. [53] As noted in the Introduction, the Taihō Statutes established a simple system of rural governance in which each administrative village (*ri, sato,* and later *gōri*) comprised 50 households. The administrative village functioned along with the unit of mutually responsible families (*gobo*) to extend the power of the court throughout Japan.

Compare the Japanese system with its Tang counterpart (see Table 23). Japanese rulers borrowed only the artificial units of local control from the Chinese codes. The court failed to adopt the natural divisions listed in the Tang codes because nothing in Japan corresponded to the large, compact villages of Tang China.[54] The preference of Japanese lawmakers underlines the mobility of the population and its tendency to settle in a dispersed fashion.

Table 23. Local Administration in Tang China and Early Japan

A. *Tang China*

Artificial Units	*Natural Units*	
	Country	City
Country and city	Country	City
Greater village (*xiang*)	Village (*cun*)	Block (*fang*)
Lesser village (*li*)	Neighborhood (*lin*)	Neighborhood (*lin*)
Co-responsible unit (*bao*)		

B. *Nara Japan*

Artificial Units		*Natural Units*
		None
Country	Capital	None
Village (*ri*)	Block (*bō*)	
Co-responsible unit (*gobo*)	Co-responsible unit (*gobo*)	

Source: Yoshida Takashi, "Kōchi kōmin," pp. 440–442. By permission of Yoshikawa kōbunkan and Yoshia Takashi.

Local administration in *ritsuryō* Japan probably did have a parallel in China: the system of the Northern Wei. Land tenure arrangements corresponded more closely to the institution of the Northern Wei than any other Chinese dynasty; *ritsuryō* local government followed the same model. Northern Wei local government was organized to facilitate the conscription of troops for the defense of the kingdom. The origin and purpose of village administration may have been similar in early Japan.[55] The correspondence between village machinery and military organization emphasizes the gravity of the foreign threat courtiers believed faced their country in the early 700s.

Village layout seems to have changed by the medieval period. Geographers claim that Otogi (southern Nara prefecture), a thirteenth-century *shōen*, was the first example of a compact settlement.[56] The dwellings at Otogi were set close together and surrounded by a moat. The change in settlement patterns may have been associated with population growth, a change in social relations, and an increase in agricultural productivity that accompanied the medieval agricultural revolution.

Conclusion

Previous historians have described Japan's period of apprenticeship to Chinese civilization in two ways. The first interpretation, which might be called the "theory of inapplicability," holds that a Chinese-style centralized state was inherently unworkable on Japanese soil. This hypothesis suggests that the *ritsuryō* system was merely a copy of Sui and Tang institutions, which had evolved from conditions unique to China, and in a way to fit the Chinese character and way of life. Only drastic modifications, which would undermine the very nature of the *ritsuryō* system, would make these institutions appropriate to Japan. The theory of inapplicability was most popular in prewar scholarship in Japan and the West, but still occasionally crops up in more recent works in English.

A second, more recent position proposes that the failure of a Chinese-style centralized state lay in its inability to cope with economic growth. According to this interpretation, growth within the *ritsuryō* system sowed the seeds of its decline. As new institutions were implemented, economic conditions improved and population started to increase. The new government mandated the opening of new fields to support the growing population, but in fact could only motivate developers by the promise of permanent tenure.

The assurance of permanent ownership meant that these developers—greedy nobles, corrupt officials, and rich temples—no longer had a stake in the proper operation of *ritsuryō* institutions. Census-taking, land allocation, and the collection of head taxes became

141

increasingly unworkable. Power flowed from the very groups that had undermined the centralized state and into the hands of local magnates who became a major political force in the late Heian period. This explanation, which could be labeled the "theory of internal growth," is based on accounts of in-migration and over-crowding in the Kinai region, and is most evident in studies written since 1945.

In contrast to these views, I have presented an "economic backwardness interpretation." My argument is composed of four parts. The first and most critical factor in *ritsuryō* Japan's poor economic performance was the debilitating effect of infectious disease. The great impact of pestilence on medieval Europe has been emphasized by William McNeill in *Plagues and Peoples* and rests on a firm foundation of Western scholarship. I believe McNeill's model is also applicable to Japan. Virulent epidemics of heavy mortality entered Japan from the continent approximately every generation, and seriously retarded population growth. Plagues of smallpox, measles, and other viruses killed off young adults, who had no resistance to infection and who were also the primary source of labor. The smallpox pestilence that lasted from 735 to 737 is the most completely documented example of such an epidemic. It reached Japan from Korea, and carried off from 25 to 35 percent of the populace with disastrous economic and political consequences.

Between epidemics, population growth was vigorous. Census data suggest that population was expanding at a moderately rapid pace in 702. An imperial edict describes temporary rural over-crowding in the 720s. But to assume from this evidence that increase was constant over 250 years ignores one variable in the demographic equation, and the most important one at that. Fairly high rates of growth at the beginning of the eighth century only deepened the demographic depression of the late 730s.

A second essential element in the economic backwardness thesis is a new view of land clearance. In 1967, Toda Yoshimi, a social and economic historian of the Heian era, noted that the opening of new parcels of land in the tenth and eleventh centuries was often followed, after some years of cultivation, by abandonment. A critical examination of court edicts and land records from the large body of material surviving from the *ritsuryō* age corroborates Toda's observation. Instead of constant expansion, the opening of new lands was counterbalanced by the abandonment of old fields. Gains in land under cultivation, when they occurred at all, were slow, and at times some areas even suffered a net loss. The cyclical pattern in agricultural development matched demographic trends.

Historians have tended to overestimate the acreage brought into permanent cultivation between 645 and 900. In some cases, conversion of wilderness into rice paddies was not even attempted; rulers regularly decried those who enclosed a tract of land and then failed to clear it. In other cases, once-rich fields were deserted and whole projects were ruined. For example, the state temple Tōdaiji controlled paddies scattered throughout Japan in the eighth century. By the tenth century, many of its most productive lands had reverted to wasteland.

A major reason for the usual rosy picture of agricultural development is a misconception about farming in the early period. Modern readers ordinarily think of wet-rice cropping as being an intensive type of cultivation, requiring large investments of labor and sophisticated irrigation technology. If it is assumed that *ritsuryō* peasants practiced the kind of intensive techniques later used in the Tokugawa era, the clearance of large tracts of land would signify great growth in the rural economy. While these assumptions become increasingly applicable to later periods, in the early period, wet-rice farming was generally an extensive regime, in which labor and technology were employed sparingly over a wide expanse of land.[1]

A third bottleneck was the poor distribution of farming technology. The *ritsuryō* period saw the introduction of numerous improvements, but few refinements filtered down to peasants in their fields. Michael Postan has noted a similar phenomenon for medieval Europe:

As I shall have to emphasize over and over again the real problem of medieval technology is not why new technological knowledge was not forthcoming, but why the methods, or even the implements, known to medieval man were not employed, or not employed earlier or more widely, than they in fact were.[2]

Technological problems were at least as inhibiting as demographic ones.

Examples of inadequate technological diffusion have been cited throughout this book. Even in the advanced Kinai region where the capital was located, there were far too few irrigation ponds to supply sufficient water for wet-rice agriculture. The plan to utilize the water wheel never progressed beyond a lawmaker's dream. Lack of adequate technology also hampered cultivators in the Kantō, where iron tools were essential for cropping wet-rice in heavier, more fertile soils. Even in the year 900, archaeological evidence suggests that iron-tipped hoes and shovels and iron sickles were held by only about 5 to 15 percent of the populace. Faced with these problems, cultivators often resorted to dry or swidden farming and planted barley, millet, or soya beans.

Evidence on disease, land clearance, and technology is corroborated by a fourth factor, the nature of rural settlement. It was once believed that *ritsuryō* peasants inhabited dense, compact villages, like those that dotted the countryside during the Tokugawa period and after. Analysis of *shōen* maps, local gazetteers, and archaeological sites, however, has shown that most people did not dwell in compact villages, but in dispersed settlements, hamlets, and isolated homesteads. Migration was common in a society ravaged by epidemics and afflicted with shifting patterns of agriculture. Peasants also moved to avoid taxation.

These four factors together create a picture of economic backwardness in the *ritsuryō* period. The interaction of the variables might be diagramed as in Figure 7. Of course, any schema can provide only a general and abstract guide to the economic realities of *ritsuryō* Japan. But it does serve as a visual aid to understanding "the vicious circle of sparse population and primitive techniques" that my evidence suggests trapped cultivators throughout the era from 645 to 900.[3]

The vicious circle also imprisoned *ritsuryō* lawgivers; the necessary economic base of a stable population farming permanent fields simply did not exist to sustain a Chinese-style centralized state over the long run. Despite institutional advances and a new elite culture which enhanced the lives of capital aristocrats, prosperity was elusive for most Japanese. The population debacle and sorry state of farming meant that the division of labor lagged and no merchant class was formed. Except for imperial capitals, no metropolitan centers developed in Japan until near the end of the Heian era.

A new view of population and agriculture in the early period

Figure 7. The Ritsuryō *Economic Process*

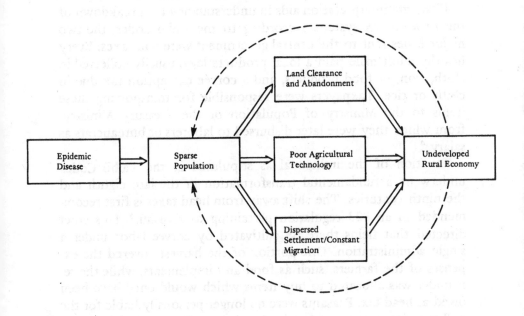

need not diminish the contributions of earlier interpretations. Elements of the "theory of inapplicability" and the "hypothesis of internal growth" continue to have an important role to play in explaining the decline of the centralized state. Key points would include the rise of selfish noble interests and the lack of administrative sophistication, especially at the local level. But the abandonment of land, mobility of cultivators, and the impact of disease also made for a much less workable system. The variables of technology and pestilence work in tandem with institutional and political factors.

The precise way in which demographic and agricultural conditions related to institutions in early Japan is a complex subject.

Analyzing such topics as the evolution of *shōen* and *kokugaryō*, trends in Kyoto politics, or the increasing power of provincial officials in light of my findings could easily fill volumes. Here I would like to touch upon three areas where some interconnections are clear, and raise a few questions for future research.

First, my interpretation aids in understanding the breakdown of the *ritsuryō* tax system. According to the Taihō Codes, the two major levies sent to the central government were poll taxes. Every healthy adult male paid a local products levy, usually collected in cloth, iron, or food products, and a corvée exemption tax due in cloth or rice. Taxpayers were responsible for transporting these items to the Ministry of Population or the Treasury Ministry, from which they were later disbursed to laborers or bureaucrats as salary.[4]

Taxation of the individual as stipulated in the Taihō Codes underwent a fundamental transformation in the late eighth and the ninth centuries. The shift away from head taxes is first recommended in an 823 regulation pertaining to Kyushu.[5] This edict directed that fields there be cultivated by corvée labor under a single administration. One portion of the harvest covered the expenses of the farmers, such as food and implements, while the remainder was allocated to buy items which would once have been owed as head tax. Peasants were no longer personally liable for the poll tax, but rather paid a rice levy which the provincial government could use to purchase cloth, iron, and foodstuffs to send to the capital. The greater power of taxation concentrated in local government paved the way for the Heian system of tax farming based on provincial quotas.

The authors of the 823 edict designed their program to maintain government income under harsh conditions. Epidemics had ravaged the Kyushu populace for several consecutive years; harvests had failed as well. In the same month as the edict appeared, a court history states: "The empire suffered greatly from an epidemic; many have died. The Saikaidō [Kyushu] was hit the hardest."[6] Lawgivers recognized that revenues raised on the basis of land, rather than population, made more sense in unsettled conditions. The Kyushu experiment is a well-known example of the link between tax policy and demographic conditions, but surely similar instances await the attention of discerning historians.

Second, an appreciation of the demographic and agricultural

realities of *ritsuryō* Japan lends a new perspective to an old problem: the rise of the local magnate. Under the Taihō Codes, local men of influence were appointed as district officials, and they served as vital links between the central government and the peasantry. Beginning in the late 700s, competition for posts at the district level seems to have intensified; references to local magnates become more numerous. Toda Yoshimi has interpreted the increased visibility of local magnates to signify the formation of a new class, which he labels "the rich." Toda sees the rise of the rich as a central cause for the decline of the *ritsuryō* state in the 800s.[7]

Where was the wealth to support the new class coming from? One way in which local magnates gained wealth was from private rice loans. Advances of rice were made in the spring to needy peasants and came due in the fall at 50 or 100 percent interest. Demand for such loans was naturally greatest in hard times, particularly during famines and plagues. At the time of the Great Smallpox Epidemic in 737, the central government banned private loans to protect the poor from profiteers.[8] Other edicts controlling private rice loans appeared in the early and mid-ninth century, a period of repeated outbreaks of pestilence.[9] Under the unstable demographic and agricultural conditions outlined in this book, opportunities to take advantage of desperate peasants must have been numerous. The precise relation between social structure and epidemics provides ample ground for further investigation.

Third, my analysis raises questions about economic development in later eras. The evolution of Japan's premodern economy is a complex subject; many variables not treated in this volume come into play. A complete picture can be obtained only by a detailed investigation of the period after 900, which is beyond the scope of this work. But, in studying the *ritsuryō* age, I have found indications that the Japanese economy began a fundamental transformation during the late Heian and Kamakura periods. I have coined the term "medieval agricultural revolution" to describe the changes that commenced at this time.

Hallmarks of the medieval agricultural revolution have been mentioned throughout this book. It was at this time that measles and smallpox first showed signs of becoming endemic. More constant population growth multiplied the number of mouths to feed, and provided more adult laborers to farm the land. Land abandonment slowed considerably, and techniques permitting more

intensive cultivation, such as the construction of water wheels and
"saucer ponds," came into use. Double-cropping first appeared in
the Kinai and dry farming became a profitable endeavor. The
dispersed, isolated settlements of the *ritsuryō* era became more
compact.

The new array of forces working to boost the economy, as I
presently see it, is illustrated below in Figure 8:

Figure 8. The Medieval Agricultural Revolution

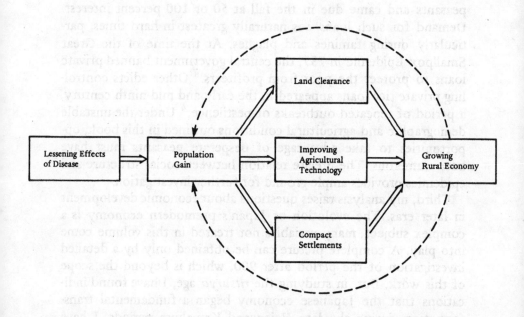

My brief description of the medieval agricultural revolution
leaves many points unclear. Three areas warrant special attention.
First, how does one view the middle Heian era (900–1050)? Was
it a time of gradual transition to endemic disease and better

technology, or did population and agriculture continue to follow the *ritsuryō* pattern? Second, what was the process by which Japan escaped the vicious circle? Did technological improvements precede demographic growth, or vice versa? Third, how is this economic transformation linked to institutions? In particular, what role did the ascendant warrior class have to play?

Before a medieval agricultural revolution could occur, the restraints of the *ritsuryō* age had to be overcome. Until epidemic disease became endemic, population could not grow constantly and settlements could not coalesce. Farmers could open land on a more permanent basis only after gaining sure access to water, iron tools, and sophisticated cropping techniques. The history of the *ritsuryō* period is the story of Japan's struggle to escape the vicious circle of demographic and economic backwardness, and is an essential prelude to the dawn of a new age.

Appendix

Table A (*Chapter 1*). Extant Population Records of the Nara and Heian Periods[a]

No.	Date	(Reign Period)	Provenance[b]	Publication
1	702	(Taihō 2)	Mino, Ahachima, Kasuga	DNK I/1–24; NI I/31–44
2	"	"	Mino, Motosu, Kurisuta	DNK I/24–40; NI I/45–54
3	"	"	Mino, Katagata, Katagata	DNK I/40–44; NI I/54–56
4	"	"	Mino, Kagami, Naka	DNK I/44–46
5	"	"	Mino, Yamagata, Miita	DNK I/48–56; NI I/57–60
6	"	"	Mino, Kamo, Hanyū	DNK I/56–96; NI I/61–84
7	"	"	Mino, unclear, unclear	DNK I/46–47
8	"	"	Mino, unclear, unclear	DNK I/47–48
9	"	"	Mino, unclear, unclear	DNK I/96
10	"	"	Chikuzen, Shima, Kawabe	DNK I/97–142; NI I/86–104
11	"	"	Buzen, Kamutsumike, Tō	DNK I/142–154; NI I/104–109
12	"	"	Buzen, Kamutsumike, Kashiguya	DNK I/155–162; NI I/110–113, 127
13	"	"	Buzen, Nakatsu, Takebe	DNK I/162–214; NI I/113–134
14	"	"	Buzen, unclear, unclear	DNK I/202, 203–204; NI I/129, 129–130
15	"	"	Bungo, unclear, unclear	DNK I/214–218
16	708	(Wadō 1)	Mutsu, unclear, unclear	DNK I/305–308; NI I/84–85
17	721	(Yōrō 5)	Shimōsa, Katsushika, Ōshima	DNK I/219–291; NI I/1–30
18	"	"	Shimōsa, Sōma, Obu	DNK I/292–301
19	"	"	Shimōsa, Katori, Ogusa	DNK I/301–303
20	724	(Jingi 1)	Ōmi, Shiga, Furuchi	DNK I/329–330
21	725	(Jingi 2)	"	DNK I/331–332
22	729	(Tempyō 1)	"	DNK I/387–389
23	730	(Tempyō 2)	"	DNK I/391–392

Table A (Continued)

No.	Date	(Reign Period)	Provenance	Publication
24	731	(Tempyō 3)	Ōmi, Shiga, Furuchi	DNK I/440–441
25	732	(Tempyō 4)	"	DNK I/450
26	733	(Tempyō 5)	"	DNK I/504–505
27	734	(Tempyō 6)	"	DNK I/621–622
28	742	(Tempyō 14)	"	DNK II/326–329
29	726	(Jingi 3)	Yamashiro, Atago, Upper Izumo	DNK I/333–352, 380; NI I/144–153, 166
30	"	"	Yamashiro, Atago, Lower Izumo	DNK I/352–380; NI I/154–166
31	732	(Tempyō 4)	Yamashiro, Atago, unclear	DNK I/505–549; NI I/167–186
32	733	(Tempyō 5)	Ukyō, 3–3	DNK I/481–490, 493–494, 501; NI I/135–139, 140, 144
33	"	"	Ukyō, 8–1	DNK I/490–493, 494–501; NI I/139–140, 140–144
34	"	"	Ukyō, unclear	DNK I/503–504
35	735	(Tempyō 7)	Yamashiro, Tsuzuki, Ōsumi (?)	DNK I/641–651; NI I/187–191
36	740	(Tempyō 12)	Echizen, Enuma, Yamashiro	DNK II/273–280; NI I/191–194
37	Before 740	(Tempyō 12)	Awa, unclear, unclear	DNK I/549–550
38	757–765	(Tempyō Hōji 1– Tempyō Jingo 1)	Unclear	DNK I/323–325
39	757–772	(Tempyō Hōji 1– Hōki 3)	Inaba, unclear, unclear	DNK I/318–323
40	757–773	(Tempyō Hōji 1– Hōki 4)	Sanuki, unclear, unclear	DNK I/317–318
41	After 785	(Enryaku 4)	Hitachi, unclear, unclear	DNK I/308–317
42	Before 863	(Jōgan 5)	Unclear	HI I/116

No.	Date	(Reign Period)	Provenance	Publication
43	902	(Engi 2)	Awa, Itano, Tanokami	HI I/225–241; DNS 1/III/123–153
44	Unclear		Awa, unclear, unclear	HI I/224–225; DNS 1/III/121–123
45	908	(Engi 8)	Suō, Kuga, Kuga	HI I/289–305; DNS 1/II/984–1020
46	998	(Chōtoku 4)	Unclear	HI IX/3489–3492; DNS 2/III/338–344
47	Unclear		Unclear	HI IX/3492–3495; DNS 2/III/344–351
48	1004	(Kankō 1)	Sanuki, Ōuchi, Nyūno	HI II/563–568; DNS 2/V/237–289

Source: Kishi Toshio, *Nihon kodai sekichō no kenkyū* (Hanawa shobō, 1973), pp. 489–496; Takeuchi Rizō, "Shōsōin koseki chōsa gaihō," *Shigaku zasshi* 68: 34–65 (March 1959); 69: 77–98 (February 1960); 69: 85–93 (March 1960).

Notes: a. This list includes only registers found in standard document collections such as *DNK*. Recently, archaeologists have uncovered several fragments preserved accidentally in lacquer buckets. See, for example, *Taga-jō urushigami monjo*, p. 48; *Kanoko C iseki urushigami monjo: bombun ben*, pp. 32, 57, 62, 67. The fragments cannot be dated.

b. Provenance of the registers is listed by province, district, and administrative village in villages, or by section, avenue, and ward in the Capital.

Table B (Chapter 2). Epidemics in Japan, 698-898

(an asterisk indicates starvation or drought)

Year/Month	Region	Government Measures	Comments
698/3	Echigo	Medicine	
4	Ōmi, Kii	"	
699/3	Shinano, Kōzuke	"	
5	Sagami	"	
700/Spring	Shinano		
12	Yamato	Medicine	
702/2	Echigo	"	
6	Kōzuke	"	
703/3	Shinano, Kōzuke	"	
5	Sagami	"	
704/3	Shinano	"	
Summer	Iga, Izu	"	
705*	20 provinces	Medicine, *shinjutsu*[a]	
706/Int. 1	Capital, Kii, Inaba, Mikawa, Suruga	Medicine, prayers	
706/4*	Kawachi, Izumo, Bizen, Aki, Awaji, Sanuki, Iyo	*Shinjutsu*	
12	Many provinces	Ritual cleansing	
707/1	Many provinces	" "	Chinese epidemic (707)
4*	Nationwide, esp. Tamba, Izumo, and Iwami	*Shinjutsu*, prayers, sutra reading	
12	Iyo	Medicine	
708/2	Sanuki	"	
3	Yamashiro, Buzen	"	
7	Tajima, Hōki	"	
709/1	Shimōsa	"	
6	Kazusa, Etchū, Kii	"	
710/2	Shinano	"	
711/5	Owari	"	
712/5	Suruga	"	
713/2	Shima	"	Korean epidemic (714)
4	Ōsumi, Yamato	"	

Year/Month	Region	Government Measures	Comments
723/4*	Hyūga, Ōsumi, Satsuma	Tax relief	
726/6	Many provinces	Medicine, *shinjutsu*	
733*	Capital and many provinces	Rice loans	
735/8*	Dazaifu	Prayers, sutra reading, medicine, grain relief (*shingō*), tax relief	Smallpox
Int. 11		Amnesty	
736/7	Unclear	Grain relief, medicine	
10	Kyushu	Tax relief	
737/4*	Kyushu	*Shinjutsu*, medicine	
6	Capital	Postponement of court business	
7	Yamato, Izu, Wakasa, Iga, Suruga	Grain relief	
747/4*	Kii	Grain relief	Korean epidemic (747)
749/2	Iwami	" "	
756/4	Kinai	Dispatch of doctors	Korean epidemic (755)
760/3	Ise, Ōmi, Mino, Wakasa, Hōki, Iwami, Harima, Bitchū, Bingo, Aki, Suō, Kii, Awaji, Sanuki, Iyo	Grain relief	
4	Shima	" "	
5	Unclear	*Shinjutsu*	
762/8	Mutsu	Grain relief	Chinese epidemic (762)
763/4	Iki		
5	Iga	Grain relief	
6	Settsu, Yamashiro	" "	*Nihon kiryaku* also lists Owari, Echizen, Noto, Yamato and Mino.

Table B (Continued)

Year/Month	Region	Government Measures	Comments
8*	Unclear	Tax relief	
764/3	Shima	Grain relief	
4	Awaji	" "	
8*	Provinces of the San'yōdō and Nankaidō		*Nihon kiryaku* also lists Iwami.
770/6*	Kinai	Religious festival, grain relief	
7	Kinai	Sutra reading	
7	Tajima	Grain relief	
772/6	Sanuki	" "	
773/5	Iga	Medicine	
7	Many provinces	Religious festival	
774/2	Many provinces	Sutra reading	
4	Many provinces	Medicine ineffective, sutra reading	
780/3*	Suruga	Grain relief	
5	Izu	" "	
782/7	Unclear	Amnesty	
785/5*	Suō	Grain relief	Korean epidemic (785)
790/9*	Kinai	Tax relief	Chinese epidemic (790) Smallpox
791/5*	Many provinces	Cancellation of imperial ceremony	
794/8	Awa		
807/12	Dazaifu	Replacement of Buddhist statue	Chinese epidemic (806)
12	Capital	Grain relief	
808/1	Capital	Grain relief, medicine, burial of corpses, sutra reading, doles of grain, soy bean paste (*miso*), cloth	
2*	Many provinces	Burial of corpses, prayers	

Year/Month	Region	Government Measures	Comments
3	Many provinces	Sutra reading	
3	Capital	" "	
5	Unclear	Cancellation of tournament	
5*	Nationwide	Dispatch of doctors	
6	Tōsandō		
809/9*	Many provinces	Tax relief	
812/7*	Unclear	Prayers	Smallpox
813/6	Capital	Prohibition of abandonment of the sick	
822/7	Kai	Grain relief	
823/2	Nationwide, esp. sea routes		
3		Buddhist ritual	
5	Iga	Grain relief	
5	Capital	Cancellation of sumō tournament	
5	Kinai	Grain relief	
7*	Nagato	Tax relief	
7	Mino, Awa	Grain relief	
7	Mikawa, Tōtōmi	Tax relief	
8	Ōmi	Grain relief	
12*			
824/3*	Mino	Grain relief	
4*	Unclear	Sutra reading	
5	Unclear	Prayers	
826/8*	Capital	Grain relief	
829/4	Many provinces	Ordination of 100 monks	
830/3	Kyushu, Mutsu	Sutra reading	
3	Dewa	Prohibition of killing	
5	Unclear	Sutra reading	
832/5*	Many provinces	" "	Bubonic plague? Chinese (832) and Korean (833) epidemics
833/3*	Unclear	Sutra reading	

Table B (Continued)

Year/Month	Region	Government Measures	Comments
3*	Tōtōmi	Grain relief	
5*	Nationwide		
834/4	Capital	Sutra reading	
835/8*	Sado	*Shinjutsu*	
12*	Noto	Grain relief	
836/5	Capital	" "	
7	Unclear	Sutra reading	
8*	Dazaifu		
8	Capital	Sutra reading	
837/6	Unclear	Sutra reading	
10*	Capital	Enrollment of sick	
840/6*	Many provinces		Chinese (840) and Korean (841) epidemics
843/1	Capital	Sutra reading	
849/2	Unclear	Prayers	
853/2	Nationwide		Smallpox
860/8	Nagato	Grain relief	
861/8	Capital		Smallpox
862/1	Nationwide		Influenza
7*	Hitachi	Tax relief	
863/1	Capital	Ritual cleansing, grain relief	Influenza
2*	Yamato, Izumi	Grain relief	
4*	Unclear		
864/7	Kaga, Izumo		
12*	Suruga		
865/2*	Izumo		
866/Int. 3	Mimasaka	Grain relief	
5*	Ise	Cancellation of ceremony	
5*	Bizen	Rice loans	
6*	Ise, Inaba, Shima	Grain relief	
10*	Bitchū	Tax relief	
867/5	Capital	Ritual cleansing	Korean epidemic (867)

Year/Month	Region	Government Measures	Comments
870/10*	Hōki		Chinese (869) and Korean (870, 873) epidemics
872/1	Capital		Influenza
876/7*	Tamba, Mimasaka	Grain relief	
898/3	Capital	Sutra reading	
4	Capital	Prayers	
6	Nationwide	Religious ritual	
7	Capital	Cancellation of sumō tournament	
12*	Many provinces		

Source: Fujikawa Yū, *Nihon shippei shi,* new edition by Matsuda Michio, pp. 12–25, with corrections and additions by the author. Evidence on Chinese and Korean epidemics from Denis Twitchett, "Population and Pestilence in T'ang China," in Franz Steiner, ed., *Studia Sino-Mongolica: Festschrift für Herbert Franke,* pp. 43–44.

Note: a. *Shinjutsu* is a general term that means "to take pity on." It may include grants of grain or medicine to widows, orphans, or the elderly.

Table C (Chapter 3). Agricultural Development in Etchū Province, 759 and 767

Date		Imizu district, Kubota	Imizu district, Suka	Imizu district, Naruto	Imizu district, Sbikada
Tempyō Hōji 3/11/14 (759)	Area[a]	130.8.192	35.1.224	58.3.010	29.3.100
	Fields	34.0.192	28.5.314	33.3.010	22.4.220
Tempyō Jingo[b] 3/5/7 (767)	Area	130.8.192	85.1.224	58.3.010	29.3.100
	Fields	44.0.192	30.8.074	51.6.210	29.3.100
	Abandoned	17.3.322	16.3.092	4.3.320	—
Jingo Keiun 1/11/16 (767)	Area	157.2.160	56.7.294	58.3.260	30.3.020
	Fields	53.6.220	37.4.186	51.4.040	22.8.200
	Abandoned	24.0.270	22.7.066	0.8.260	—

Date		Imizu district, Hasetsukabe	Niigawa district, Ōyabu	Tonami district, Ikarugi	Tonami district, Kinabiru
Tempyō Hōji 3/11/14 (759)	Area	84.0.212	150.0.000	100.0.000	—
	Fields	36.4.090	—	—	—
Tempyō Jingo 3/5/7 (767)	Area	84.0.232	150.0.000	—	37.7.098
	Fields	84.0.232	18.0.000	—	37.7.098
	Abandoned	—	—	—	12.5.266
Jingo Keiun 1/11/16 (767)	Area	84.0.212	150.0.000	100.0.000	58.5.056
	Fields	76.3.290	19.1.060	0.8.340	42.1.234
	Abandoned	—	—	—	19.6.060

Table C (*Chapter 3*). (Continued)

Date		Tonami district, Iyama	Tonami district, Isbiawa	TOTAL
Tempyō Hōji 3/11/14 (759)	Area	—	—	587.7.018
	Fields	—	—	154.6.046
Tempyō Jingo 3/5/7 (767)	Area	120.0.000	112.0.000	807.4.136
	Fields	47.0.085	97.2.336	439.9.077
	Abandoned	—	32.2.314	82.9.234
Jingo Keiun 1/11/16 (767)	Area	120.0.000	119.5.196	934.8.118
	Fields	47.0.085	95.2.012	446.1.227
	Abandoned	—	38.2.250	105.5.186

Source: Takeuchi Rizō, *Nara chō jidai ni okeru jiin keizai no kenkyū*, pp. 222–225. By permission of Ōokayama shoten.

Notes: a. Areas are given in *chō.tan.bu.*

b. This report lists total area of Tōdaiji's holdings in Etchū as 757.4.116 and its productive fields as 427.3.127, both incorrect figures.

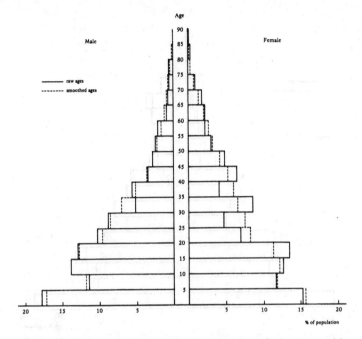

Appendix Figure A (Chapter 1) The Mino Population Pyramid

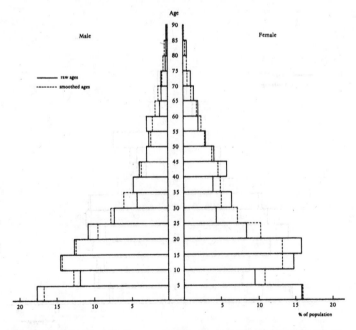

Appendix Figure B (Chapter 1) The Hanyū Population Pyramid

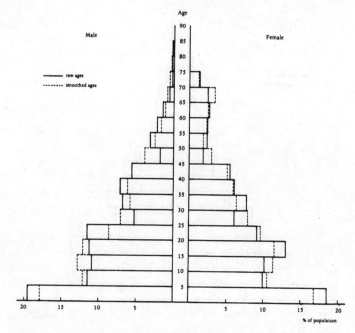

Appendix Figure C (Chapter 1) The Kyushu Population Pyramid

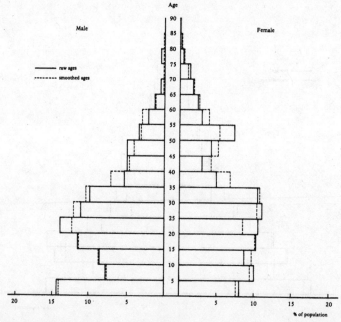

Appendix Figure D (Chapter 1) The Shimōsa Population Pyramid

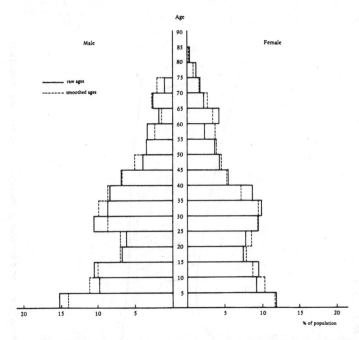

Appendix Figure E (Chapter 1) The Yamashiro Population Pyramid

Note: The smoothed data often continued to show small percentages after the raw data had reached 100% (i.e., after the oldest member of the population had been counted). For purposes of these figures, the smoothed data were assumed to equal 100% when the raw data totaled 100%.

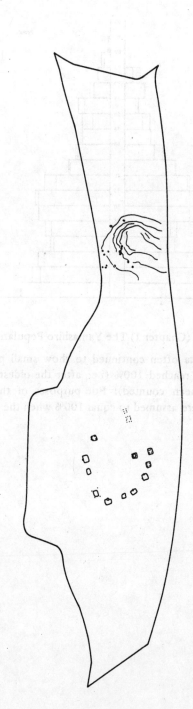

Appendix Figure F (Chapter 5)

a. Settlement Plan for Yamada Mizunomi, 700.

Squares made of solid lines were pit dwellings, while those with dotted lines were buildings located on or above the surface.

A = valley

Source: Yamada Mizunomi no iseki: kōsatsu ben bessatsu, p. 872. By permission of Kōbun sha.

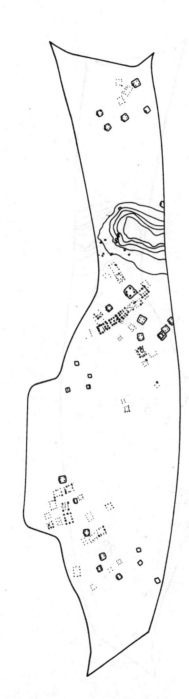

Appendix Figure G (Chapter 5).
b. Yamada Mizunomi, 750.

Squares made of solid lines were pit dwellings, while those with dotted lines were buildings located on or above the surface. Darkened squares were pit dwellings rebuilt between 725 and 750.

A = valley

Source: Yamada Mizunomi, p. 875. By permission of Kōbun sha.

Appendix Figure H (Chapter 5)
c. Yamada Mizunomi, 850–900.

Source: Yamada Mizunomi, p. 880. By permission of Kōbun sha.

Abbreviations Used in Notes

DNK   *Dai Nihon komonjo.* 25 vols. Tokyo daigaku shuppan kai, 1901.

DNS   *Dai Nihon shiryō,* Series 1, III; Series 2, III, V. Shiryō hensan kakari, 1925–1934.

HI   *Heian ibun.* Takeuchi Rizō, ed. 13 vols. Tokyodō, 1965.

NI   *Nara ibun.* Takeuchi Rizō, ed. 3 vols. Tokyodō, 1962.

NKBT   *Nihon koten bungaku taikei,* II, IV–VII. Iwanami shoten, 1958–1967.

SZKT   *Shintei zōho kokushi taikei,* I–VI, X, XI, XXII, XXIV, XXIX. Yoshikawa kōbunkan, 1929–1966.

TM   *Tōnan'in monjo* in *Dai Nihon komonjo, Iewake* 18. 4 vols. Tokyo daigaku shuppan kai, 1944–1954.

Notes

Introduction

1. A list of basic works without which this study could not have been undertaken includes Fujikawa Yū, *Nihon shippei shi*, new edition by Matsuda Michio; Furushima Toshio, *Furushima Toshio chosaku zenshū 6 Nihon nōgyō gijutsu shi*; John Hall, *Government and Local Power in Japan, 500 to 1700*; Iyanaga Teizō, *Nara jidai no kizoku to nōmin*; Sawada Goichi, *Nara chō jidai minsei keizai no sūteki kenkyū*; Takigawa Masajirō, *Ritsuryō jidai no nōmin seikatsu*; Torao Toshiya, *Handen shūju hō no kenkyū*; Yoshida Takashi, "Ritsuryō sei to sonraku," *Iwanami kōza Nihon rekishi 3 Kodai 3*, pp. 141-200.

2. William McNeill, *Plagues and Peoples*; Emmanuel LeRoy Ladurie, "Un Concept: l'Unification Microbienne du Monde (XIVᵉ-XVIIIᵉ Siècles)," *Schweizerische Zeitschrift für Geschichte* 23:627-696 (1973).

3. Yamanouchi Sugao, "Jōmon bunka no shakai," *Nihon to sekai no rekishi*, I, 94.

4. Serizawa Chōsuke, *Sekki jidai no Nihon*, p. 152.

5. Kanaseki Hiroshi and Sahara Makoto, eds., *Kodai shi hakkutsu 4 Inasaku no hajimari*, p. 30. This work updates Wajima Seiichi, ed., *Nihon no kōkogaku 3 Yayoi jidai*.

6. Kanaseki and Sahara, *Inasaku no hajimari*, pp. 87-89.

7. Ibid., pp. 59, 69.

8. Kanaseki and Sahara, "The Yayoi Period," *Asian Perspectives* 19:22 (1976).

9. Henry Lewis, *Ilocano Rice Farmers*, pp. 49-65.

10. The development of wet-rice agriculture in the Yayoi and tomb periods is still a matter of uncertainty. For example, Kanaseki and Sahara, *Inasaku no hajimari*, p. 42, define three stages in the Yayoi era. In the first, cultivators cropped only waterlogged lands near the ocean or rivers; tools were made of wood and stone; no sluices or dikes were constructed. In the

second stage, farmers opened fields further inland at higher elevations, using dams and channels and perhaps even some metal-covered tools. In the final stage, large-scale clearance projects were undertaken and the decreasing variety of wooden hoes and spades is interpreted to mean the adoption of iron implements. Yet, it is important to note that Kanaseki and Sahara never attach dates to their stages and cite Toro, which was located in a swamp and has produced no metal tools, as an example of rice farming of the third stage. Later in the same volume (pp. 104–116), Kawakoshi Tetsushi contends that only wooden and stone farm implements were employed by Yayoi farmers, except in northern Kyushu.

Problems also abound in the interpretation of tomb-period agriculture. Tsude Hiroshi, "Nōgu tekkika no futatsu no kakki," *Kōkogaku kenkyū* 51:36–51 (1967), and Hachiga Susumu, "Kodai ni okeru suiden kaihatsu," *Nihon shi kenkyū* 96:1–24 (1968), set forth the standard view, creating a three-stage model based on soils and iron tools. They extend a similar first stage through the second century A.D. Their second division lasts until A.D. 500, and is characterized by the use of crude iron tools for breaking soils which are "part swamp, part dry." In Tsude and Hachiga's third stage, which lasts into the seventh century, iron implements are employed to turn thick clay soils high above the natural water table. This schema is plagued by some methodological difficulties, particularly Hachiga's assumption that current and prehistoric soil compositions were the same.

A more satisfactory model of the development of Japan's wet-rice agriculture must await more evidence and more systematic, scientific analysis. Even then, differences of opinion are likely to persist. In general, I have followed the views of Tsude and Hachiga.

See Chapter 4 for a more detailed discussion of agricultural technology.

11. Kanaseki and Sahara, *Inasaku no hajimari*, p. 116.

12. *SZKT, Nihon shoki*, Nintoku 11/4/6–11/10, 298; *Nihongi, Chronicles of Japan from the Earliest Times to A.D. 697*, tr. William Aston, I, 280–281.

13. Nishioka Toranosuke, "Chikō jidai yori teibō jidai e no tenkai," *Shien* 3:25–30 (October 1929).

14. Onoyama Setsu, ed., *Kodai shi hakkutsu 6 Kofun to kokka no naritachi*, pp. 16, 56–57.

15. Ibid., p. 57.

16. Conversation with Maekawa Kazuya of the Research Institute for Humanistic Studies at Kyoto University. The Statutes on Stables and Pastures (*Kumoku-ryō*) do not describe the method by which livestock are to be raised. A careful examination of the laws, especially *SZKT, Kumoku-ryō no gige, bokushi bagyū no jō*, p. 272, suggests that herds were much smaller than in China, and that mating was controlled by separation of male and female cattle and horses (not by castration).

17. Mori Kōichi, "Gunshū fun to kofun no shūmatsu," *Iwanami kōza*

Nihon rekishi 2 *Kodai* 2, pp. 97–99. For varying interpretations of sixth-century tumuli, see Wajima Seiichi, "Kofun bunka no henshitsu," *Iwanami kōza Nihon rekishi* 2 *Kodai* 2 (1962), pp. 137–138.

18. For estimates of ancient Japanese population, see Ryoichi Ishii, *Population Pressure and Economic Life in Japan*, p. 4. Recently, archaeologists have uncovered a lacquer-saturated document which provides further insight into early Japanese population (see *Kanoko c iseki*, pp. 105-110). According to this record, the total population of Hitachi province (located in the eastern Kanto) around 800 was about 190,000, a figure that corresponds closely to the estimate made for this province by Sawada Goichi. Because Sawada used the same method to estimate both provincial and national population, one could view the new discovery as corroborating his calculation of Japan's total population (about 6 million in the early ninth and mid-tenth centuries). It therefore seems likely that the higher figure of 5.5 million in 645 is more accurate, but, given the dramatic short-term fluctuations that undoubtedly occurred in the Nara and Heian periods, it seems more reasonable to list a range of possibilities for any estimate of early Japanese population. For population in early medieval Europe, see Georges Duby, *The Early Growth of the European Economy*, tr. Howard Clarke, pp. 12-13.

19. Inoue Mitsusada, "Taika no kaishin to higashi Ajia," *Iwanami kōza Nihon rekishi* 2 *Kodai* 2 (1975), pp. 134–139.

20. Only Sakamoto Tarō, *Taika kaishin no kenkyū*, still believes that the Reform Edict was written entirely in 646. Most scholars follow Inoue Mitsusada, "Taika no kaishin," in rejecting large parts of the proclamation as a forgery by editors of the *Nihon shoki*. Some Japanese historians, such as Hara Hidesaburō, "Taika no kaishin ron hihan josetsu," *Nihon shi kenkyū* 86:25-45 (September 1966); 88:23-48 (January 1967), and Kadowaki Teiji, "*Taika no kaishin*" ron, believe that the entire edict was a fabrication of eighth-century courtiers.

21. *SZKT, Nihon shoki*, Saimei 5/7/3, 271; *Nihongi*, II, 262.

22. *SZKT, Nihon shoki*, Tenji 2/8/17, 286; *Nihongi*, II, 279–280.

23. *SZKT, Nihon shoki*, Tenji 4/8/17, 289; *Nihongi*, II, 283–284.

24. *SZKT, Nihon shoki*, Tenji 3/2/9, 287-288; *Nihongi*, II, 280-282. Controversy surrounds Tenji's 664 reforms. For a summary of current views, see Inoue Mitsusada, "Taika no kaishin," pp. 41–43.

25. *SZKT, Nihon shoki*, Tenji 9/2, 297; *Nihongi*, II, 292.

26. Inoue Mitsusada, *Nihon kodai shi no shomondai*, pp. 239–320. For a variant interpretation, see Hayakawa Shōhachi, "Ritsuryō sei no keisei," *Iwanami kōza Nihon rekishi* 2 *Kodai* 2 (1975), pp. 236–240.

27. Prince Ōama's motives in the Civil War of 672 have been widely discussed. Most historians agree the war was essentially a succession dispute. Kawasaki Tsuneyuki, *Temmu Tennō*, pp. 46-52, sees personal reasons for Prince Ōama's actions: his revulsion at elder brother Tenji's cruelty and

romantic rivalry over Princess Nukata. Prince Ōama is also portrayed, pp. 112–117, as worried about Tenji's slow progress in centralization since the Battle of the Paekch'ŏn River. Seki Akira and Naoki Kōjirō argue that Ōama's decision to fight was related to the nature of his political support. Seki and Naoki's views, as well as other analyses of the Civil War of 672, are cogently summarized in Hoshino Ryōsaku, *Jinshin no ran*, pp. 268–288.

28. Temmu was also motivated by domestic concerns in his drive for centralization, as were all leaders throughout the late sixth and the seventh centuries. He was anxious that his soon-to-be-designated heir (Prince Kusakabe, 662–689) not be subjected to the fate that befell Prince Ōtomo in the Civil War of 672. Imperial succession in early Japan was not fixed; a ruler's brother could succeed to the throne almost as easily as his son. Several of the Emperor Tenji's offspring were still alive. While international pressures and the need to curb local magnates motivated Temmu's establishment of a more despotic system, family and political considerations also played a role. This viewpoint is expressed in Kitayama Shigeo, *Temmu chō*, pp. 3–13.

29. The following is intended merely as a general sketch of the Emperor Temmu's reforms. For a more detailed treatment see Kawasaki, *Temmu*, pp. 132–175, and Kitayama, *Temmu*, pp. 123–188. Both authors divide Temmu's activities into two periods: 675–677 and 681–686.

30. *SZKT, Nihon shoki*, Temmu 4/2/15, 336; *Nihongi*, II, 327.

31. Hayakawa, "Ritsuryō sei," pp. 240–242.

32. Ibid., pp. 222–232.

33. *SZKT, Nihon shoki*, Temmu 1/7/22, 325; *Nihongi*, II, 319; Mayuzumi Hiromichi, "Kokushi sei no seiritsu," *Ritsuryō kokka no kiso kōzō*, pp. 124–125.

34. *Rissho zampen* in *Shintei zōho shiseki shūran*, ed. Tsunoda Bun'ei, IV, 178.

35. Hayakawa Shōhachi, "Ritsuryō dajōkan sei no seiritsu," *Zoku Nihon kodai shi ronshū*, I, 513–584.

36. Some historians maintain that Emperor Tenji compiled and implemented the Ōmi Codes, but I follow Aoki Kazuo, "Kiyomihara ryō to kodai kanryō sei," *Kodai gaku* 3:115–133 (June 1954), who argues that the Ōmi Codes were a collection of imperial edicts, not a systematic set of statutes.

37. The best explanation of both the Kiyomihara and Taihō systems of bureaucratic evaluation and promotion appears in Nomura Tadao, *Kodai kanryō no sekai*.

38. Mayuzumi, pp. 139–142.

39. *SZKT, Ruijū sandai kyaku*, Kōnin 13/Int. 9/20, Order of the Council of State, pp. 279–280.

1. Fertility, Mortality, and Life Expectancy in the Early Eighth Century

1. Susan Hanley and Kozo Yamamura, *Economic and Demographic Change in Preindustrial Japan, 1600-1868*, pp. 199-225. For a general introduction to stable population analysis, see Henry Shryock and Jacob Siegel, *The Methods and Materials of Demography*, 3rd printing, pp. 526-531, 810-836.

2. The most distinguished name in Nara population studies is Sawada Goichi, who wrote *Nara chō jidai minsei keizai no sūteki kenkyū*. His calculation of sex ratios, smoothing of age structures, and comparison of early Japanese age pyramids with modern structures prefigured this study (see especially pp. 49-73, 687-692). But he was unaware that the printed version of the document fragments he used was grossly inaccurate, and had no access to sophisticated demographic techniques.

Publication of Sawada's book stimulated more research on *ritsuryō* census records. Most research that followed Sawada focused on the nature of the "living units" appearing in the census records, and on the quality of the documents themselves. Takigawa Masajirō was Sawada's greatest rival, and he wrote several articles in which he contradicted Sawada's view of the Nara household. See his *Ritsuryō jidai*, pp. 32-41, for details. The debate over the nature of the household and village heated up in the 1940s and early 1950s. By the mid-1950s, two camps had formed. One view (*jittai setsu*), held by Ishimoda Shō and Tōma Seita, argued that the households recorded in the registers reflected social reality. A second interpretation (*gisei setsu*), offered by Kishi Toshio and Okamoto Kenji, proposed that neither the *ritsuryō* household nor village mirrored living conditions accurately, but, instead, were administrative fictions created by the central government. Work on the *ritsuryō* household and village continued throughout the 1960s. A major contributor was Takamure Itsue, *Nihon kon'in shi*, pp. 67-74, who analyzed marital institutions as observed in the household registers.

See Urata Akiko, "Henko sei no igi," *Shigaku zasshi* 81:29-39 (February 1972) and Yoshida Takashi, "Ritsuryō sei to sonraku," pp. 141-200, for concise summaries of the most important research on these topics. Chapter 5 of this book also contains many references to other works on the village.

Although I agree with Kishi and others who have grave doubts about how well *ritsuryō* census documents reflect social organization, these suspicions should not preclude the thoughtful use of age and sex data for demographic analysis as attempted in this chapter.

3. *Shiki kaichū kōshō*, ed. Takigawa Kitarō, II, 109. For a Western language version of this passage, see *Les Mémoires Historiques de Se Ma Ts'ien*, tr. Edouard Chavannes, p. 240. For a discussion of population registration in pre-Qin times, see Robin Yates, "The City Under Siege: Technology and Organization as seen in the Reconstructed Text of the Military Chapters of *Mo-tzu*."

4. *Han shu*, 28B, 1640.

5. Ikeda On, *Chūgoku kodai sekichō kenkyū*, pp. 146–148.

6. *Samguk saigi*, in *Chōsen shi*, IV, Annals of King Shinmun 9/1, 77; Annals of King Sŏngdŏk 21/8/1, 129. The first citation marks Silla's adaptation of a stipend system, for which nationwide taxation and a census were important. The second reference is to Silla's implementation of state land allocation, for which a census was necessary. See also Inoue Hideo, *Kodai no Chōsen*, pp. 222–227.

7. Nomura Tadao, "Shiryō shōkai: Shōsōin yori hakken sareta Shiragi no minsei monjo ni tsuite," *Shigaku zasshi* 62:58–68 (April 1953).

8. *SZKT, Nihon shoki*, Kimmei 1/8, p. 51.

9. The authenticity of the 646 and 652 commands to register the populace is closely tied to the debate over the Taika Reform Edict. See Introduction, n20. Miyamoto Tasuku, "Ritsuryōteki tochi seido," in Takeuchi Rizō, ed., *Taikei Nihon shi sōsho 6 Tochi seido* 1, p. 85, notes that the 652 census is considered spurious by most Japanese historians, although he accepts its validity.

10. Hayashi Rokurō, *Jōdai seiji shakai no kenkyū*, pp. 345–404; Torao Toshiya, *Handen shūju hō no kenkyū*, pp. 291–340.

11. *SZKT, Ko-ryō no gige, Zō koseki no jō*, pp. 96–97. The degree to which this provision and the others that follow were enforced is difficult to ascertain. Law always serves as a social ideal that may not be fully realized. But the fragmentary evidence Japanese historians have been able to collect suggests surprisingly strict adherence to the Taihō Codes. Many examples are cited throughout the text and notes of this chapter, such as the upcoming discussions of the evolution of the tax register or the dates on which tax and household registers were due in the capital. Other instances of enforcement would include the notation of the province, district, and administrative village on each seam of the Chikuzen household register, the compilation of audits of household registers (*kanjaku*) covered in Chapter 5, and entries in provincial fiscal ledgers providing expenses to officials charged with collecting draft returns for tax registers. A welcome addition to this knowledge was the discovery of a record from the Kanto province of Kōzuke. (*HI*, IX, 3511–3541.) This document states that in 1208, long after the system of census-taking had ceased to function, 550 scrolls of household registers were still on hand in the provincial offices, including 90 scrolls from the 670 census. Further reading would include the extensive explanation of the Yōrō articles on household and tax registers written by Yoshida Takashi in Inoue Mitsusada et al., eds., *Nihon shisō taikei 4 Ritsuryō*, pp. 555–559. See also Hayashi, *Jōdai seiji*, and Torao, *Handen shūju*, cited in n10 above.

12. *SZKT, Ko-ryō no gige, Zō koseki no jō*, p. 97.

13. *SZKT, Den-ryō no gige*, Handen no jō, p. 365.

14. *SZKT, Shoku Nihongi*, Wadō 6/5/12, pp. 52–53.

15. *SZKT, Ko-ryō no gige, Zō keichō no jō*, p. 96.

16. This discussion is based on Kamata Motokazu, "Keichō seido shiron," *Shirin* 55:1-43 (September 1972).

17. *SZKT, Shoku Nihongi*, Yōrō 1/5/22, p. 69.

18. *SZKT, Engi shukei shiki, Daichō no jō*, pp. 627-642.

19. *HI*, I, 301-302.

20. The Heian registers have been analyzed by Hirata Kōji, "Heian jidai no koseki ni tsuite," in *Nihon kodai chūsei shi no chihōteki tenkai*, pp. 59-96.

21. The printed versions of these records are inaccurate. The household registers were reconstructed in compliance with guidelines established by a group of scholars headed by Takeuchi Rizō. See Takeuchi Rizō, "Shōsōin koseki chōsa gaihō," *Shigaku zasshi* 68:34-65 (March 1959); 69:77-98 (February 1960); 69:85-93 (March 1960). The Yamashiro tax registers were restored according to the opinion of Kishi Toshio, who was a member of Takeuchi's group and examined the records in the original. I wish to express my appreciation to Professor Kishi Toshio for his generous help throughout this project.

22. Kishi Toshio, "Kodai kōki no shakai kikō," in *Shin Nihon shi kōza: Kodai kōki*, p. 9.

23. Ibid., pp. 11-12.

24. Hirano Kunio, *Taika zendai shakai soshiki no kenkyū*, pp. 364-376.

25. The only reference to the Ordinance of 715 is included in *NKBT, Izumo fudoki*, pp. 96-97. For a translation of this gazetteer, see *The Izumo fudoki*, tr. Michiko Aoki, p. 81.

26. This edict is mentioned in *SZKT, Ko-ryō no shūge, Ōbun no jō*, "one writer" cited in *Koki*, p. 293.

27. Of course, populations with sex ratios lying outside the 90 to 105 range may still be used in demographic analysis. Sex ratios for many Tokugawa villages in the eighteenth century are as high as 130, and yet the populations are frequently subjected to analyses similar to the one conducted in this chapter. Still, sex ratios which lie appreciably outside this range must be accounted for in some way. In the Tokugawa case, female infanticide is usually the answer; for my data, evasion of registration by taxable males probably gave rise to the feminine ratios. (Conversation with Professor Hayami Akira, 28 October 1983.)

28. For a more complete explanation of Myers's blended method, see *Manual II: Methods of Appraisal of Quality of Basic Data for Population Estimates*, pp. 41-42. Myers's index measures only preference for final digits, and should not be considered a definitive test of overall age accuracy. It is therefore not as valuable a yardstick of data reliability as the sex ratio or percentage of children under age 15.

29. Sawada Goichi, *Nara chō jidai*, p. 52.

30. Kishi Toshio, *Nihon kodai sekichō no kenkyū*, pp. 111-139.

31. Nambu Noboru, "Kōgo nenjaku to saikaidō koseki museisha," *Kodai shi ronsō*, I, 606–632. It is interesting to note that a similar problem also appears in early Tokugawa census data and the first counts of the Ainu in the modern age. Preferences are for ages ending in 0 and 5, while registrants shy away from the final digits 4 and 7, which are homonymous with the Japanese words for death and suffering, respectively. (Private conversation with Professor Hayami Akira of Keio University, 28 October 1983.)

32. Kishi, *Sekichō*, p. 128.

33. Another calculation provides further insight into the quality of the 702 data. Sex ratios for the Mino, Hanyū, and Kyushu sets for the heaped ages ending in digits 0, 2, and 7 are 58.1, 68.5, and 61.5 respectively. These results suggest that the census-takers of 670 and 690 not only rounded off registrants' ages, but also allowed many males to escape registration or be enrolled as females. Such highly unbalanced sex ratios imply serious underlying problems, even in relatively good records like the Mino or Hanyū registers. But, because the overall sex ratios were acceptable, I proceeded with the analysis.

34. Kishi, *Sekichō*, pp. 73–81. For a reply to Kishi, see Torao Toshiya, "Mitabi Kiyomihara ryō no handen hō ni tsuite," in *Zoku Nihon kodai shi ronshū*, III, 491–500.

35. I am deeply indebted to Professor Kobayashi Kazumasa, a demographer now retired from the Southeast Asian Research Center at Kyoto University, for his guidance at this stage of the project. Dr. Harashima Akira of the National Institute for Environmental Studies at Tsukuba wrote the computer programs for this study.

36. *DNK*, I, 24.

37. For an explanation of Greville's technique, see Hugh Wolfenden, *Population Statistics and Their Compilation*, rev. ed., pp. 141–155; Thomas Greville, "The General Theory of Osculatory Interpolation," *Transactions of the Actuarial Society of America* 45:202–265 (1944).

38. For example, the number of people in the 5-year interval 23 to 27 (P_{23-27}) was derived as follows:

$$P_{23-27} = \frac{P_{8-17}}{\left(\dfrac{P_{8-17}}{P_{28-37}}\right)^{\frac{1}{4}} + 1}$$

The number of persons in 5-year interval 18 to 22 was obtained by subtracting P_{23-27} from the total number of persons in the 10-year interval 18 to 27.

39. A computer tape showing the smoothing of male and female data for the 5 sets of documents will be provided upon request.

40. Stable population analysis is not ordinarily undertaken without the use of an independent variable such as the growth or birth rate. However, calculation of vital statistics from the sex and age distribution of a population is

common in archaeology. See Kenneth Weis, "On the Systematic Bias in Skeletal Sexing," *American Journal of Physical Anthropology* 37:239–249 (September 1972). Professor David Herlihy of Harvard University has also analyzed medieval European populations using stable population techniques without an independent variable.

Professor Kitō Hiroshi, a student of Hayami Akira (Japan's leading demographer), has recently inferred life expectancy from the age structure of the Mino population. See his *Nihon nisen nen no jinkō shi*, p. 60. Without reference to model life tables, Kitō estimated life expectancy at about 17 or 18 years.

41. Sawada, *Nara chō jidai*, pp. 49–61, also suspected inaccuracy in the Shimōsa and Yamashiro data.

42. I should like to thank Ansley Coale of the Office of Population Research at Princeton University for his analysis of the failure of the test on Mino males. He has suggested that the inadequate registration of older males was responsible for the poor results. His analysis is also pertinent to the problem of high birth rates discussed later. Private correspondence with Ansley Coale, 25 November 1981.

43. On the birth rates in the Tokugawa period, see Hanley and Yamamura, pp. 199–205.

44. Takamure, *Kon'in shi*, pp. 69–70. These percentages are not derived from exactly the same data used in this study. Takamure uses evidence of separate registration of spouses to bolster her argument that early Japanese kinship was bilateral and marriage residence duolocal. Although I generally endorse Takamure's conclusion, it is important to note that other historians do not. For support of the patrilocal perspective, see Nunomura Kazuo, "Sekichō ni okeru fukeiteki kyōdaiteki kazoku kyōdōtai," *Rekishi gaku kenkyū* 429:24–34 (February 1976). For additional discussion of kinship, see Chapter 5, n 34.

45. Jane Menken, James Trussell, and Susan Watkins, "The Nutrition Fertility Link: An Evaluation of the Evidence," *The Journal of Interdisciplinary History* 11:425–441 (Winter 1981).

46. See n 40, above.

47. Harry Miskimin, *The Economy of Early Renaissance Europe, 1300–1460*, pp. 26–27.

48. Hanley and Yamamura, pp. 320–334. It is important to note that many Japanese demographers believe life expectancy in the Tokugawa period to have been far below the Hanley estimate. Hayami Akira has tabulated life expectancy in some late-seventeenth-century villages as being as low as 29 years from birth. The difference between the two estimates is based on a discrepancy in the number of newborn actually registered in Edo census records. If one accepts Hayami's estimates for the Edo period, calculations of Nara-period life expectancy in this book may even be somewhat high. See also n 40 above.

49. Torao, *Handen shūju*, pp. 53–80.

50. Kōchi Shōsuke, "Taihō ryō handen shūju seido kō," *Shigaku zasshi* 86:29–30 (March 1977).

51. Kishi, *Sekichō*, p. 274.

52. *SZKT, Shoku Nihongi*, Yōrō 7/4/17, p. 96.

53. *SZKT, Shoku Nihongi*, Yōrō 7/11/12, p. 97.

54. Miyamoto Tasuku, "Ritsuryōteki tochi seido," pp. 94–95.

55. *SZKT, Shoku Nihongi*, Tempyō 1/3/23, p. 116.

56. Iyanaga Teizō, "Mino no kuni, Kamo no kōri, Hanyū no sato no ko-seki no kochi ni tsuite," *Chihō shi kenkyū* 56.57:1–24 (April, June 1962). One *chō* = approximately 3 acres or 1.2 hectares.

2. Population Trends and Epidemic Disease

1. McNeill, *Plagues and Peoples*, p. 125.

2. Some outstanding medical historians have studied disease in the early period, including Fujikawa Yū, *Nihon shippei shi*, and Hattori Toshirō, *Nara jidai igaku no kenkyū*. But their work does not really treat the social, economic, or political effects of pestilence. Recently, such historians as Iya-naga Teizō and Morita Tei have begun to emphasize the role of epidemics.

3. The following explanation is drawn from McNeill, pp. 14–131.

4. J. C. Russell, *British Medieval Population*, pp. 54, 146, 246, 269–270. Not all scholars believe that English population stagnated in the medieval period. For example, see Michael Postan, "Medieval Agrarian Society in its Prime: England," in Michael Postan, ed., *The Cambridge Economic History of Europe:* I, *The Agrarian Life of the Middle Ages*, 2nd ed., pp. 560–570. But Postan does not deny that epidemic outbreaks inflicted great losses on English population. For a general debate on the effects of epidemics in European agrarian history, see Robert Brenner, "Agrarian Class Structure and Economic Development," *Past and Present* 70:30–75 (February 1976); Michael Postan and Emmanuel LeRoy Ladurie, "Symposium: Agrarian Class Structure and Economic Development in Pre-Industrial Europe," *Past and Present* 78:55–59 (February 1978).

5. *SZKT, Kushiki-ryō no gige, Koku yū zui no jō*, p. 255.

6. *SZKT, Kushiki-ryō no shūge, Koku yū zui no jō*, Ato ki, p. 866.

7. *SZKT, Kushiki-ryō no gige, Koku yū kyūsoku no jō*, p. 284.

8. *Daidō ruijū hō*, cited in *Iryō uta haisai*, comp. by Furuhayashi Kenchō. Archives of Dr. Fujikawa Yū at Kyoto University, Vol. I, leaf 16, recto and verso.

9. *Honchō seiki*, cited in Fujikawa, *Shippei*, p. 101.

10. *Zoku kojidan* in *Kokushi sōsho*, X, 270.

11. *Ainōshō* in *Nihon koten zenshū*, XV, 107–108.

12. Denis Twitchett, "Population and Pestilence in T'ang China," in Franz

Steiner, ed., *Studia Sino-Mongolica: Festschrift für Herbert Franke*, p. 42.

13. *SZKT, Shoku Nihongi*, Tempyō 4/8/27, p. 129. The exact relationship between resistance to disease and diet is controversial. See Andrew Appleby, "Nutrition and Disease: The Case of London, 1550-1750," *The Journal of Interdisciplinary History* 6:1-22 (Summer 1975). Experiments suggest that well-fed monkeys resist many viruses better than starving ones.

14. *SZKT, Ko-ryō no gige, Sō suikan no jō*, p. 106.

15. *SZKT, Shoku Nihongi*, Jingi 3/6/5, p. 105. Note the use of *shinjutsu* and not the legal term *shingō*.

16. Shōmu had used the amnesty in a similar manner before. Cf. *SZKT, Shoku Nihongi*, Tempyō 4/7/5, pp. 128-129.

17. *Samguk sagi*, p. 139. Japanese sources contain no references to the invasion.

18. *NKBT, Man'yōshū*, IV, #3668, pp. 78-79. I express my gratitude to Professor Edwin Cranston of Harvard University for assistance with this translation.

19. *NKBT, Man'yōshū*, IV, #3688, pp. 85-86. Translation from *The Man'-yōshū*, Nippon gakujutsu shinkō kai, ed., p. 248, with slight alteration.

20. The *Shoku Nihongi* does not state where Ōtomo stayed while he battled smallpox; it merely says he was not permitted entry into the capital with the rest of the party in the 1st month of 737. At the end of the 3rd month, Ōtomo and a group of 40 people finally paid court. Aoki Kazuo, *Nihon no rekishi 3 Nara no miyako*, pp. 305-307, believes Ōtomo recovered from the sickness in Tsushima.

21. *SZKT, Ruijū fusen shō*, pp. 90-91.

22. *SZKT, Kushiki-ryō no gige, Tenshi shinji no jō*, p. 282.

23. *SZKT, Engi dajōkan shiki, Nai gein no jō*, pp. 326-327.

24. Hattori, *Nara igaku*, pp. 181-182.

25. Barbara Tuchman, *A Distant Mirror*, pp. 101-103.

26. Hattori, *Nara igaku*, p. 175.

27. Fujikawa, *Shippei*, p. 103.

28. *SZKT, Chōya gunsai*, pp. 482-483. One *ryō* = 14 grams and 1 *shō* = 0.24 liter.

29. *SZKT, Engi shuzei shiki, Shōzei chō no jō*, pp. 671-685.

30. *SZKT, Shoku Nihongi*, Yōrō 1/5/22, p. 69.

31. *SZKT, Seiji Yōryaku*, pp. 415, 430.

32. *SZKT, Engi shuzei shiki, Kan zeichō no jō*, p. 643.

33. Hayakawa Shōhachi, "Kugai tō seido no seiritsu," *Shigaku zasshi* 69:22-25 (March 1960).

34. For example, see *SZKT, Nihon shoki*, Ankan 2/9/3, p. 43.

35. *SZKT, Nihon shoki*, Temmu 4/4/9, p. 337.

36. *DNK*, II, 247-252.

37. Numerous entries in the *Shoku Nihongi* support this definition. For example, see Tempyō 1/8/5, p. 120.

38. Hayakawa, "Kugai tō," p. 32.

39. Establishing the relationship between the proportion of non-payment in rice sheaves and mortality is difficult. The samples are small (in Satsuma, consisting of only 135 sheaves and 11 people), and some historians have cast doubt upon the reliability of the default entries. Funao Yoshimasa, "Suiko no jittai ni kansuru ichi kōsatsu," *Shirin* 56:74–102 (September 1973), has argued that local notables in Bitchū took out large loans under the names of dead peasants; thus, remission rates noted on this record would be fraudulent. The information provided in the *shōzei chō* is too cursory to permit an analysis like Funao's to be carried out.

A more pressing problem involves social class. In the late seventh century, an edict of the Emperor Temmu states that rice loans should be allotted mostly to households of poor to moderate means. These households presumably would have been more likely to have been malnourished and susceptible to disease, and also probably would have accumulated large debts to provincial officials. Both phenomena would tend to make the default statistics overrepresent total mortality. However, the average loan taken out by the peasants who died in 737 was 20.1 sheaves, which is by no means excessive. Figures from Sawada Goichi, pp. 178–184, suggest that, in Mutsu, adult males borrowed about 37 sheaves per person in the early ninth century, when the system of rice loans had clearly become a tax every adult male was required to pay. Even in the 730s, the rice loans were evolving toward the status of a tax, and the average loan per person leaves no reason to assume that only the indigent were represented.

40. Several unknowns make this procedure a tricky business. Exact figures are available for only 4 of the 15 provinces known to have been afflicted (see Map 4). Other provinces undoubtedly suffered from the disease but failed to report to the capital (e.g., Bungo). And trade and travel routes make other provinces likely candidates for outbreaks (e.g., Chikugo, Ōmi). Relative population densities for Japan's 66 provinces were computed by Sawada, but his estimates apply to the tenth century, when 200 years of migration had greatly increased the population of eastern Japan. For these reasons, a precise province-by-province tabulation of mortality involves too many assumptions to be reliable. Further research into *ritsuryō* travel and migration routes and the nature of smallpox may allow a more precise calculation in the future.

41. McNeill, p. 180.

42. *SZKT, Ruijū sandai kyaku*, Daidō 3/9/26 Order of the Council of State, pp. 395–396. Also see Sawada Goichi, *Nara chō jidai*, pp. 169–177, for a discussion of the object of *suiko* loans.

43. MacFarlane Burnet and David White, *The Natural History of Infectious Disease*, pp. 99–100.

44. Maurice Beresford, *The Lost Villages of England.*

45. See Hayakawa Shōhachi, "Tempyō rokunen Izumo no kuni keikai chō no kenkyū," in *Nihon kodai shi ronshū,* II, 297–298.

46. *SZKT, Ruijū sandai kyaku,* Tempyō 12/8/4 Order of the Council of State cited in Daidō 3/8/3 Order, p. 349.

47. *SZKT, Shoku Nihongi,* Tempyō 17/10/5 and Tempyō 17/11/27, pp. 184–185. The best analysis of the new system is Hayakawa, "Kugai tō," pp. 1–20.

48. *SZKT, Shoku Nihongi,* Tempyō 4/7/5, pp. 128–129.

49. *SZKT, Shoku Nihongi,* Tempyō 7/5/23, p. 138.

50. For example, see Torao Toshiya, *Handen shūju hō no kenkyū,* pp. 406–408, 423–426; Kozo Yamamura, "The Decline of the *Ritsuryō* System: Hypothesis on Economic and Institutional Change," *Journal of Japanese Studies* 1:18 (Autumn 1974). For a contrasting view, see Yoshida Takashi, "Konden eisei shizai hō no henshitsu," in *Nihon shakai keizai shi kenkyū: Kodai chūsei hen,* pp. 61–91. Chapter 3 contains a detailed discussion of the 743 law.

51. *SZKT, Ruijū sandai kyaku,* Tempyō 8/2/25 Edict, p. 385.

52. For example, see Iyanaga Teizō, "Hasseiki no Nihon," in *Nihon to sekai no rekishi,* V, 40; Yoshida Takashi, "Ritsuryō sei to sonraku," p. 189.

53. Kishi Toshio, *Nihon kodai seiji shi kenkyū,* pp. 276–277.

54. Ernest Jawetz et al., eds., *Review of Medical Microbiology,* pp. 431–434.

55. *SZKT, Nihon Montoku tennō jitsuroku,* Ninju 3/2, p. 49.

56. *SZKT, Ruijū fusen shō,* pp. 89–90.

57. *SZKT, Ruijū kokushi,* Daidō 2/12/1, pp. 258–259.

58. *SZKT, Ruijū sandai kyaku,* Kōnin 14/2/21, Remonstrance of the Council of State, pp. 434–437. For the classic study of this new policy, see Akamatsu Toshihide, "Kueiden o tsūjite mitaru shoki shōen sei no kōzō ni tsuite," *Rekishi gaku kenkyū* 7:1–28 (May 1937). Also note Morita Tei, "Kodai chihō gyōsei kikō ni tsuite no ichi kōsatsu," *Rekishi gaku kenkyū* 401:15–27 (October 1973).

59. *SZKT, Shoku Nihongi,* Enryaku 9/Kono toshi no jō, p. 550.

60. Twitchett, "Population and Pestilence," p. 48.

61. Ibid., pp. 35–68.

62. *SZKT, Nihon shoki,* Bidatsu 14/3/30, p. 115. Translation from *Nihongi,* II, 104.

63. Hattori Toshirō, "Jōko shi iji kō," *Nihon ishi gaku zasshi* 1312:64–76 (February 1943).

64. *SZKT, Hyakuren shō,* Kangen 1/5/19 (smallpox), p. 199; Gennin 1/4/13 (measles), p. 161. Cited in Fujikawa, *Shippei,* pp. 37–38.

3. Land Clearance

1. Abe Takeshi, *Nihon shōen seiritsu shi no kenkyū*, p. 57.

2. Studies of land clearance in Japanese history are very numerous. As a potential source of Abe's thesis in the prewar era, note Honjō Eijirō and Kokushō Iwao, *Nihon keizai shi*, pp. 157-159, 186-187. As examples of the best postwar works which also share Abe's assumption about the link between population growth and the creation of new fields, I cite: Furushima Toshio, *Furushima Toshio chosaku zenshū* 6 *Nihon nōgyō gijutsu shi*, pp. 94-105, 139-142, 153-157, 241-248; Yasuda Motohisa, *Nihon shōen shi gaisetsu*, pp. 14-26; George Sansom, *A History of Japan to 1334*, p. 88; John Hall, *Government and Local Power in Japan, 500 to 1700*, pp. 103-105 (Hall's work was based on the studies of Yasuda and Furushima); and, most recently, Miyamoto Tasuku, "Ritsuryōteki tochi seido," pp. 110-116.

3. *SZKT, Den-ryō no shūge, Kōbai no jō*, pp. 370-372. For the corresponding Tang statute, see *Tōrei shūi*, comp. Niida Noboru, p. 614. For an English translation of the Chinese article, see Denis Twitchett, *Financial Administration under the T'ang Dynasty*, p. 131. The related concepts of state and private land set forth in the law codes vary considerably from modern ideas. The simplest rule of thumb to distinguish the concepts is that, in general, only private land was liable for the 3% rice tax (*denso*). For a concise summary of work on the distinction between state and private land, see Miyamoto, "Ritsuryōteki tochi seido," pp. 77-84. Iyanaga Teizō, "Ritsuryōseiteki tochi shoyū," *Iwanami kōza Nihon rekishi* 3 *Kodai* 3 (1962), pp. 39-53, and Yoshida Takashi's explanatory notes in Inoue Mitsusada et al., eds., *Nihon shisō shi taikei* 4 *Ritsuryō*, pp. 578-579, provide an excellent introduction to study of this statute.

4. Torao Toshiya, "Ritsuryō jidai no konden hō ni kansuru ni san no mondai," *Hirosaki daigaku jimbun shakai* 15:65-69 (1958). For a dissenting opinion, see Fukuoka Takeshi, "Kūkan chi no eishuken o meguru shomondai," *Rekishi gaku kenkyū* 285: 1-10 (Februrary 1962).

5. *SZKT, Shoku Nihongi*, Wado 4/12/6, p. 47. Miyamoto, "Ritsuryōteki tochi seido," p. 60, believes that this law, and not the Taihō Codes, first granted peasants the right to clear wilderness.

6. Obstructing peasants was a punishable offense. See *SZKT, Zō-ryō no gige, Kokunai no jō*, p. 334.

7. *SZKT, Shoku Nihongi*, Keiun 3/3/14, p. 26.

8. *SZKT, Shoku Nihongi*, Yōrō 6/Int. 4/25, pp. 92-93. One *koku* = about 24 liters.

9. This interpretation was originally proposed by Murao Jirō, *Ritsuryō zaisei shi no kenkyū*, pp. 499-544. Haneda Minoru, "Sanze isshin hō ni tsuite," *Hisutoria* 30:38-40 (June 1961), believes that the law applied to all Japan, but agrees with Murao that the scheme focused on dry fields as a precaution

against drought. Haneda's argument for the nationwide applicability of this order seems weak; he does not adequately explain how the 722 law can apply to the whole nation when the other orders issued on the same day (Yōrō 6/Int. 4/25) are either directed explicitly to Mutsu officials or discuss conditions unique to Mutsu, such as the raising of military expeditions. As Haneda also remarks, if the 722 law is seen as an attempt to increase paddy fields on a nationwide scale, then it must not have been too effective, because it was replaced in only one year. See also Abe Takeshi, *Shōen seiritsu*, p. 65, who has calculated that, at 100 men per *chō*, the Mutsu project would have required 100 million workers and 7 million *koku* of rice for provisions. For still other views, see Miyamoto, "Ritsuryōteki tochi seido," pp. 61-62.

10. *SZKT, Shoku Nihongi*, Yōrō 5/2/17; Yōrō 5/3/7, p. 85.

11. *SZKT, Shoku Nihongi*, Yōrō 7/3/17, p. 96.

12. Tokinoya Shigeru, "Den-ryō to konden hō," *Rekishi kyōiku* 4:33-35 (May 1956); 5:50-51 (June 1956); Torao, "Konden hō," pp. 73-75. For a critique of Tokinoya, see Haneda, "Sanze isshin hō," pp. 40-44; Iyanaga, "Ritsuryō tochi," pp. 47-49. Haneda and Iyanaga argue that Tokinoya's view contradicts ninth-century legislation like the Tenchō 1/8/20 Order of the Council of State, which specifically guarantees lifelong tenure to peasants who return abandoned land to productivity. Even though they dispute Tokinoya's argument that the 723 law included reopened deserted fields within its purview, Iyanaga and Haneda share his emphasis on the importance of abandoned fields in the *ritsuryō* period.

13. *SZKT, Shoku Nihongi*, Tempyō 15/5/27, p. 174. The "previous regulation" referred to appears in *SZKT, Shoku Nihongi*, Tempyō 1/11/7, p. 121, and reiterates the duties of provincial governors as specified in the law codes.

Also see *SZKT, Shoku Nihongi*, Tempyō Jingo 1/3/5, p. 319, for revocation of the 743 law and Hōki 3/10/14, p. 406, for its resurrection.

14. *SZKT, Ruijū sandai kyaku*, Tempyō 15/5/27 Edict, p. 441.

15. A thorough discussion of this edict is found in Yoshida Takashi, "Konden eisei shizai hō no henshitsu," pp. 61-91. A similar view was also proposed by Maruyama Tadatsuna, "Konden eisei shizai hō ni tsuite," *Hōsei shigaku* 13:28-48 (1960). See Yasuda, *Shōen shi*, pp. 19-20, for a brief but more traditional interpretation.

16. *SZKT, Ruijū sandai kyaku*, Kampyō 8/4/2 Order of the Council of State, pp. 486-487.

17. *DNK*, II, 258-271; *NI*, I, 281-288. Close scrutiny shows that the report did not reflect conditions in Hamana perfectly. See Torao Toshiya, *Handen shūju hō no kenkyū*, pp. 429-455, who argues that figures used for each peasant's parcel are suspiciously uniform, and that officials at the provincial offices may have manipulated numbers to profit from reduced tax rates.

Although irregularities in the Tōtōmi report are disturbing, figures used for the entire district are probably accurate. See Nakano Hideo, "Tōtōmi no kuni Hamana no kōri yuso chō no kisoteki kōsatsu," *Nihon rekishi* 219:67–89 (August 1972); and Ōyama Seiichi, "Tempyō jūninen Tōtōmi no kuni, Hamana no kōri yuso chō no shiryō sei ni kansuru ichi kōsatsu," *Nihon rekishi* 306:111–120 (November 1973). Also see Torao's corrections of the inaccurate text.

18. Hayashiya Tatsusaburō, *Kodai kokka no kaitai*, pp. 48–51, discusses the terrain at Hamana, while *SZKT, Nihon Montoku tennō jitsuroku*, Kashō 3/8/3, p. 16, reports flooding.

19. *DNK*, II, 335–337.

20. *NI*, II, 343.

21 Clifford Geertz, *Agricultural Involution*, p. 29.

22. *SZKT, Shoku Nihongi*, Tempyō 15/10/15, p. 175.

23. *Tōdaiji yōroku*, ed. Tsutsui Hidetoshi, pp. 13–14.

24. *SZKT, Shoku Nihongi*, Tempyō Shōhō 1/4/1, pp. 197–200.

25. Kishi Toshio, *Nihon kodai seiji shi kenkyū*, p. 378; *DNK*, I, 316–317.

26. *NI*, II, 690; *DNK*, IV, 49–50. For a translation of this document, see Kan'ichi Asakawa, *Land and Society in Medieval Japan*, pp. 84–85.

27. *SZKT, Shoku Nihongi*, Tempyō Shōhō 6/1/7, p. 219.

28. *NI*, II, 690–693; *DNK*, IV, 52–58; Asakawa, pp. 85–88.

29. *NI*, II, 690–697; *DNK*, IV, 52–58, 111–114, 219–221, 246–250; Asakawa, pp. 85–92. A more accurate version of the final report is contained in *TM*, II, 149–154. Since Asakawa's translation is based on *DNK*, IV, 246–250, it is incorrect.

30. *NI*, II, 698; *DNK*, IV, 250–252; *TM*, II, 155–157. Ten *shaku* = 1 *jō*. One *shaku* = 29.7 centimeters (11.75 inches).

31. Hara Hidesaburō, "Hasseiki ni okeru kaihatsu ni tsuite," *Nihon shi kenkyū* 61:5 (July 1962).

32. Kinda Akihiro, "Tōdaiji ryō shōen no keikan to kaihatsu," in Asaka Toshiki, ed., *Kodai no chihō shi*, IV, 204–205. My analysis of Kuwabara follows Kinda's reading of the topography.

33. *NI*, II, 717; *DNK*, V, 547; *TM*, II, 256. Elizabeth Sato has stated in "The Early Development of the Shōen," in John Hall and Jeffrey Mass, eds., *Medieval Japan: Essays in Institutional History*, p. 98, that "by far the majority of cases" of land abandonment were produced by local sabotage. It is not clear whether she is referring to Kuwabara, Echizen, or all of the Tōdaiji *shōen* of the Nara era. Although her statement may be true for individual *shōen*, especially in Echizen, it does not hold for many other Tōdaiji projects. In addition, even when local sabotage was the main cause of land abandonment, it should be viewed in the context of the poor agricultural technology of the eighth century, a topic Sato neglects. See, for example, Nagahara Keiji, *Nihon keizai shi*, p. 63, who lists poor irrigation as the principal cause for the decline of the early *shōen*. Also see Iyanaga, "Ritsuryō tochi," p. 45, who puts poor farming techniques ahead of social factors in his analysis of field

desertion. Even if Sato were correct in her belief that sabotage was the major cause, it would not contradict the theme of this chapter, which is the impermanence of land clearance.

34. Maruyama Yoshihiko, "Tōdaiji ryō shōen no hensen," in Yagi Atsuru, ed., Kodai no chihō shi, II, 233-260.

35. NI, II, 737; DNK, V, 525-527; TM, II, 418-419.

36. HI, I, 63-67; TM, II, 283-293. For a detailed analysis of the clearance of the original 68 chō, see Maruyama Yoshihiko, pp. 240-243, 245-248, 255-256.

37. Maruyama Yoshihiko, pp. 244-245.

38. NKBT, Man'yōshū, III, #4085, pp. 274-275.

39. SZKT, Shoku Nihongi, Jingo Keiun 1/3/20, p. 342.

40. NI, II, 723-730, 731-736; DNK, IV, 275-292; V, 662-666, 685-691; TM, II, 295-325. The most accurate and accessible compilation is TM, IV. One map made of paper is not in the Shōsōin collection.

41. For example, Takeuchi Rizō, Nara chō jidai ni okeru jiin keizai no kenkyū, pp. 225-226; Yonezawa Yasushi, Etchū kodai shi no kenkyū, pp. 167-192.

42. Arai Kikuo, Iyanaga Teizō, and Kameda Takashi, "Etchū no kuni Tōdaiji ryō shōen ezu ni tsuite," Shoku Nihongi kenkyū 5:2-22 (February 1958).

43. These views are summarized in Kinda, "Shōen no keikan," pp. 199-201.

44. NI, II, 730-731; DNK, V, 640-645; TM, II, 350-355.

45. HI, I, 386.

46. HI, II, 511-513.

47. In general, Japanese historians put the early shōen (shoki shōen) in a different class from later Heian and Kamakura projects. A major characteristic of all early shōen is that they disappeared, or at least became less productive, in the ninth and tenth centuries. See Miyamoto, "Ritsuryōteki tochi seido," pp. 128-131. Of course, a few of Tōdaiji's shōen survived, primarily because they were located in the Kinai region near the temple. But, even if all of Tōdaiji's shōen in the Kinai had continued to be productive into the mid-Heian era, they would have amounted to no more than 6 to 10% of the temple's once vast holdings. In contrast, the failed projects in Echizen and Etchū tallied almost half of Tōdaiji's land. For another example of a shōen that made the transition into the tenth and eleventh centuries, see Elizabeth Sato's analysis of Tōji's Ōyama shōen in "Early Development," pp. 101-107.

How well the early shōen of Tōdaiji might represent all land clearance projects in the ritsuryō era is open to debate. Tōdaiji itself was a unique institution; its shōen were established more hurriedly and later than those of other temples, and the paddies were located in marshy terrain. But Iyanaga Teizō, Nara jidai no kizoku to nōmin, pp. 109-110, notes that developing land in swampy areas was common throughout the early period. While other projects of the *ritsuryō* era were undoubtedly more successful than most of Tōdaiji's *shōen*, I have examined Tōdaiji's projects in some detail because the pattern of land clearance and desertion matches the trend seen in legal records and elsewhere. Again, see Iyanaga, *Kozoku to nōmin*, pp. 55–56.

48. *SZKT, Ruijū sandai kyaku*, Tenchō 1/8/20 Order of the Council of State, p. 322.

49. Iyanaga Teizō, "Ritsuryō tochi," pp. 45–49; Kikuchi Yasuaki, *Nihon kodai tochi shoyū no kenkyū*, pp. 310–328; Sakamoto Shōzō, *Nihon ōchō kokka taisei ron*, pp. 140–164.

50. *SZKT, Ruijū sandai kyaku*, Jōwa 8/5/5 Order of the Council of State cited in Jōgan 12/12/25 Order, p. 322.

51. Exposition of the Eizanji case follows Toda Yoshimi, *Nihon ryōshu sei seiritsu shi no kenkyū*, pp. 167–190. Toda reserves judgment on 1 *chō* of land.

52. The topic of fallow systems in early Japan is controversial. The Land Statutes contained a provision permitting peasants tilling poor soil to farm a greater area than the legal standard, but this provision was not applied until the early ninth century (*SZKT, Ruijū sandai kyaku*, Kōnin 12/6/4 for Kawachi province and Tenchō 4/6/2 for Izumi). Could the belated implementation of the statute on fallow fields signify the increasing exhaustion of the land? If so, laws on fallow land may be related to the regulations on land clearance and abandonment cited in this chapter. Works on the fallow system include Torao Toshiya, "Kōden o meguru futatsu no mondai," in *Ritsuryō kokka to kizoku shakai*, pp. 279–289, and Miyahara Takeo, *Nihon kodai no kokka to nōmin*, pp. 308–314. Also see Takashige Susumu, *Kodai chūsei no kōchi to sonraku*, pp. 56–83.

53. Furushima, *Nihon nōgyō*, pp. 241–242.

54. Toda, *Ryōshu sei seiritsu*, pp. 168–169.

55. Yoshia Takashi, "Ritsuryō sei to sonraku," pp. 170–171.

56. Although the traditional date for compilation of the *Shūgai shō* is 1341, it would be more accurate to say that the work reflected conditions of the middle Kamakura era, or perhaps even earlier. See Iyanaga Teizō, "*Shūgai shō* oyobi *Kaitō shokoku ki* ni arawareta shokoku no denseki shiryō ni kansuru oboegaki," *Nagoya daigaku bungaku bu kenkyū ronshū* 41:8–11 (1966), for a detailed analysis of this text.

57. Inagaki Yasuhiko, "Chūsei no nōgyō keiei to shūshu keitai," *Iwanami kōza Nihon rekishi 6 Chūsei* 2 (1975), pp. 175–182.

4. Land Use and Agricultural Technology

1. See, for example, Kan'ichi Asakawa, *Land and Society in Medieval Japan*, pp. 219–230. Many Japanese historians treat only the institutional framework within which early agriculture operated, without making a de-

tailed study of concrete factors such as technology, soil, topography, or land use. For instance, see Kameda Takashi, *Nihon kodai yōsui shi no kenkyū*, and Torao Toshiya, *Handen shūju hō no kenkyū*. Of course, there are also many excellent works that examine early farming technology in a concrete way, such as Furushima Toshio, *Furushima Toshio chosaku zenshū 6 Nihon nōgyō gijutsu shi*, Iyanaga Teizō, *Nara jidai no kizoku to nōmin*, and Toda Yoshimi, *Nihon ryōshu sei seiritsu shi no kenkyū*.

It may be true that wet-rice technology gives an impression of inertia when viewed over the long run. A few basic implements, like the hoe or conduit, appear to have changed little in a thousand years; social factors like the organization of manpower probably played a greater role in the overall development of rice farming than did the invention of new technology. Even in the Nara and Heian periods, certain areas controlled by wealthy temples or aristocrats may have been farmed in a more intensive manner resembling medieval or early modern cultivation. Although I accept these points, the evidence presented in this chapter still suggests that projecting our knowledge of Tokugawa or other rice regimes back into the Nara and Heian eras is not appropriate.

2. *SZKT, Nihon shoki*, Ōjin 7/9, p. 272; *Nihongi*, I, 257.

3. Tsude Hiroshi, "Nōgu tekkika no futatsu no kakki." Also see Introduction, n 10.

4. *DNK*, I, 399–400, 410–411; *NI*, I, 197, 203. On the topic of seed rice and yields, see Sawada Goichi, pp. 527–535. Sawada notes that yields in the Nara period were less than 60% of yields in the Tokugawa era, while Tokugawa cultivators also used less seed rice in planting. He also showed that the range of yields from rice paddies was much greater in the early period; his conclusions about the extensive character of *ritsuryō* agriculture match the conclusions in Chapters 3 and 4 of this book. Also see Kozo Yamamura, "The Decline of the Ritsuryō System."

5. Georges Duby, *The Early Growth of the European Economy.*

6. *SZKT, Ruijū sandai kyaku*, Enryaku 19/9/6 Order of the Council of State cited in Tenchō 1/5/5 Regulation, p. 505.

7. *SZKT, Ruijū sandai kyaku*, Tenchō 1/5/5 Order of the Council of State, pp. 505–506.

8. Kinda Akihiro, "Heian ki no Yamato bonchi ni okeru jōri jiwari naibu no tochi riyō," *Shirin* 61:96–112 (May 1978). Dating ponds according to their relationship to the *jōri sei* is a risky business because place-names frequently change. Kinda is fully aware of his assumptions and discusses potential problems. See especially pp. 97–101.

9. This *tsubo* should not be confused with the modern unit of area, which is only 3.31 square meters (3.95 square yards).

10. *Tsurezuregusa*, in *Nihon koten bungaku zenshū*, p. 133.

11. *Sejŏng sillok*, in *Chosŏn wangjo sillok*, Sejŏng 11/12, p. 207.

12. *SZKT, Ruijū sandai kyaku*, Tenchō 6/5/27 Order of the Council of State, p. 323.

13. *SZKT, Ruijū sandai kyaku,* Kōnin 12/4/21 Order of the Council of State, pp. 606–607.

14. *SZKT, Ruijū sandai kyaku,* Enryaku 19/2/3 Order of the Council of State, p. 500.

15. *NKBT, Man'yōshū,* VI, #2244, pp. 130–131. These poems are cited in Naoki Kōjirō, *Nara jidai shi no shomondai,* p. 55.

16. *NKBT, Man'yōshū,* V, #1624, pp. 340–341.

17. Furushima, *Nihon nōgyō,* pp. 106–107.

18. Stone blades are still employed in the Philippines and other countries in East Asia. See Lewis, pp. 55–64. The stone knives uncovered in Japan all date from the Yayoi period, but it should also be noted that sickles can be used to harvest rice in sheaf form. See Kanaseki and Sahara, p. 109.

19. For example, *NKBT, Man'yōshū,* II, #1634, pp. 344–354; IV, #4122, pp. 296–299.

20. In *SZKT, Den-ryō no shūge, Kyōden no jō,* pp. 372–373, and *Zaige shoshi no jō,* pp. 375–376, legal commentators imply that transplanting was a common practice on government lands, but their writings do not rule out cultivation by direct sowing.

21. Harashima Reiji, *Nihon kodai shakai no kiso kōzō,* pp. 307–347.

22. Kitō Kiyoaki, "Hasseiki no shakai kōsei shiteki tokushitsu," *Nihon shi kenkyū* 172:9–18 (December 1976); Tsude Hiroshi, "Shohyō to shōkai: Harashima Reiji cho *Nihon kodai shakai no kiso kōzō,*" *Nihon shi kenkyū* 107:66–71 (August 1969).

23. *NKBT, Man'yōshū,* VI, #2999, pp. 286–287.

24. Yamamoto Takeo, "Rekishi no nagare ni sou Nihon to sono shūhen no kikō hensen," *Chigaku zasshi* 75:119–141 (March 1967).

25. Yoshinori Yasuda, "Early Historical Forest Clearance around the Ancient Castle Site of Tagajo, Miyagi Prefecture, Japan," *Asian Perspectives* 19:52 (1976).

26. David Herlihy, "Ecological Conditions and Demographic Change," in Richard DeMolen, ed., *One Thousand Years: Western Europe in the Middle Ages,* pp. 13, 35.

27. Kagami Kanji, "Owari no kuni Tan'yō mura no tochi jiwari," *Jimbun chiri* 4:20–29 (January 1952).

28. Kinda Akihiro, "Shōen sonraku no keikan," in Toda Yoshimi, ed., *Nihon shi 2 Chūsei 1,* 127–158.

29. The earliest evidence for the *shimahata* is found in *Shimpen Ichinomiya shi shi: Shiryō hen 5,* ed. Iyanaga Teizō, pp. 202–203.

30. *Nihon shōen ezu shūsei,* ed. Nishioka Toranosuke, I, 31.

31. Kinda, "Tochi riyō," pp. 79–85.

32. *SZKT, Ruijū sandai kyaku,* Yōrō 7/8/28 Order of the Council of State, p. 327.

33. These orders are found in *SZKT, Ruijū sandai kyaku,* pp. 326–329. The *Ruijū sandai kyaku* lists the date of the 715 order as 713.

34. For the 693 order, see *SZKT, Nihon shoki,* Jitō 7/4/17, pp. 418–419, prayer for rain; for the 715 command, see *SZKT, Shoku Nihongi,* Wadō 7/6/23, p. 56, prayer for rain; for the 723 order, see Chapter 3, n10; for the 820 law, see *SZKT, Nihon kiryaku,* Kōnin 9/3/19, p. 306, description of drought; the 840 law explicitly lists a great drought as a factor in its formulation (the issuance of the 839 law is probably connected to the same drought). It is also important to note that dry crops like wheat and barley were considered to have great nutritional value for starving people, and that this belief may have also played a role in the decision to order the planting of these crops.

35. Kinda, "Shōen sonraku no keikan," p. 148. Also note *SZKT, Ruijū sandai kyaku,* Jōwa 7/5/2 Order of the Council of State, p. 328, for an example of some peasants' preference for dry over rice cropping.

36. Kikuchi Yasuaki, pp. 188–191. The reader should be advised that only 9 bills of sale of dry fields exist for the period 766 through 1076, a small sample on which to base conclusions.

37. *SZKT, Nihon shoki, Shindai jō,* 11–12; *Nihongi,* I, 21.

38. J. R. McEwan, "Shifting Cultivation in Tsushima in the Eighteenth Century," *Asia Major* 5:208–229 (February 1956).

39. Robert Hall and Toshio Noh, "*Yakihata,* Burned-field Agriculture in Japan, with its Special Characteristics in Shikoku," *Papers, Michigan Academy of Science, Arts, and Letters* 38:315–322 (1953).

40. *SZKT, Gumbō-ryō no gige, Hōhō no jō,* p. 203.

41. *SZKT, Zō-ritsu, Shitsuka oyobi hiji shō den ya no jō,* p. 162.

42. *NKBT, Man'yōshū,* V, #1336, pp. 250–251; *The Man'yōshū,* tr. Nippon gakujutsu shinkō kai, p. 292.

43. *NKBT, Man'yōshū,* IV, #199, pp. 108–109; *Man'yōshū,* pp. 39–40.

44. *NKBT, Man'yōshū,* IV, #230, pp. 126–129; *Man'yōshū,* p. 104.

45. *DNK,* IV, 227.

46. *DNK,* V, 622–623.

47. *SZKT, Nihon shoki,* Temmu 5/5 *Kono toshi no jō,* p. 341; *Nihongi,* II, 332.

48. *SZKT, Nihon sandai jitsuroku,* Jōgan 9/3/25, p. 214.

49. Sasaki Kōmei, *Inasaku izen,* pp. 97–102.

50. Conklin and Freeman, cited in Geertz, p. 26.

51. Sawada Goichi, pp. 143–177.

52. *SZKT, Den-ryō no shūge, Denchō no jō,* pp. 345–347. The following discussion only touches the surface of Japanese research on the *jōri sei.* See Watanabe Hisao, *Jōri sei no kenkyū,* for a detailed summary of the history of studies in this field. For a recent bibliography, see Ochiai Shigenobu, *Jōri sei.* Fujioka Kenjirō, ed., *Nihon rekishi chiri sōsetsu 2 Kodai hen,* reconstructs field patterns for selected areas in the early period.

53. John Hall, pp. 86–88; Takeuchi Rizō, *Ritsuryō sei to kizoku seiken,* I, 46–84.

54. Kishi Toshio, "Asuka to hōkaku jiwari." Kishi has recently come to

doubt the value of this study due to the large element of coincidence: anything can appear to fit into a grid if enough lines are drawn.

55. *Shōen ezu*, pp. 45–47.

56. Conversation with Iyanaga Teizō in March 1978. I was accompanying Professor Iyanaga on a survey of the area just north of Nara.

57. *SZKT, Ruijū sandai kyaku*, Engi 2/3/13 Order of the Council of State, p. 427.

58. This brief summary does not pretend to be a thorough discussion of the state land system or the question of its enforcement. The best analysis of the institution can be found in Torao, *Handen shūju*. Also see the explanatory notes of Yoshida Takashi in Inoue Mitsusada et al., eds., *Nihon shisō taikei 4 Ritsuryō*, pp. 570–572, 576–678. For a recent bibliography of work on this system, see Murayama Kōichi, *Handen shūju*, pp. 317–330.

59. This argument is the work of Yoshida Takashi, "Kōchi kōmin ni tsuite," in *Zoku Nihon kodai shi ronshū*, II, 411–426. The interpretation of Chinese land systems follows Ikeda On, "Kindensei," in *Kodai shi kōza 8 Kodai no tochi seido*, pp. 137–174.

5. Rural Settlement

1. For example, see Okuda Shinkei, "Shōen zen sonraku no kōzō ni tsuite," *Shigaku zasshi* 58:24–48 (March 1949); Iyanaga Teizō, *Nara jidai no kizoku to nōmin*. For a concise summary of this view by a non-specialist, see Conrad Totman, *Japan before Perry*, p. 57. Work in this field is examined fully in Kinda Akihiro, "Nara Heian ki no sonraku keitai ni tsuite," *Shirin* 54:50–52 (May 1971).

2. *SZKT, Ko-ryō no shūge, Kyokyō no jō*, pp. 278–279. For a brief discussion of the application of this provision, see the explanatory notes by Yoshida Takashi in Inoue Mitsusada et al., eds., *Nihon shisō taikei 4 Ritsuryō*, pp. 553–555.

3. *SZKT, Ko-ryō no shūge, Ko tōsō no jō*, pp. 268–270. A like statute was included in Tang codes; see *Tōrei shūi*, p. 230. On the application of this provision, see n2, above.

4. *SZKT, Ko-ryō no shūge, Zetsugan no jō*, pp. 280–281. See *Tōrei*, p. 238, for the Tang article. The Taihō Codes used two terms, *tōbō* and *furō*, to describe persons who migrated without official permission. The former word was applied to those who were untaxed, while those who were of taxable age were called *furōnin* (*SZKT, Homō-ritsu, Hibō furō tasho no jō*, pp. 169–170, and *SZKT, Ko-ryō no shūge, Zetsugan no jō*, first *Koki*, p. 281). In practice, these two terms, which may be rendered "runaway" and "vagrant" respectively, were used interchangeably. On the application of this provision, see n2, above.

5. Nagayama Yasutaka, *Ritsuryō futan taikei no kenkyū*, pp. 178-184.

6. Kamata Motokazu, "Ritsuryō kokka no futō taisaku," in *Akamatsu Toshihide kyōju taikan kinen kokushi ronshū*, pp. 179-183.

7. *SZKT, Nihon shoki*, II, Tenji 9/2, p. 297.

8. *SZKT, Nihon shoki*, II, Jitō 3/Int. 8/10, pp. 402-403. *Nihongi*, II, 394.

9. *SZKT, Shoku Nihongi*, Wadō 2/10/14, p. 40.

10. The text of this edict in the *Shoku Nihongi* is corrupt. I follow Kamata in substituting the text included in *SZKT, Ruijū sandai kyaku*, Kōnin 2/8/11 Order of the Council of State, p. 519.

11. Hayakawa Shōhachi, *Nihon no rekishi 4 Ritsuryō kokka*, pp. 286-287.

12. *SZKT, Nihon shoki*, Temmu 6/9/27, p. 345.

13. *SZKT, Shoku Nihongi*, Yōrō 4/3/17, p. 80.

14. *SZKT, Ruijū sandai kyaku*, Yōrō 5/4/27 Regulation in Tempyō 8/2/25 Edict, p. 385.

15. This interpretation of the 721 legislation is derived from an 811 regulation. See *SZKT, Ruijū sandai kyaku*, Kōnin 2/8/11 Order of the Council of State, p. 519.

16. *SZKT, Ruijū sandai kyaku*, Tempyō 8/2/25 Edict, p. 385.

17. Naoki Kōjirō, *Nara jidai shi no shomondai*, p. 15.

18. *SZKT, Ruijū sandai kyaku*, Kōnin 2/8/11 Order of the Council of State, p. 519.

19. *SZKT, Ruijū sandai kyaku*, Hōki 11/10/26 Order of the Council of State, p. 384; Kōnin 2/8/11 Order of the Council of State, p. 519.

20. *SZKT, Ruijū sandai kyaku*, Enryaku 4/6/24 Order of the Council of State, pp. 384-385.

21. Miskimin, p. 46.

22. Kitayama Shigeo, *Nara chō no seiji to minshū*, p. 89. Also see Harashima, pp. 473-524, which has been largely superseded by Nagayama, pp. 158-193.

23. This analysis is drawn from Naoki, *Shomondai*, pp. 19-20. Demographers have invented several methods to measure migration, the most common being the rate of mobility, which is defined as the number of movers divided by the population at risk for a set interval of time. Unfortunately, *ritsuryō* records do not provide enough information to permit calculation of the mobility rate, which would require intercensal figures for one region and/or the whole country, or the registration of births and deaths. See Shryock and Siegel, pp. 616-640.

24. *DNK*, I, 360-361. Historians are uncertain why the Yamashiro tax registers continued to record "runaways" long after the time that the law codes required that their names be expunged. It may well be that this provision of the Household Statutes simply became a dead letter. It is also unclear why the registers note the province and district to which the runaway

had fled. If officials knew where the peasant had run off to, why not send him home? For a recent discussion of these entries, see Nagayama, pp. 166–178.

25. *DNK*, I, 517.

26. *DNK*, I, 334–335. This argument follows Nagayama, pp. 172–173.

27. *DNK*, I, 343.

28. *NI*, II, 535–537 and *DNK*, XXV, 137. The analysis of these documents follows Yoshida Akira, *Nihon kodai shakai kōsei shi ron*, pp. 165–191.

29. *SZKT, Ruijū sandai kyaku*, Enryaku 9/4/16 Order of the Council of State, p. 625.

30. *Heijō-kyū mokkan: Kaisetsu*, II, pp. 59–62. Also see Tateno Kazushi, "Ritsuryō sei ka no kōtsū to jimmin shihai," *Nihon shi kenkyū* 211:61–62, 67 (March 1980).

31. *DNK*, XV, 165–166.

32. *SZKT, Shoku Nihongi*, Tempyō Shōhō 4/1/3, p. 213.

33. Habara Yūkichi, *Nihon kodai gyogyō keizai shi*, pp. 151–190.

34. Pioneering studies of early Japanese marital institutions have been written by Takamure Itsue, *Nihon kon'in shi*, and William McCullough, "Japanese Marriage Institutions in the Heian Period," *Harvard Journal of Asiatic Studies* 27:103–167 (1967). For a recent summary, see Sekiguchi Yūko, "Nihon kodai kazoku no kiteiteki ketsuen chūtai ni tsuite," in *Kodai shi ronsō*, II, 417–491; Yoshida Takashi, "Ritsuryō sei to sonraku," *Iwanami kōza Nihon rekishi 3 Kodai 3*, pp. 156–161. Also see Chapter 1, n43.

35. Robin Fox, *Kinship and Marriage*, p. 83.

36. *DNK*, XV, 441.

37. My discussion follows Kishi Toshio, *Nihon kodai sekichō no kenkyū*, p. 379. It should be noted that, while Kishi's argument seems to suggest that Komi and Tamiya were dispersed settlements, he draws no conclusions, and it is also possible that dwellings were more compactly arranged.

38. Nishijima Sadao, *Chūgoku keizai shi kenkyū*, pp. 657–672.

39. *NKBT, Man'yōshū*, V, #1556, pp. 322–323.

40. *NKBT, Man'yōshū*, VI, #2550, pp. 132–133.

41. *SZKT, Ruijū sandai kyaku*, Daidō 4/9/16 Order of the Council of State, p. 428.

42. Kinda, "Sonraku keitai," pp. 83–85. For definitions of hamlet, solitary homestead, and dispersed and compact settlement, see ibid., p. 53.

43. On the Hiraide excavation, see *Hiraide*. Many geographers hesitate to apply their techniques to archaeological sites, because of the difficulties in reconstructing the topography with precision.

44. My discussion is taken from *Yamada Mizunomi no iseki: kōsatsu hen bessatsu*. Also see Ishii Noritaka, *Kodai no shūraku*, pp. 181–194, for a discussion of Yamada Mizunomi. Ishii argues that Yamada was a *kaihatsu sonraku*, or "land development village." This interpretation would seem to

support conclusions about the fluidity of settlement and shifting character of *ritsuryō* farming made in this and earlier chapters.

45. *NKBT, Man'yōshū*, II, #892, pp. 100-101. *The Man'yōshū*, tr. Nippon gakujutsu shinkō kai, p. 206.

46. Narasaki Shōichi and Yokoyama Kōichi, eds., *Kodai shi hakkutsu 10 Miyako to mura no kurashi*, pp. 45-49.

47. Kinda, "Sonraku keitai," p. 86.

48. Mutō Tadashi, "Nihon kodai no sonraku keitai ni kansuru ichi kōsatsu," *Shirin* 52:112-124 (June 1969).

49. *NKBT, Harima fudoki*, pp. 290-293.

50. Historical geographers have posited a relationship between farming practices and rural settlement. For example, see Alan Mayhew, *Rural Settlement and Farming in Germany*. It is important to note that this relationship has been most firmly established for European dry agriculture. Other forms, such as wet-rice planting or swidden cropping, may not be so exclusively identified with particular settlement patterns. Worldwide surveys of slash-and-burn cultivation, for example, indicate that it may be found with both dense and dispersed settlements. But my argument is based on historical evidence for early Japan, which suggests that the pattern of shifting cultivation and dispersed settlement were indeed related.

51. Maurice Beresford and John Hurst, eds., *Deserted Medieval Villages*, pp. 169-181, 229-244.

52. Thomas Smith, *The Agrarian Origins of Modern Japan*, p. 60.

53. The following interpretation has been argued by Yoshida Takashi, "Kōchi kōmin ni tsuite," in *Zoku Nihon kodai shi ronshū*, II, 436-451. Yoshida has based his analysis of Chinese institutions on the work of Miyazaki Ichisada, *Ajia shi kenkyū*, IV, 486-487. Also see John Hall, p. 83, for a brief treatment of rural settlement and administration that essentially agrees with Yoshida.

54. Yoshida Takashi, "Ritsuryō sei to sonraku," pp. 175-176.

55. Urata Akiko, "Henko sei no igi."

56. Kinda, "Sonraku keitai," p. 91.

Conclusion

1. Takeuchi Rizō, "Kokudo no kaihatsu," in Takeuchi Rizō, ed., *Kodai no Nihon 1 Yōsetsu*, p. 188.

2. Michael Postan, *The Medieval Economy and Society*, p. 42.

3. Ester Boserup, *The Conditions of Agricultural Growth*, pp. 70-76.

4. For a detailed discussion of government finance from 700 to 925, see Hayakawa Shōhachi, "Ritsuryō zaisei no kōzō to sono henshitsu," in Iyanaga Teizō, ed., *Nihon keizai shi taikei 1 Kodai*, pp. 221-280. See especially the diagram on p. 259.

5. The regulation appears in *SZKT, Ruijū sandai kyaku*, Kōnin 14/2/21, Remonstrance of the Council of State, pp. 434–437. Studies of this order include Akamatsu Toshihide, "Kueiden o tsūjite mitaru shoki shōen sei no kōzō ni tsuite"; Murai Yasuhiko, *Kodai kokka kaitai katei no kenkyū*, pp. 61–118; Nagayama Yasutaka, pp. 246–284.

6. *SZKT, Nihon kiryaku*, Kōnin 14/2/*Kono tsuki no jō*, p. 314.

7. Toda Yoshimi, pp. 13–44.

8. *SZKT, Ruijū sandai kyaku*, Tempyō 9/9/21 Edict, p. 403.

9. *SZKT, Ruijū sandai kyaku*, Jōwa 7/2/11 Order of the Council of State, p. 399. Also note the contents of the Kōnin 10/2/20 Order of the Council of State included therein.

Bibliography

The place of publication is not given for Japanese works published in Tokyo.

Primary Sources

Ainōshō 塵嚢抄 (A bag of remnants), in Nihon koten zenshū 日本古典全集 (A collection of Japanese classics), Vol. XV. Nihon koten zenshū kankō kai, 1936.

Chōya gunsai 朝野群載 (Collected documents from court and country), in Shintei zōho kokushi taikei 新訂増補国史大系 (A library of Japanese history, revised edition), Vol. XXIX. Yoshikawa kōbunkan, 1938.

Dai Nihon komonjo 大日本古文書 (Documents of Japan). 25 vols. Tokyo daigaku shuppan kai, 1901.

Dai Nihon shiryō 大日本史料 (Historical materials of Japan) Series 1, Vol. III; Series 2, Vols. III, V. Shiryō hensan kakari, 1925-1934.

Engi shiki 延喜式 (The ordinances of Engi), in Shintei zōho kokushi taikei, Vol. XXVI. Yoshikawa kōbunkan, 1973.

Fudoki 風土記 (Gazetteers), in Nihon koten bungaku taikei 日本古典文学大系 (A library of classical Japanese literature). Ed. Akimoto Kichirō 秋本吉郎, Vol. II. Iwanami shoten, 1958.

Han shu 漢書 (History of the Former Han), Vol. IV. Peking, Zhong-hua shu-ju.

Heian ibun 平安遺文 (Documents from the Heian period). Ed. Takeuchi Rizō 竹内理三, 13 vols. Tokyodō, 1965.

Heijō-kyū mokkan 平城宮木簡 (Wooden tablets from Heijō Palace), Vol. II. Kyoto, Shin'yō sha, 1975.

Hiraide 平出 . Asahi shimbun kan, 1955.

Hyakuren shō 百錬抄 (Manuscript of one hundred smeltings), in *Shintei zōho kokushi taikei*, Vol. XI. Yoshikawa kōbunkan, 1929.

Iryō uta haisai 医療歌配剤 (Medical prescriptions). Comp. Furuhayashi Kenchō 古林見桃 . 2 vols. Archives of Dr. Fujikawa Yū 富士川游 at Kyoto University, 1772.

Kanoko C iseki urushigami monjo: hombun hen 鹿ヶ子 C 遺跡 漆紙文書 本文編 (Lacquer documents from Kanoko C Site: Text) Ibaraki ken kyōiku zaidan, 1983.

Kōnin shiki 弘仁式 (The ordinances of Kōnin), in *Shintei zōho kokushi taikei*, Vol. XXVI. Yoshikawa kōbunkan, 1937.

Man'yōshū 万葉集 (Collection of a myriad leaves), in *Nihon koten bungaku taikei*. Ed. Gomi Tomohide 五味智英 et al., Vols. VII-X. Iwanami shoten, 1959.

Nara ibun 寧楽遺文 (Documents from the Nara period). Ed. Takeuchi Rizō. 3 vols. Tokyodō, 1962.

Nihon kiryaku 日本紀略 (Abbreviated Japanese annals), in *Shintei zōho kokushi taikei*, Vols. X-XI. Yoshikawa kōbunkan, 1929.

Nihon kōki 日本後紀 (Latter chronicles of Japan), in *Shintei zōho kokushi taikei*, Vol. III. Yoshikawa kōbunkan, 1934.

Nihon Montoku tennō jitsuroku 日本文徳天皇実録 (The veritable records of the Emperor Montoku), in *Shintei zōho kokushi taikei*, Vol. III. Yoshikawa kōbunkan, 1934.

Nihon sandai jitsuroku 日本三代史録 (The veritable records of Three Reigns), in *Shintei zōho kokushi taikei*, Vol. IV. Yoshikawa kōbunkan, 1934.

Nihon shōen ezu shūsei 日本莊園絵図集成 (A collection of maps from Japanese estates). Ed. Nishioka Toranosuke 西岡虎之介 . 2 vols. Tokyodō, 1976.

Nihon shoki 日本書紀 (Chronicles of Japan), in *Shintei zōho kokushi taikei*, Vol. I. Yoshikawa kōbunkan, 1951.

Rissho zampen 律書残篇 (Fragments from commentaries on the penal codes), in *Shintei zōho shiseki shūran* 新訂増補 史籍集覧 (A collection of historical materials). Ed. Tsunoda Bun'ei 角田文衞 , Vol. IV. Kyoto, Rinsen shoten, 1967.

Ritsu 律 (The penal codes), in *Shintei zōho kokushi taikei,* Vol. XXII. Yoshikawa kōbunkan, 1939.

Ritsuryō 律令 (The law codes). Ed. Inoue Mitsusada 井上光貞 et al., in *Nihon shisō taikei* 日本思想大系 (A library of Japanese thought), Vol. IV. Iwanami shoten, 1976.

Ruijū fusen shō 類聚符宣抄 (Assorted orders), in *Shintei zōho kokushi taikei,* Vol. XXVII. Yoshikawa kōbunkan, 1933.

Ruijū kokushi 類聚国史 (Assorted national histories), in *Shintei zōho kokushi taikei,* Vols. V-VI. Yoshikawa kōbunkan, 1933-1934.

Ruijū sandai kyaku 類聚三代格 (Assorted regulations from Three Reigns), in *Shintei zōho kokushi taikei,* Vol. XXV. Yoshikawa kōbunkan, 1936.

Ryō no gige 令義解 (Interpretations of the administrative codes), in *Shintei zōho kokushi taikei,* Vol. XXII. Yoshikawa kōbunkan, 1939.

Ryō no shūge 令集解 (Collected commentaries on the administrative codes), in *Shintei zōho kokushi taikei,* Vol. XXIV. Yoshikawa kōbunkan, 1966.

Samguk sagi 三国史記 (History of the Three Kingdoms), in *Chōsen shi* 朝鮮史 (The history of Korea), Vol. IV. Seoul, Chōsen insatsu kabushiki kaisha, 1932.

Seiji Yōryaku 政事要略 (A handbook of government), in *Shintei zōho kokushi taikei,* Vol. XXVIII. Yoshikawa kōbunkan, 1935.

Sejŏng sillok 世宗實錄 (The veritable records of King Sejŏng), in *Chosŏn wangjo sillok* 朝鮮王朝實錄 (The veritable records of Korea), Vol. II. Seoul, Tongguk munhwa sa, 1955.

Shiki kaichū kōshō 史記会註考証 (Commentaries on the *Records of the Grand Historian (Shih Chi)*). Ed. Takigawa Kitarō 瀧川亀太郎 Vol. II. Tokyo daigaku tōyō bunka kenkyūjo, 1956.

Shimpen Ichinomiya shi shi: Shiryō hen 新編一宮市史資料編 (History of Ichinomiya City, revised: Historical materials). Ed. Iyanaga Teizō 彌永貞三 . Vol. V. Osaka, Dai Nihon insatsu kabushiki kaisha, 1963.

Shoku Nihongi 続日本紀 (Chronicles of Japan, continued), in *Shintei zōho kokushi taikei,* Vol. II. Yoshikawa kōbunkan, 1935.

Shoku Nihon kōki 續日本後紀 (The latter chronicles of Japan, continued), in *Shintei zōho kokushi taikei*, Vol. III. Yoshikawa kōbunkan, 1934.

Sui shu 隋書 (History of the Sui dynasty), Vol. VI. Peking, Zhonghua shuju, 1973.

Taga-jō urushigami monjo 多賀城漆紙文書 (Lacquer documents from Ft. Taga). Miyagi ken bunka zai hogo kyōkai, 1979.

Tōdaiji yōroku 東大寺要録 (Essential records of Tōdaiji). Ed. Tsutsui Hidetoshi 筒井英俊. Tosho kankō kai, 1971.

Tōnan'in monjo 東南院文書 (Records from the Tōnan'in), in *Dai Nihon komonjo, Iewake* 大日本古文書家わけ (Documents of Japan) 18. 4 vols. Tokyo daigaku shuppan kai, 1944-1954.

Tōrei shūi 唐令拾遺 (Remnants of the Tang codes). Comp. Niida Noboru 仁井田陞. Tōhō bunka gakuin kenkyūjo, 1933.

Tsurezuregusa 徒然草 (Essays in idleness), in *Nihon koten bungaku zenshū* 日本古典文学全集 (A collection of Japanese literature), Vol. XXVII. Shōgakkan, 1971.

Yamada Mizunomi no iseki: Kōsatsu hen bessatsu 山田水呑の遺跡考察篇別冊 (The Yamada Mizunomi site: Considerations). Kōbun sha, 1977.

Zoku kojidan 続古事談 (A discussion of ancient matters—continued), in *Kokushi sōsho* 国史叢書 (Historical texts), Vol. X. Kokushi kenkyū kai, 1915.

Secondary Sources

Abe Takeshi 阿部猛. *Nihon shōen seiritsu shi no kenkyū* 日本荘園成立史の研究 (The establishment of the estate). Yūsankaku, 1960.

Akamatsu Toshihide 赤松俊秀. "Kueiden o tsūjite mitaru shoki shōen sei no kōzō ni tsuite" 公営田を通じて見たる初期庄園制の構造について (The structure of the early estate as seen in state farms), *Rekishi gaku kenkyū* 7:1-28 (May 1937).

Aoki Kazuo 青木和夫. "Kiyomihara ryō to kodai kanryō sei" 浄御原令と古代官僚制 (The Kiyomihara administrative codes and the ancient bureaucratic system), *Kodai gaku* 3:115-133 (June 1954).

————. *Nihon no rekishi 3 Nara no miyako* 日本の歴史 3 奈良の都 (A history of Japan: Nara). Chūō kōron sha, 1965.

Appleby, Andrew. "Nutrition and Disease: The Case of London, 1550-1750," *The Journal of Interdisciplinary History* 6:1-22 (Summer 1975).

Arai Kikuo 新井喜久夫 , Iyanaga Teizō 彌永貞三 , and Kameda Takashi 亀田隆之 . "Etchū no kuni Tōdaiji ryō shōen ezu ni tsuite" 越中国東大寺領庄園絵図について (The maps of Tōdaiji's Etchū estates), *Shoku Nihongi kenkyū* 5:2-22 (February 1958).

Asakawa, Kan'ichi. *Land and Society in Medieval Japan.* Tokyo, Society for the Promotion of Science, 1965.

Beresford, Maurice. *The Lost Villages of England.* New York, Philosophical Library, 1954.

————, and John Hurst, eds. *Deserted Medieval Villages.* London, Lutterworth, 1971.

Boserup, Ester. *The Conditions of Agricultural Growth.* Chicago, Allen & Unwin, 1965.

Brenner, Robert. "Agrarian Class Structure and Economic Development," *Past and Present* 70:30-75 (February 1976).

Burnet, MacFarlane, and David White. *The Natural History of Infectious Disease,* 4th ed. Cambridge, Cambridge University Press, 1972.

Coale, Ansley, and Paul Demeny. *Regional Model Life Tables and Stable Populations.* Princeton, Princeton University Press, 1966.

Duby, Georges. *The Early Growth of the European Economy.* Tr. Howard Clarke. Ithaca, Cornell University Press, 1974.

Fox, Robin. *Kinship and Marriage.* Harmondsworth, Penguin Books, 1967.

Fujikawa Yū 富士川游 . *Nihon shippei shi* 日本疾病史 (A history of disease in Japan). New Edition by Matsuda Michio 松田道雄 . Heibon sha, 1969.

Fujioka Kenjirō 藤岡謙二郎 , ed. *Nihon rekishi chiri sōsetsu 2*

Kodai hen 日本歴史地理総説古代篇 (Japanese historical geography: Ancient). Yoshikawa kōbunkan, 1975.

Fukuoka Takeshi 福岡猛志 . "Kūkan chi no eishuken o meguru shomondai" 空閑地の営種権をめぐる諸問題 (Problems concerning the cultivation of wilderness), *Rekishi gaku kenkyū* 285:1-10 (February 1962).

Funao Yoshimasa 舟尾好正 . "Suiko no jittai ni kansuru ichi kōsatsu" 出挙の実態に関する一考察 (The reality of rice loans), *Shirin* 56:74-102 (September 1973).

Furushima Toshio 古島敏雄 . *Furushima Toshio chosaku zenshū 6 Nihon nōgyō gijutsu shi* 古島敏雄著作全集 6 日本農業技術史 (The complete works of Furushima Toshio: The history of Japanese agricultural technology). Tokyo daigaku shuppan kai, 1975.

Geertz, Clifford. *Agricultural Involution.* Berkeley, University of California Press, 1963.

Greville, Thomas. "The General Theory of Osculatory Interpolation," *Transactions of the Actuarial Society of America* 45:202-265 (1944).

Habara Yūkichi 羽原又吉 . *Nihon kodai gyogyō keizai shi* 日本古代漁業経済史 (An economic history of ancient Japanese fishing). Kaizō sha, 1951.

Hachiga Susumu 八賀晋 . "Kodai ni okeru suiden kaihatsu" 古代における水田開発 (The development of rice paddies in the ancient period), *Nihon shi kenkyū* 96:1-24 (March 1968).

Hall, John. *Government and Local Power in Japan, 500 to 1700.* Princeton, Princeton University Press, 1966.

Hall, Robert, and Toshio Noh. "*Yakihata*, Burned-field Agriculture in Japan, with its Special Characteristics in Shikoku," *Papers, Michigan Academy of Sciences, Arts, and Letters* 38:315-322 (1953).

Haneda Minoru 羽田稔 . "Sanze isshin hō ni tsuite" 三世一身法について (On the 723 law), *Hisutoria* 30:38-51 (June 1961).

Hanley, Susan, and Kozo Yamamura. *Economic and Demographic Change in Preindustrial Japan, 1600-1868.* Princeton, Princeton University Press, 1977.

Hara Hidesaburō 原秀三郎 "Hasseiki ni okeru kaihatsu ni

tsuite" 八世紀における開発について (Land clearance in the eighth century), *Nihon shi kenkyū* 61:1-27 (July 1962).

————. "Taika no kaishin ron hihan josetsu" 大化改新論批判序説 (A critical introduction to the debate over the Taika Reforms), *Nihon shi kenkyū* 86:25-45 (September 1966); 88:23-48 (January 1967).

Harashima Reiji 原島礼二. *Nihon kodai shakai no kiso kōzō* 日本古代社会の基礎構造 (The basic structure of ancient Japanese society). Mirai sha, 1968.

Hattori Toshirō 服部敏良. "Jōko shi iji kō" 上古史医事考 (Thoughts on medicine in high antiquity), *Nihon ishi gaku zasshi* 1312:64-76 (February 1943).

————. *Nara jidai igaku no kenkyū* 奈良時代医学の研究 (Medicine in the Nara period). Tokyodō, 1945.

Hayakawa Shōhachi 早川庄八. "Kugai tō seido no seiritsu" 公廨稲制度の成立 (Establishment of the system of provincial tax-farming), *Shigaku zasshi* 69:1-53 (March 1960).

————. *Nihon no rekishi 4 Ritsuryō kokka* 日本の歴史千律令国家 (A history of Japan: The *ritsuryō* state). Shōgakkan, 1974.

————. "Ritsuryō dajōkan sei no seiritsu" 律令太政官制の成立 (Establishment of the Council of State), in *Zoku Nihon kodai shi ronshū* 続日本古代史論集 (Essays in ancient Japanese history, continued), Vol. I. Yoshikawa kōbunkan, 1972.

————. "Ritsuryō sei no keisei" 律令制の形成 (The formation of the *ritsuryō* system), in *Iwanami kōza Nihon rekishi 2 Kodai 2*. 岩波講座日本歴史 2 古代 2 (Iwanami lectures in Japanese history: The ancient period). Iwanami shoten, 1975.

————. "Ritsuryō zaisei no kōzō to sono henshitsu" 律令財政の構造とその変質 (The structure and evolution of *ritsuryō* finance), in Iyanaga Teizō 彌永貞三 ed., *Nihon keizai shi taikei 1 Kodai* 日本経済史大系 1 古代 (A library of Japanese economic history: Ancient). Tokyo daigaku shuppan kai, 1965.

————. "Tempyō rokunen Izumo no kuni keikai chō no kenkyū" 天平六年出雲国計会帳の研究 (Research on the official log of Izumo province from Tempyō 6 [734], in *Nihon kodai shi ronshū* 日本古代史論集 (Essays in ancient Japanese history), Vol. II. Yoshikawa kōbunkan, 1962.

Hayashi Rokurō 林陸郎. *Jōdai seiji shakai no kenkyū* 上代

政治社会の研究 (Ancient politics and society). Yoshikawa kōbunkan, 1969.

Hayashiya Tatsusaburō 林屋辰三郎 . *Kodai kokka no kaitai* 古代国家の解体 (The decline of the ancient state). Tokyo daigaku shuppan kai, 1955.

Herlihy, David. "Ecological Conditions and Demographic Change," in Richard De Molen, ed., *One Thousand Years: Western Europe in the Middle Ages.* Boston, Houghton Mifflin, 1973.

Hirano Kunio 平野邦雄 . *Taika zendai shakai soshiki no kenkyū* 大化前代社会組織の研究 (Research on pre-Taika social organization). Yoshikawa kōbunkan, 1969.

Hirata Kōji 平田耿二 . "Heian jidai no koseki ni tsuite" 平安時代の戸籍について (Household registers of the Heian period), in *Nihon kodai chūsei shi no chihōteki tenkai* 日本古代中世史の地方的展開 (Regional development in ancient and medieval Japanese history). Yoshikawa kōbunkan, 1973.

Honjō Eijirō 本庄栄治郎 and Kokushō Iwao 黒正巖 . *Nihon keizai shi* 日本経済史 (An economic history of Japan). Nihon hyōron sha, 1929.

Horio Hisashi 堀尾尚 and Iinuma Jirō 飯沼二郎. *Nōgu* 農具 (Agricultural implements). Hōsei daigaku shuppan kyoku, 1976.

Hoshino Ryōsaku 星野良作 . *Jinshin no ran* 壬申の乱 (The Civil War of 672). Yoshikawa kōbunkan, 1973.

Ikeda On 池田温 . *Chūgoku kodai sekichō kenkyū* 中国古代籍帳研究 (Research on ancient Chinese tax and household registers). Tokyo daigaku tōyō bunka kenkyūjo, 1979.

————. "Kindensei" 均田制 (The equal-field system), in *Kodai shi kōza 8 Kodai no tochi seido* 古代史講座 8 古代の土地制度 (Lectures in ancient history: The land system). Gakusei sha, 1963.

Inagaki Yasuhiko 稲垣泰彦 . "Chūsei no nōgyō keiei to shūshu keitai" 中世の農業経営と収取形態 (Medieval agriculture and the system of exploitation), in *Iwanami kōza Nihon rekishi 6 Chūsei 2* 岩波講座日本歴史 6 中世 (Iwanami lectures in Japanese history: The medieval period). Iwanami shoten, 1975.

Inoue Hideo 井上秀雄 *Kodai no Chōsen* 古代の朝鮮 (Ancient Korea). NHK bukkusu, 1972.

Inoue Mitsusada 井上光貞. *Nihon kodai shi no shomondai* 日本古代史の諸問題 (Problems in ancient Japanese history). Shisaku sha, 1949.

———. "Taika no kaishin to higashi Ajia" 大化の改新と東アジア (The Taika Reforms and East Asia), in *Iwanami kōza Nihon rekishi 2 Kodai 2*. Iwanami shoten, 1975.

Ishii Noritaka 石井則孝. *Kodai no shūraku* 古代の集落 (The ancient village). Kyōiku sha, 1982.

Ishii, Ryoichi. *Population Pressure and Economic Life in Japan*. Chicago, University of Chicago Press, 1937.

Iyanaga Teizō 彌永貞三. "Hasseiki no Nihon" 八世紀の日本 (Eighth-century Japan), in *Nihon to sekai no rekishi* 日本と世界の歴史 (Japan and world history), Vol. V. Gakushū kenkyū sha, 1970.

———. "Mino no kuni, Kamo no kōri, Hanyū no sato no koseki no kochi ni tsuite" 御野国加毛郡半布里戸籍の故地について (The ancient landscape at Hanyū administrative village, Kamo district, Mino province), *Chihō shi kenkyū* 56.57:1-24 (April, June 1962).

———. *Nara jidai no kizoku to nōmin* 奈良時代の貴族と農民 (Peasant and aristocrat in the Nara period). Jibundō, 1956.

———. "Ritsuryōseiteki tochi shoyū" 律令制的土地所有 (Land tenure under the *ritsuryō* system), in *Iwanami kōza Nihon rekishi 3 Kodai 3*. Iwanami shoten, 1962.

———. "*Shūgai shō* oyobi *Kaitō shokoku ki* ni arawareta shokoku no denseki shiryō ni kansuru oboegaki" 拾芥抄及び海東諸国記に現れた諸国の田積史料に関する覚え書き (A memo on the historical sources for provincial arable land figures as seen in the *Shūgai shō* and *Kaitō shokoku ki*), *Nagoya daigaku bungaku bu kenkyū ronshū* 名古屋大学文学部研究論集 (Research Papers of the Faculty Letters at Nagoya University) 41:11-28 (1966).

The Izumo fudoki. Tr. Michiko Aoki. Tokyo, Sophia University, 1971.

Jawetz, Ernest, et al., eds. *Review of Medical Microbiology*. Los Altos, Lange Medical Publications, 1978.

Kadowaki Teiji 門脇禎二 . *"Taika no kaishin" ron* 大化改新論 (The debate over the "Taika Reforms"). Tokuma shoten, 1967.

Kagami Kanji 鏡味完二. "Owari no kuni Tan'yō mura no tochi jiwari" 尾張国丹陽村の土地地割リ (Land division in Tan'yō village, Owari province), *Jimbun chiri* 4:2-29 (January 1952).

Kamata Motokazu 鎌田元一 . "Keichō seido shiron" 計帳制度試論 (An essay on the tax register), *Shirin* 55: 1-43 (September 1972).

————. "Ritsuryō kokka no futō taisaku" 律令国家の浮逃対策 (Policy toward vagrants and runaways), in *Akamatsu Toshihide kyōju taikan kinen kokushi ronshū* 赤松俊秀教授退官記念国史論集 (Essays in Japanese history commemorating the retirement of Professor Akamatsu Toshihide). Kyoto, Bunkō sha, 1972.

Kameda Takashi 亀田隆之 . *Nihon kodai yōsui shi no kenkyū* 日本古代用水史の研究 (The history of ancient Japanese irrigation). Yoshikawa kōbunkan, 1973.

Kanaseki, Hiroshi, and Makoto Sahara. "The Yayoi Period," *Asian Perspectives* 19:15-26 (1976).

Kanaseki Hiroshi 金関恕 and Sahara Makoto 佐原誠 , eds. *Kodai shi hakkutsu 4 Inasaku no hajimari* 古代史発掘4稲作の始まり (Excavations in ancient history: The origins of rice cultivation). Kōdan sha, 1975.

Kawasaki Tsuneyuki 川崎庸之. *Temmu tennō* 天武天皇 (The Emperor Temmu). Iwanami shoten, 1952.

Kidder, J. E. *Early Buddhist Japan.* New York, Praeger, 1972.

Kikuchi Yasuaki 菊地康明 . *Nihon kodai tochi shoyū no kenkyū* 日本古代土地所有の研究 (Land tenure in ancient Japan). Tokyo daigaku shuppan kai, 1969.

Kinda Akihiro 金田章裕 . "Heian ki no Yamato bonchi ni okeru jōri jiwari naibu no tochi riyō" 平安期の大和盆地における条里地割内部の土地利用 (Land use in the Yamato Basin during the Heian period), *Shirin* 61:75-112 (May 1978).

————. "Nara Heian ki no sonraku keitai ni tsuite" 奈良平安期の村落形態について (Settlement patterns in the Nara and Heian periods), *Shirin* 54:49-117 (May 1971).

————. "Shōen sonraku no keikan" 荘園村落の景観 (The

landscape of estate villages), in Toda Yoshimi 戸田芳実 , ed., *Nihon shi 2 Chūsei 1* 日本史２中世１ (Medieval Japanese history). Yūhikaku, 1978.

———. "Tōdaiji ryō shōen no keikan to kaihatsu" 東大寺領庄園 の景観と開発 (The landscape and clearance of Tōdaiji's estates), in Asaka Toshiki 浅香年木 , ed., *Kodai no chihō shi* 古代の地方史 (Local history of ancient Japan), Vol. IV. Asakura shoten, 1978.

Kishi Toshio 岸俊男 . "Asuka to hōkaku jiwari" 飛鳥と 方格地割り (Asuka and the regular division of land), *Shirin* 53:1-41 (July 1970).

———. "Kodai kōki no shakai kikō" 古代後期の社会機構 (Social structure in the late ancient period), in *Shin Nihon shi kōza: Kodai kōki* 新日本史講座 古代後期 (New lectures in Japanese history: The latter part of the ancient period). Chūō kōron sha, 1952.

———. *Nihon kodai seiji shi kenkyū* 日本古代政治史研究 (Ancient Japanese politics). Hanawa shobō, 1966.

———. *Nihon kodai sekichō no kenkyū* 日本古代籍帳の 研究 (Ancient Japanese registers). Hanawa shobō, 1973.

Kitayama Shigeo 北山茂夫 . *Nara chō no seiji to minshū* 奈良 朝の政治と民衆 (Politics and the people in the Nara period). Kyoto, Takagiri shoin, 1948.

———. *Temmu chō* 天武朝 (The Temmu Court). Chūō kōron sha, 1978.

Kitō Hiroshi 鬼頭宏 . *Nihon nisen nen no jinkō shi* 日本 二千年の人口史 (Two thousand years of Japanese population). PHP Paperbacks, 1983.

Kitō Kiyoaki 鬼頭清明 . "Hasseiki no shakai kōsei shiteki tokushitsu" 八世紀の社会構成史的特質 (The historical characteristics of eighth-century social structure), *Nihon shi kenkyū* 172:3-28 (December 1976).

Kōchi Shōsuke 河内祥輔. "Taihō ryō handen shūju seido kō" 太宝令班田収授制度考 (The system of state land allocation in the Taihō Codes), *Shigaku zasshi* 86:1-39 (March 1977).

LeRoy Ladurie, Emmanuel. "Un Concept: l'Unification Microbienne du Monde (XIVe-XVIIIe Siècles)," *Schweizerische Zeitschrift für Geschichte* 23:627-696 (1973).

Les Mémoires Historiques de Se Ma Ts'ien. Tr. Edouard Chavannes. Paris, E. Leroux, 1897.

Lewis, Henry. *Ilocano Rice Farmers.* Honolulu, University of Hawaii Press. 1971.

McCullough, William. "Japanese Marriage Institutions in the Heian Period," *Harvard Journal of Asiatic Studies* 27:103-167 (1967).

McEwan, J. R. "Shifting Cultivation in Tsushima in the Eighteenth Century," *Asia Major* 5:208-229 (February 1956).

McNeill, William. *Plagues and Peoples.* Garden City, Doubleday, 1976.

Manual II: Methods of Appraisal of Quality of Basic Data for Population Estimates. New York, United Nations, 1955.

The Man'yōshū. Tr. Nippon gakujutsu shinkō kai. New York, Columbia University Press, 1965.

Maruyama Tadatsuna 丸山忠綱. "Konden eisei shizai hō ni tsuite" 墾田永世私財法について (The 743 law permitting the permanent private possession of newly opened lands), *Hōsei shigaku* 13:28-48 (1960).

Maruyama Yoshihiko 丸山幸彦. "Tōdaiji ryō shōen no hensen" 東大寺領庄園の変遷 (The vicissitudes of Tōdaiji's estates), in Yagi Atsuru 八木充, ed., *Kodai no chihō shi,* II. Asakura shoten, 1977.

Mayhew, Alan. *Rural Settlement and Farming in Germany.* London, Batsford, 1973.

Mayuzumi Hiromichi 黛弘道. "Kokushi sei no seiritsu" 国司制の成立 (The establishment of the provincial office), in *Ritsuryō kokka no kiso kōzō* 律令国家の基礎構造 (The basic structure of the ritsuryō state). Yoshikawa kōbunkan, 1960.

Menken, Jane, James Trussell, and Susan Watkins. "The Nutrition Fertility Link: An Evaluation of the Evidence," *The Journal of Interdisciplinary History* 11:425-441 (Winter 1981).

Miskimin, Harry. *The Economy of Early Renaissance Europe, 1300-1460.* Cambridge, Cambridge University Press, 1975.

Miyahara Takeo 宮原武夫. *Nihon kodai no kokka to nōmin* 日本古代の国家と農民 (Peasants and state in ancient Japan). Hōsei daigaku shuppan kai, 1973.

Miyamoto Tasuku 宮本救. "Ritsuryōteki tochi seido" 律令的土地制度 (The land system of the ritsuryō period), in

Takeuchi Rizō, ed., *Taikei Nihon shi sōsho 6 Tochi seido* 1. Yamakawa shuppan sha, 1973.

Miyazaki Ichisada 宮崎市定 . *Ajia shi kenkyū* アジア史研究 (History of Asia), Vol. IV. Kyoto, Tōyō shi kenkyū kai, 1964.

Mori Kōichi 森浩一 . "Gunshū fun to kofun no shūmatsu," 群集墳と古墳の終末 (Groups of tombs at the end of the tomb period), in *Iwanami kōza Nihon rekishi 2 Kodai* 2. Iwanami shoten, 1975.

Morita Tei 森田悌 . "Kodai chihō gyōsei kikō ni tsuite no ichi kōsatsu" 古代地方行政機構についての一考察 (The structure of ancient local government), *Rekishi gaku kenkyū* 401:15–27 (October 1973).

Murai Yasuhiko 村井康彦 . *Kodai kokka kaitai katei no kenkyū* 古代国家解体過程の研究 (The decline of the ancient state). Iwanami shoten, 1965.

Murao Jirō 村尾次郎 . *Ritsuryō zaisei shi no kenkyū* 律令財政史の研究 (Finances in the *ritsuryō* period). Yoshikawa kōbunkan, 1961.

Murayama Kōichi 村山光一 . *Handen shūju* 班田収授 (The state land allocation system). Yoshikawa kōbunkan, 1978.

Mutō Tadashi 武藤直 . "Nihon kodai no sonraku keitai ni kansuru ichi kōsatsu" 日本古代の村落形態に関する一考察 (Ancient Japanese settlement patterns), *Shirin* 52:112–124 (June 1969).

Nagahara Keiji 長原慶二 . *Nihon keizai shi* 日本経済史 (An economic history of Japan). Iwanami shoten, 1980.

Nagayama Yasutaka 長山泰孝 . *Ritsuryō futan taikei no kenkyū* 律令負担体係の研究 (The *ritsuryō* tax system). Hanawa shobō, 1976.

Nakano Hideo 中野栄夫 . "Tōtōmi no kuni Hamana no kōri yuso chō no kisoteki kōsatsu" 遠江国浜名郡輸租帳の基礎的考察 (The land tax report from Hamana district, Tōtōmi province), *Nihon rekishi* 291:67–86 (August 1972).

Nambu Noboru 南部昇 . "Kōgo nenjaku to Saikaidō koseki museisha" 甲午年籍と西海道戸籍無姓者 (The registers of 670 and people without surnames in the Kyushu household registers), in *Nihon kodai shi ronsō* 日本古代史論叢 (Essays in ancient Japanese history), Vol. I. Yoshikawa kōbunkan, 1978.

Naoki Kōjirō 直木孝次郎 . *Nara jidai shi no shomondai* 奈良時代史の諸問題 (Problems in Nara history). Hanawa shobō, 1968.

———. *Nihon no rekishi 2 Kodai kokka no seiritsu* 日本の歴史 2 古代国家の成立 (A history of Japan: The establishment of the ancient state). Chūō kōron sha, 1965.

Narasaki Shōichi 楢崎彰一 and Yokoyama Kōichi 横山浩 一 , eds. *Kodai shi hakkutsu 10 Miyako to mura no kurashi* 古代史発掘 10 都と村の暮し (Excavations in ancient history: Life in the capital and village). Kōdan sha, 1974.

Nihongi, Chronicles of Japan from the Earliest Times to A.D. 697. Tr. William Aston. 2 vols. London, Kegan, Paul, Trench, Trubner, 1896.

Nishijima Sadao 西島定生 . *Chūgoku keizai shi kenkyū* 中国経済史研究 (An economic history of China). Tokyo daigaku bungakubu, 1965.

Nishioka Toranosuke 西岡虎之介 . "Chikō jidai yori teibō jidai e no tenkai" 池溝時代より堤防時代への展開 (From ponds and ditches to dams), *Shien* 3:23-58 (October 1929).

Nomura Tadao 野村忠夫 . *Kodai kanryō no sekai* 古代官僚 の世界 (The world of the ancient bureaucrat). Hanawa shobō, 1969.

———. "Shiryō shōkai: Shōsōin yori hakken sareta Shiragi no minsei monjo ni tsuite" 史料紹介 正倉院より発見された 新羅の民政文書について (Introducing new historical materials: The administrative record from Silla discovered in the Shōsōin), *Shigaku zasshi* 62:58-68 (April 1953).

Nunomura Kazuo 布村一夫 . "Sekichō ni okeru fukeiteki kyō-daiteki kazoku kyōdōtai" 籍帳における父系的兄弟的 家族共同体 (Paternal fraternal family communities as seen in the registers), *Rekishi gaku kenkyū* 429:23-34 (1976).

Ochiai Shigenobu 落合重信 . *Jōri sei* 条里制 (The *jōri sei*). Yoshikawa kōbunkan, 1967.

Okuda Shinkei 奥田真啓 . "Shōen zen sonraku no kōzō ni tsuite" 庄園前村落の構造について (The structure of the village before the appearance of estates), *Shigaku zasshi* 58:24-48 (March 1949).

Onoyama Setsu 小野山節 , ed. *Kodai shi hakkutsu 6 Kofun to kokka no naritachi* 古代史発掘 6 古墳と国家の成り立ち

(Excavations in ancient Japanese history: Tombs and the establishment of the state). Kōdan sha, 1975.

Ōyama Seiichi 大山誠一 . "Tempyō jūninen Tōtōmi no kuni Hamana no kōri yuso chō no shiryō sei ni kansuru ichi kōsatsu" 天平十二年遠江国浜名郡輸租帳の史料性に関する 一考察 (The historical value of the land tax report of Hamana district, Tōtōmi province from Tempyō 12 [740] , *Nihon rekishi* 306:111–120 (November 1973).

Postan, Michael. "Medieval Agrarian Society in its Prime: England," in Michael Postan, ed. *The Cambridge Economic History of Europe* I, *The Agrarian Life of the Middle Ages*, 2nd. ed. Cambridge, Cambridge University Press, 1966.

———. *The Medieval Economy and Society*. Berkeley, University of California Press, 1972.

———, and Emmanuel LeRoy Ladurie. "Symposium: Agrarian Class Structure and Economic Development in Pre-Industrial Europe," *Past and Present* 78:55–59 (February 1978).

Russell, J.C. *British Medieval Population*. Albuquerque, University of New Mexico Press, 1948.

Sakamoto Shōzō 坂本賞三 . *Nihon ōchō kokka taisei ron* 日本王朝国家体制論 (A discourse on the Japanese dynastic state system). Tokyo daigaku shuppan kai, 1972.

Sakamoto Tarō 坂本太郎 . *Taika kaishin no kenkyū* 大化 改新の研究 (The Taika Reforms). Jibundō, 1938.

Sansom, George. "Early Japanese Law and Administration," *Transactions of the Asiatic Society of Japan* (Series 2), 9:67–109 (1932); 11:117–149 (1934).

———. *A History of Japan to 1334*. Stanford, Stanford University Press, 1958.

Sasaki Kōmei 佐々木高明 . *Inasaku izen* 稲作以前 (Before wet-rice cultivation). NHK bukkusu, 1971.

Sato, Elizabeth. "The Early Development of the Shōen," in John Hall and Jeffrey Mass, eds., *Medieval Japan: Essays in Institutional History*. New Haven, Yale University Press, 1974.

Sawada Goichi 沢田吾一 . *Nara chō jidai minsei keizai no sūteki kenkyū* 奈良朝時代民政経済の数的研究 (Statistical research on the Nara economy and population). Fusanbō, 1927.

Sekiguchi Yūko 関口裕子 . "Nihon kodai kazoku no kiteiteki ketsuen chūtai ni tsuite" 日本古代家族の規定的血縁粗帯について (Restrictive blood ties within the ancient Japanese family), in *Kodai shi ronsō*, Vol. II. Yoshikawa kōbunkan, 1978.

Serizawa Chōsuke 芹沢長介 . *Sekki jidai no Nihon* 石器時代の日本 (Japan in the stone age). Tsukiji shokan, 1960.

Shryock, Henry, and Jacob Siegel. *The Methods and Materials of Demography*, 3rd printing. 2 vols. Washington, D.C., U.S. Bureau of the Census, 1975.

Smith, Thomas. *The Agrarian Origins of Modern Japan*. Stanford, Stanford University Press, 1959.

Takamure Itsue 高群逸枝 . *Nihon kon'in shi* 日本婚姻史 (A history of marriage in Japan). Jibundō, 1963.

Takashige Susumu 高重進 . *Kodai chūsei no kōchi to sonraku* 古代中世の耕地と村落 (Ancient and medieval farmland and villages). Daimei dō, 1975.

Takeuchi Rizō 竹内理三 . "Kokudo no kaihatsu" 国土の開発 (The opening of the nation's lands), in Takeuchi Rizō, ed., *Kodai no Nihon* 1 *Yōsetsu* 古代の日本 1 軍説 (Ancient Japan: Essays). Kadokawa shoten, 1971.

———. *Nara chō jidai ni okeru jiin keizai no kenkyū* 奈良朝時代における寺院経済の研究 (Temple finances in the Nara period). Ōokayama shoten, 1932.

———. *Ritsuryō sei to kizoku seiken* 律令制と貴族政権 (The *ritsuryō* system and aristocratic power), Vol. I. Ochanomizu shobō, 1957.

———. "Shōsōin koseki chōsa gaihō" 正倉院戸籍調査概報 (Report on the investigation of household registers of the Shōsōin), *Shigaku zasshi* 68:34–65 (March 1959); 69:77–98 (February 1960); 69:85–93 (March 1960).

Takigawa Masajirō 滝川政次郎 . *Ritsuryō jidai no nōmin seikatsu* 律令時代の農民生活 (Peasant life in the *ritsuryō* period). Kangen sha, 1953.

Tateno Kazushi 館野和巳 . "Ritsuryōseika no kōtsū to jimmin shihai," 律令制下の交通と人民支配 (The *ritsuryō* transportation system and control of the people), *Nihon shi kenkyū* 211:54–82 (March 1980).

Toda Yoshimi 戸田芳実 . *Nihon ryōshu sei seiritsu shi no kenkyū* 日本領主制成立史の研究 (The establishment of the Japanese domain system). Iwanami shoten, 1967.

Tokinoya Shigeru 時野谷滋 . "Den-ryō to konden hō" 田令と墾田法 (The law codes and legislation on land clearance), *Rekishi kyōiku* 4:28–35 (May 1956); 5:50–55 (June 1956).

Torao Toshiya 虎尾俊哉 . *Handen shūju hō no kenkyū* 班田収授法の研究 (The system of state land allocation). Yoshikawa kōbunkan, 1961.

———. "Kōden o meguru futatsu no mondai" 公田をめぐる二つの問題 (Two problems regarding state lands), in *Ritsuryō kokka to kizoku shakai* 律令国家と貴族社会 (The *ritsuryō* state and the aristocracy). Yoshikawa kōbunkan, 1969.

———. "Mitabi Kiyomihara ryō no handen hō ni tsuite" 三たび浄御原令の班田法について (The land system of the Kiyomihara Codes—a third essay), in *Zoku Nihon kodai shi ronshū*, Vol. III. Yoshikawa kōbunkan, 1972.

———. "Ritsuryō jidai no konden hō ni kansuru ni san no mondai" 律令時代の墾田法に関する二、三の問題 (Two or three problems regarding laws on land clearance in the *ritsuryō* period), *Hirosaki daigaku jimbun shakai* 15:61–88 (1958).

Totman, Conrad. *Japan before Perry*. Berkeley, University of California Press, 1981.

Tsude Hiroshi 都出比呂志 . "Nōgu tekkika no futatsu no kakki" 農具鉄器化の二つの画期 (Two epochs in the spread of iron technology), *Kōkogaku kenkyū* 51:36–51 (1967).

———. "Shohyō to shōkai: Harashima Reiji cho *Nihon kodai shakai no kiso kōzō*" 書評と紹介栗島礼二著日本古代社会の基礎構造 (Reviews and introductions: Harashima Reiji's *Basic Structure of Ancient Japanese Society*), *Nihon shi kenkyū* 107:66–71 (August 1969).

Tuchman, Barbara. *A Distant Mirror*. New York, Ballantine Books, 1978.

Twitchett, Denis. *Financial Administration under the T'ang Dynasty*, rev. ed. Cambridge, Cambridge University Press, 1970.

———. "Population and Pestilence in T'ang China," in *Studia Sino-Mongolica: Festschrift für Herbert Franke*. Ed. Wolfgang Bauer. Wiesbaden, Franz Steiner, 1979.

Urata Akiko 浦田明子 . "Henko sei no igi" 編戸制の意義 (The significance of the household system), *Shigaku zasshi* 81:28-76 (February 1972).

Wajima Seiichi 和島誠一 . "Kofun bunka no henshitsu" 古墳文化の変質 (The transformation of tomb culture), in *Iwanami kōza Nihon rekishi 2 Kodai* 2. Iwanami shoten, 1962.
———, ed. *Nihon no kōkogaku 3 Yayoi jidai* 日本の考古学 3 弥生時代 (Japanese archaeology: The Yayoi period). Kawade shobō, 1966.

Watanabe Hisao 渡辺久雄 . *Jōri sei no kenkyū* 条里制の研究 (The *jōri sei*). Osaka, Shōgen sha, 1968.

Weis, Kenneth. "On the Systematic Bias in Skeletal Sexing," *American Journal of Physical Anthropology* 37:239-249 (September 1972).

Wolfenden, Hugh. *Population Statistics and Their Compilation*, rev. ed. Chicago, University of Chicago Press, 1954.

Yamamoto Takeo 山本武夫 . "Rekishi no nagare ni sou Nihon to sono shūhen no kikō hensen" 歴史の流れに沿う日本とその周辺の気候変遷 (Historical climatic changes in Japan and vicinity), *Chigaku zasshi* 75:119-141 (March 1967).

Yamamura, Kozo. "The Decline of the *Ritsuryō* System: Hypotheses on Economic and Institutional Change," *Journal of Japanese Studies* 1:3-37 (Autumn 1974).

Yamanouchi Sugao 山内清男 . "Jōmon bunka no shakai" 縄文文化の社会 (Society in the Jōmon period), in *Nihon to sekai no rekishi*, Vol. I. Gakushū kenkyū sha, 1969.

Yasuda Motohisa 安田元久 . *Nihon shōen shi gaisetsu* 日本庄園史概説 (An outline of the history of Japanese estates). Yoshikawa kōbunkan, 1957.

Yasuda, Yoshinori. "Early Historical Forest Clearance around the Ancient Castle Site of Tagajo, Miyagi Prefecture, Japan," *Asian Perspectives* 19:42-58 (1976).

Yates, Robin. "The City Under Siege: Technology and Organization as seen in the Reconstructed Text of the Military Chapters of *Mo-tzu*." PhD dissertation, Harvard University, 1980.

Yonezawa Yasushi 米沢薫 . *Etchū kodai shi no kenkyū*

越中古代史の研究(The ancient history of Etchū). Toyama Prefecture, Etsuhi bunka kenkyū kai, 1965.

Yoshida Akira 吉田晶 . *Nihon kodai shakai kōsei shi ron* 日本古代社会構成史論 (The structure of ancient Japanese society). Hanawa shobō, 1968.

Yoshida Takashi 吉田孝 . "Kōchi kōmin ni tsuite" 公地公民 について (State control of the people and land), in *Zoku Nihon kodai shi ronshū*, Vol. II. Yoshikawa kōbunkan, 1972.

———. "Konden eisei shizai hō no henshitsu" 墾田永世私財法の変質 (The transformation of the law permitting private possession of newly cleared lands), in *Nihon shakai keizai shi kenkyū: Kodai chūsei hen* 日本社会経済史研究 古代中世編 (Social and economic history of Japan: The ancient and medieval periods). Yoshikawa kōbunkan, 1967.

———. "Ritsuryōsei to sonraku" 律令制と村落 (The village and the *ritsuryō* system), in *Iwanami kōza Nihon rekishi 3 Kodai 3*. Iwanami shoten, 1975.

Glossary of Japanese, Chinese, and Korean Terms

Well-known geographical names have been omitted.

Abe no Ason Tsugumaro
阿倍朝臣継麻呂
Abiko 我孫子
Ahachima, Kasuga 味蜂間, 春部
Akae 赤江
Aki 阿伎
Aki no Suguri Tariiwa
阿伎勝足石
ama 海人
Amabe 海部
Arahaka 荒伯
Asauchi 麻打
Asuka 飛鳥
Asuwa 足羽
Atago, Upper Izumo
愛宕、雲上
Atago, Lower Izumo
愛宕、雲下
Ato 跡
Ato no Sō 阿刀僧
Ato no Sukune Otari
安都宿禰雄足
阿刀男足
阿刀小足
Awa 阿波

Awata 粟田
Awata no Hitomaro
粟田人麻呂

bao 保
Bian Zhuo 扁鵲
Bitchū 備中
bō 坊
bu 歩
Bungo 豊後
Bungo, Kuzu 豊後, 球珠
Bungo, Nahori 豊後, 直入
Buzen, Kamutsumike, Kashi-
  guya 豊前, 上三毛,
  加自久也
Buzen, Kamutsumike, Tō
  豊前, 上三毛, 塔
Buzen, Nakatsu, Takebe 豊前,
  仲津, 丁

Chikuzen, Shima, Kawabe
  筑前, 嶋, 川辺
Chimori 道守
chō (area) 町
chō (report) 牒

chō (tax) 調
chō shi 調使
Ch'ŏngae Somun 泉蓋蘇文
chōshū shi 朝集使
Chuyu 州柔
cun 村

daichō shi 大帳使
dainagon 大納言
Dazaifu 大宰府
Den-ryō 田令
denso 田租
Dōkyō 道鏡
dōyō goku 動用穀

Echi no Takutsu 朴市田来津
Echigo 越後
Echizen 越前
Eizanji 永山寺
eki 疫
ekishitsu 疫疾
Engi 延喜
Enryaku 延暦
entōsō 豌痘瘡
Enuma 江沼
Etchū 越中

fang 坊
Fuchi 敷智
fudō goku 不動穀
fudoki 風土記
Fujiwara 藤原
Fujiwara no Fubito
藤原不比等
藤原史
Fujiwara no Ason Fujitsugu
藤原朝臣藤嗣
Fujiwara no Ason Tsunanushi
藤原朝臣縄主
fukanden den 不堪佃田

Fukuro 福留
furō 浮浪
furōnin chō 浮浪人帳
Furuchi 古市
[Fujiwara no] Fusasaki 房前

Gakuanji 額安寺
gegeko 下下戸
Genshō 元正
geseiko 下政戸
gisei setsu 擬制説
gō 郷
goho 五保
gōri 郷里
Gufukuji 弘福寺
gunji 郡司

Hamana 浜名
Han 韓
handen sei 班田制
Hani-yama-hime 埴山姫
Hanyū 半布
haori 半折
Harima 播磨
Hata no Otogimi
秦茅君　秦茅公
秦乙君　秦乙公
Hata no Tachihito 秦立人
Hata no Tarihito 秦足人
Hatabito no Hiromoto
秦人広本
Heiei 平栄
Hida 斐陀　飛騨
Hiraide 平出
Hirose 広瀬
Hitachi 常陸
Hizen 肥前
hokubi gari 穂首刈り
Hokurikudō 北陸道
Horie 堀江

hōsō 疱瘡
Hosokawa 細川
hottate bashira jūkyo
堀立柱住居

Ichinomiya 一宮
Iga 伊賀
iho 廬
Ikue no Omi Azumabito
生江臣東人
Ikue no Omi Yasumaro
生江臣安麻呂
Inaba, Takakusa 因幡, 高草
Ise 伊勢
Ishiyamadera 石山寺
Isobe 磯部
Isogami 石上
Itokomaro 伊刀古麻呂
Iyo 伊予
Izanagi no Mikoto 伊弉諾尊
Izanami no Mikoto
伊弉冉尊
Izu 伊豆
Izumi, Hine 和泉, 日根
Izumo 出雲
Izumo no Omi Hanime
出雲臣覇通売
Izumo no Omi Matari
出雲臣真足
Izumo no Omi Omimaro
出雲臣意美麻呂
Izumo no Omi Ōshima
出雲臣大島

jikimaki 直播き
Jitō 持統
jittai setsu 実態説
jō 丈
jōden 乗田
jōkōden 常荒田

Jōmon 縄文
jōri sei 条里制
Junna 淳和

Kaga 加賀
Kagu-tsuchi 軻遇突智
kaihatsu sonraku 開発村落
Kamitsukenu no Ason Hirohito
上毛野朝臣広人
Kamo, Hanyū 加毛, 半布
kanjaku 勘籍
kari ho 借廬
Karu 軽
Kasa no Ason Yasu
笠阿曽弥安
Kasugabe no Suguri Mayame
春日部主村麻夜売
Katagata, Katagata 肩県, 肩々
Katsushika, Ōshima 葛飾, 大島

Kawachi 河内
Kawaradera 川原寺
keichō 計帳
keichō shi 計帳使
kenin 家人
Ki no Ason 紀朝臣
Kii 紀伊
Kim Sang-jŏng 金相貞
Kinabiru 析名蛭
Kinai 畿内
Kiyomihara 浄御原
Kiyowara no Mabito Natsuno
清原真人夏野
ko 戸
Kodera 古照
Kōgo nenjaku 甲午年籍
Koguryŏ 高句麗
Kōgyoku 皇極
kōhaiden 荒廃田
Koki 古記

koku 石

kokubunji 国分寺

kokugaryō 国衙領

Komi　子見

Kōmyō 光明

Kōnin 弘仁

Koryŏ 高麗

Ko-ryō 戸令

koseki 戸籍

Kōtoku 孝徳

kubunden 口分田

Kuga 玖珂

kūkanchi 空閑地

Kumoku-ryō 廐牧令

kuni 国

kuni no miyatsuko 国族

Kuni no Miyatsuko Katsuiwa
　国族難磐

Kura no Komaro 倉古万呂

Kurita 栗太

Kusakabe no Hirohito
　日下部広人

Kushiki-ryō 公式令

Kuwabara 桑原

Kuze 久世

Kwisil Poksin 鬼室福信

kyūkyū tō 救急稲

li 里

Li Yuan 李淵

Liaodong 遼東

lin 隣

Makimuku 纏向

makishi 蒔

makeru 蒔有

Mamuta 茨田

[Fujiwara no] Maro 麻呂

Matsuyama 松山

Mibu Tsukai no Nushi
　壬生使王

migi ōdoneri 右大舎人

Mimana 壬那

Mino 御野 or 美濃

miso 豉

Miwahito no Hiromaro
　神人広万呂

miyake 屯倉 官家
　御屯 三宅

Mizu-ha-no-me 罔象女

mogasa 裳瘡

Mommu 文武

Motosu, Kurisuta 本簀 ,
　栗栖太

mou 畝

[Fujiwara no] Muchimaro
　武智麻呂

Mutobe no Azumabito
　六人部東人

Mutsu 陸奥

nagachi 長地

Nagata (Prince) 長田

Nagato 長門

Nagato, Toyoura 長門 ,
　豊浦

Nagaya (Prince) 長屋

Naka (Prince) 中

Nakatomi no Kamatari
　中臣鎌足

Nankaidō 南海道

Nara 奈良 寧楽 平城

nawashiro 苗代

negari 根刈り

Nishikibe no Atai Nemaro
　錦部直禰麻呂

no 野

Nōne 長畝

nubi 奴婢
Nukata 額田

Ōama 大海人
ōdoneri 大舍人
Oharida 小治田
Ōmi 近江
Otogi 乙木
Ōtomo 大友
Ōtomo no Morohito
　　大友諸人
Ōtomo no Sukune Maro
　　大伴宿禰麻呂
Ōtomo no Sukune Minaka
　　大伴宿禰三中　御中
Ōtomo no Sukune Yakamochi
　　大伴宿禰家持
Ōtomo Tamba no Fubito no
　　Miyatsuko Kibimaro
　　大友但波史族吉備麻呂
Ōtsu 大津
Owari no Tsurugi
　　尾治都留伎
Ōyakeme 大宅女

Paekche 百済
Paekch'ŏn 白村

ri (block of the *jōri sei*) 里
ri (mile) 里
ri (administrative village) 里
ritsuryō 律令
ryō (bureau) 寮
ryō (ounce) 両
ryōko 陵戸

Saikaidō 西海道
Saimei 済明
Sakai 坂井

sakan 主典
sangi 参議
San'indō 山陰道
sanji 散事
Sanuki 讃岐
San'yōdō 山陽道
sara ike 皿池
sato 里
Satsuma, Takagi 薩麻, 高城
sekihansō 赤斑蒼
semmyō 宣命
Settsu 攝津
shaku 尺
shakyō sho 写経所
shi 司
shichō 仕丁
Shigaraki 紫香楽
Shikada 鹿田
shiki 職
shimahata 島畑
Shimōsa 下総
Shimotsukenu no Ason Iwa-
　　shiro 下毛野朝臣石代
shingō 賑給
shinjutsu 賑恤
shiro 代
shishō 史生
shiwabuki 志湿夫使
shō 升
shōen 庄園　荘園
shoki shōen 初期庄園
Shōmu 聖武
shōryō 少領
Shōsōin 正倉院
Shōtoku 称徳
shōzei chō 正税帳
shōzei chō shi 正税帳使
Silla 新羅
Soenokami 添上

Soga no Iruka 蘇我入鹿
shuchō 主帳
Shūgai shō 拾芥抄
shujitsu 手実
shukei-ryō 主計寮
shusei 主政
shuzei-ryō 主税寮
Sōma, Obu 倉麻，意布
Suhata no Eji Michitari
　　箐秦絵師道足
suiko 出挙
Suka 須加
Suminoe 住吉
Suō 周防
Suruga 駿河

Tachibana no Moroe 橘諸兄
Taihō 大宝
Taika 大化
tairyō 大領
Taizong 太宗
Takaba 高庭
takabata 高畑
Takamado 高円
Takaya 高屋
Takeda 竹田
Takechi no Sukune
　　武内宿禰
tamahi 多麻比
Tamiya 田宮
tan 段
Tang Changan 唐長安
tani ike 谷池
tate ana jūkyo 竪穴住居
taue 田植之
Temmu 天武
Tempyō 天平
Tempyō Hōji 天平宝字
Tenchō 天長
Tenji 天智

ten'yaku-ryō 典薬寮
tōbō 逃亡
Tōdaiji 東大寺
[Izumo no Omi] Tojime
　　出雲臣刀自売
Tōkaidō 東海道
Tonami 礪波
Tonami no Omi Shirushi
　　利波臣志留志
Toro 登呂
Tōsandō 東山道
Tōtōmi 遠江
Totori no Kunimaro
　　鳥取国万呂
tsubo 坪
Tsuki no Otomaro 調乙万呂
Tsuki no Tamatari 調玉足
Tsukimoto no Oyu 槻本老
Tsukushi 筑紫
Tsuruga 敦賀

Uchi 宇智
udaiben 右大弁
udaijin 右大臣
udaishi 右大使
Udemi 宇弖美
Ŭija 義慈
Uji 宇治
[Fujiwara no] Umakai 宇合
Urahara 蒲原
Urao 蒲生

Wa 倭
Waka-musubi 稚産霊
Wakasa 若狭
Wamyō shō 和名抄

Xiang 郷
Xian 献

yakibata 燒畑

Yamada Mizunomi 山田水呑

Yamagata, Miita 山方 ，
三井田

Yamanoue no Okura
山上憶良

Yamashiro 山城 山背

Yamato 大和 大倭
大養德

Yayoi 弥生

yō 膺

Yŏ P'ung-jang 余豐璋

yontō kan 四等官

Yōrō 養老

Yoshimine no Ason Yasuyo
良峯朝臣安世

Yoshinari 吉成

Yoshino 吉野

Yu Fu 俞附

Yuki no Muraji Yakamaro
雪連宅満

yuso chō 輸租帳

zakko 雜戶

zō Tōdaiji shi 造東大寺司

Index

Abe no Ason Tsugumaro, 56–58
Abe Takeshi, 74
Administrative village, 17, 138–139
Age-heaps: definition, 35; in Mino and Hanyū data, 35–37; in 690 census, 36–37; in 702 census, 37; in Kyushu data, 38; in Shimōsa and Yamashiro data, 38; smoothing of, 40–41, 180; in Tokugawa period data, 180; in Ainu data, 180
Ages, conversion to modern Western equivalents, 40–41
Agricultural technology: Yayoi period, 3, 173–174; iron agricultural tools, 5, 6, 95, 103–104, 174; wooden agricultural tools, 5–6, 102, 173–174, 192; as cause of land abandonment, 76, 78, 82, 87, 88, 188–189; irrigation technology, 87, 94–97; *tani ike*, 96–97; saucer ponds, 96–97; failure of, 115; and migration, 128; and settlement patterns, 137; in *ritsuryō* period, summary, 143–144; Tomb period, 174
Artificially irrigated rice farming: in mid-seventh century, 8; at Kuwabara *shōen*, 85–88; planting methods, 95; harvesting methods, 95; yields, 95; drawbacks, 95–96, 100–101
Asuka, 114, 115
Ato, 52
Average age at death over age 5: Kyushu population, 44; Hanyū population, 44; Mino population, 44

Battle of the Paekch'ŏn River, 9, 10; *Nihon shoki* account, 10–11
Bian Zhuo, 61, 62
Birth rate: Mino population, 44, 45; Hanyū population, 44; Kyushu population, 44, 45
Black Death. *See* Bubonic plague
Bubonic plague: in Europe, 51; contemporary explanations, 62; transmission of, 70; and migration, 126
Buddhism: stimulated by Great Smallpox Epidemic of 735 to 737, 68; in *Nihon shoki*, 72
Burial practices, in Tomb period, 7

Census. *See* Population registration
Census of 670, 19; reasons for, 11; rounding of ages, 36; control of migration, 121